GLOBAL EUROPE, SOCIAL EUROPE

GLOBAL EUROPE, SOCIAL EUROPE

Edited by

ANTHONY GIDDENS,
PATRICK DIAMOND AND
ROGER LIDDLE

polity

Individual chapters © their authors 2006; this collection
© Polity Press 2006

First published in 2006 by Polity Press

Polity Press
65 Bridge Street
Cambridge CB2 1UR, UK.

Polity Press
350 Main Street
Malden, MA 02148, USA

ISBN-10: 0-7456-3934-8
ISBN-13: 978-07456-3934-5
ISBN-10: 0-7456-3935-6 (pb)
ISBN-13: 978-07456-39352 (pb)

A catalogue record for this book is available from the British Library.

Typeset in 10.5 on 12 pt Sabon
by Servis Filmsetting Ltd, Manchester
Printed and bound in Great Britain by MPG Books Ltd, Bodmin, Cornwall

The publisher has used its best endeavours to ensure that the URLs for
external websites referred to in this book are correct and active at the time
of going to press. However, the publisher has no responsibility for the
websites and can make no guarantee that a site will remain live or that the
content is or will remain appropriate.

Every effort has been made to trace all copyright holders, but if any have
been inadvertently overlooked the publishers will be pleased to include any
necessary credits in any subsequent reprint or edition.

For further information on Polity, visit our website: www.polity.co.uk

Contents

About Policy Network

}{ policy network

This collection of essays is the result of a large-scale *Policy Network* project on the European Social Model in 2005 and 2006 led by Anthony Giddens, Patrick Diamond, and Roger Liddle, and managed by François Lafond. It follows from a policy pamphlet, *The Hampton Court Agenda: A Social Model for Europe*, published by *Policy Network* in March 2006.

Policy Network is an international think-tank launched in December 2000 with the support of Tony Blair, Gerhard Schröder, Giuliano Amato and Göran Persson, following the Progressive Governance Summits in New York, Florence and Berlin. In July 2003, *Policy Network* organized the London Progressive Governance Conference, which brought together 12 world leaders, and more than 600 progressive politicians, thinkers and strategists. In October 2004, *Policy Network* built on this success by organizing the Budapest Progressive Governance Conference, hosted by the Hungarian Prime Minister Ferenc Gyurcsány. In July 2005, *Policy Network* co-organized, with the Africa Institute of South Africa and the Presidency of South Africa, the first Regional African Progressive Governance Conference in Johannesburg. Most recently, *Policy Network* hosted a Progressive Governance summit on 11 and 12 February 2006, in Hammanskraal, South Africa.

A Progressive Network

Policy Network's objective is the promotion and cross fertilization of progressive policy ideas among centre-left modernizers. Acting as the secretariat to the Progressive Governance Network, *Policy Network* facilitates dialogue between politicians, policy-makers and experts across Europe and from democratic countries around the world. By providing a forum that promotes debate and shares ideas, *Policy Network* strengthens the hand of modernizers and the case for permanent renewal.

Our Common Challenge

Progressive governments and parties in Europe are facing similar problems and looking for modern social democratic responses. There are increasingly rising fears for security – economic, political and social – combined with the contradictions of reforming the traditional welfare state with employment policies, rapid change in science and technology and pressing global issues, all of which should be tackled in common, as part of the need for fundamental democratic renewal. In the past, progressives used to work independently to resolve these problems. Today, there is a growing consensus that we must engage with progressives from other countries and situate European with national responses within a broader international framework of progressive thinking, rooted in our social democratic values.

Activities

Policy Network is animated through a series of regular events, particularly the annual Spring Retreat and the 18-monthly Progressive Governance Conferences and Summits. In addition to these, we organize symposia, working groups and one-day conferences that focus on particular policy problems. Our interests in the past few years have centred on: Economic Reform, Public Services, Democratic Renewal, Community and Inequality as well as Global Governance.

During 2005 and 2006, we have concentrated our energies on the renewal of the European social model. Our programme on the European social model was launched during the UK Presidency of the European Union and has investigated the principal means through which the various models for welfare states in Europe can be adapted to meet the challenges of the twenty-first century. Fifteen working papers were commissioned and presented for discussion at a private seminar for the UK Prime Minister at 10 Downing Street one week prior to the European Summit at Hampton Court. Since then, and following an influential symposium organized at the end of November 2005, the debate has widened in a series of discussions across Europe in collaboration with other European centre-left think-tanks in Italy, the Netherlands, France, Hungary, Germany, Spain and Finland in the first half of 2006. Similar discussions also took place around the UK.

Since its inception in 2000, *Policy Network* has strived to contribute to the new policy agenda for the centre-left, not only in Europe, but also across the world. These meetings have been held in London, and also around Europe in partnership with a variety of national think-tanks such as the *Fondazione Italianieuropei*, the *Wiardi Beckman Stichting*, the *Global Progressive Forum*, the *Fundación Alternativas*, *A Gauche en Europe*, the *Friedrich-Ebert-Stiftung*, the EPC, the *Progressive Policy Institute* and the *Centre for American Progress*.

The outcome and results of these discussions are published in the three annual issues of *Policy Network*'s journal *Progressive Politics* and a series of individual pamphlets that are distributed throughout the network, placed on our website and used as the basis for discussions at *Policy Network* events.

We have always prided ourselves on being the first in the field in policy innovation, an achievement that has been greatly aided by the strength of the network of international partners we have built up.

Honorary Chair: Peter Mandelson
Director: Patrick Diamond
Executive Assistant: Suzanne Verberne-Brennan
Office Manager: Anna Bullegas
Events Manager: Joanne Burton
Head of Publications and Research Fellow: Nathaniel Copsey
Head of Research: Olaf Cramme
Policy Researchers: Johanna Juselius, Simon Latham, Robert Lorentz, Constance Motte, András Nagy

www.policy-network.net

About the Contributors

Karl Aiginger is Director of the Austrian Institute of Economic Research, WIFO. His recent publications include 'Competitiveness of the wider Europe and its impact on transatlantic relations', a paper prepared for the Second Annual Berkeley-Vienna Conference on the US and European Economies in Comparative Perspective (12–13 September 2005), and 'Labour market reforms and economic growth – the European experience in the nineties' (*Journal of Economic Studies* 32/6).

Katinka Barysch is chief economist at the Centre for European Reform in London. She previously worked at the Economist Intelligence Unit. Recent CER publications include: 'Why Europe should embrace Turkey' (2005, with Steven Everts and Heather Grabbe), 'Embracing the dragon: The EU's partnership with China' (2005, with Charles Grant and Mark Leonard) and 'The EU and Russia: Strategic partners or squabbling neighbours?' (2004).

Simon Commander is Director of the Centre for New and Emerging Markets at London Business School and Senior Adviser at the European Bank for Reconstruction and Development (EBRD). He has previously worked at the World Bank in Washington DC, and his publications are very extensive, including books, articles and working papers.

René Cuperus is Senior Research Fellow and Director for International Relations at the Wiardi Beckman Foundation, the think-tank of the Dutch Labour Party, PvdA. His recent publications include: 'Why the Dutch voted no. An anatomy of the new Euroscepticism in Old Europe' (2005), *The Challenge of Diversity. European Social Democracy Facing Migration, Integration and Multiculturalism* (ed. with K. Duffek and J. Kandel, 2003) and 'Europe and the revenge of national identity', in *Europe, a Global Player?* (2006).

Patrick Diamond is the Director of Policy Network and is a former Special Adviser in the British Prime Minister's Policy Unit. He joined the German Marshall Fund in 2005 as a Transatlantic Fellow, and is a Senior Visiting Fellow at the Centre for the Study of Global Governance at the London School of Economics and Political Science.

Maurizio Ferrera is Professor of Social and Labour Market Policies at the State University of Milan. He directs the Research Unit on European Governance (URGE) of the Collegio Carlo Alberto Fundation (Turin) and is deputy director of the POLEIS Centre for Comparative Political Studies at the Bocconi University, Milan. He is the author of *The Boundaries of Welfare: European Integration and the New Spatial Politics of Social Protection* (2005).

Anthony Giddens is the former director of the London School of Economics and Political Science. He is currently Life Fellow of King's College, Cambridge, and a member of the House of Lords. Among many other books, he is the author of *The Third Way* (1998).

Alois Guger is Research Fellow for Incomes Policy and Social Policy at the Austrian Institute of Economic Research in Vienna. His key areas of research include income distribution, incomes and wage policy, industrial relations, and employment and stabilization. Recent publications (in English) include: 'The European social model: from obstruction to advantage' (2005), 'Stagnation policy versus growth policy' (2006; with M. Marterbauer and E. Walterskirchen) and 'The ability to adapt: why it differs between the Scandinavian and the continental European models' (2006; with K. Aiginger).

Axel Heitmueller is Economic/Policy Adviser in the Prime Minister's Strategy Unit in the Cabinet Office, London. He is also employed as research associate at the Centre for New and Emerging Markets (CNEM) at the London Business School. His work has been published in journals such as the *Journal of Population Economics* and the *Scottish Journal of Political Economy*.

Anton Hemerijck is Director of the Netherlands Scientific Council for Government Policy (WRR) in The Hague and Senior Lecturer in the Department of Public Administration at Leiden University.

Jane Jenson holds the Canada Research Chair in Citizenship and Governance, departement de science politique, Université de Montréal. She is the author of, among others, *Who Cares? Women's Work, Childcare and Welfare State Redesign* (2001), with M. Sineau.

Roger Liddle is now a member of the President of the European Commission's Bureau of European Policy Advisers, having previously served as a member of the cabinet of the European Trade Commissioner, Peter Mandelson. He was for eight years European adviser to Tony Blair. He is a Visiting Fellow at the European Institute, London School of Economics and Political Science. His publications include (with Peter Mandelson) *The Blair Revolution: Can New Labour Deliver* (1996); *The New Case for Europe* (2005); and *Economic Reform in Europe: Priorities for the Next Five Years* (2005, with Maria Joao Rodrigues).

Måns Lönroth is Managing Director of Mistra, the Swedish foundation for Strategic Environmental Research. Previously, he was State Secretary at the Swedish Ministry of Environment. He is also a member of the Advisory Council for the Environment of the Swedish Government as well as a number of other Swedish organizations. Since 1999 he has also been a member of the China Council for the cooperation of environment and development, an advisory council to the Government of China. In 2002 he was appointed vice-chairman of the council.

Luc Soete is Professor of International Economics at the University of Maastricht, the Netherlands, and Director of the research institute MERIT (Maastricht Economic Research Institute on Innovation and Technology). His research interests cover the broad range of theoretical and empirical studies of the impact of technological change, in particular new information and communications technologies on employment, economic growth and international trade and investment.

John Sutton is the Sir John Hicks Professor of Economics at the London School of Economics and Political Science, where he directs the Economics of Industry Group at STICERD. He has written widely in the areas of microeconomic theory and industrial organization. His books include *Sunk Costs and Market Structure* (1981), *Technology* *and Market Structure* (1998) and *Marshall's Tendencies: What Can Economists Know?* (2000).

Loukas Tsoukalis is Professor of European Integration at the University of Athens and Visiting Professor at the Institut des Sciences Politiques, Paris, and the College of Europe, Bruges. President of the Hellenic Foundation for European and Foreign Policy (ELIAMEP), he is also special adviser to the President of the European Commission. He is the author of *What Kind of Europe?* (2005).

Laura Tyson is Dean of the London Business School and formerly Dean of the Haas School of Business at the University of California at Berkeley. She served in the Clinton Administration and was the Chair of the Council of Economic Advisers between 1993 and 1995, and the President's National Economic Adviser between 1995 and 1996. She has published books and articles on industrial competitiveness and trade and on the economies of Central Europe and their transition to market systems. Dr Tyson is a member of the Boards of the Council on Foreign Relations, the Brookings Institution, the Institute of International Economics, Bruegel, Eastman Kodak Company, Morgan Stanley Company and AT&T.

Patrick Weil is a senior research fellow at CNRS (National Centre for Scientific Research) in the university of Paris 1 – Sorbonne. His most recent books are *Qu'est ce qu'un français? Histoire de la nationalité française depuis la Révolution* [*What is a Frenchman? History of the French Nationality since the Revolution*] (2002), *La République et sa diversité* [*The Republic and its Diversity*] (2005).

List of Abbreviations

BHPS	British Household Panel Survey
ECB	European Central Bank
ECHP	European Community Household Panel
EES	European Employment Strategy
EMU	European Monetary Union
ESM	European Social Model
EU	European Union
FDI	Foreign Direct Investment
GDP	Gross Domestic Product
GDR	German Democratic Republic
ICT	Information and Communications Technology
ILO	International Labour Organization
IMF	International Monetary Fund
OECD	Organization for Economic Cooperation and Development
OMC	Open Method of Coordination
R&D	Research and Development
REACH	Registration, Evaluation and Authorization of Chemicals
RESM	Revised European Social Model
SGP	Stability and Growth Pact
SME	Small and Medium-sized Enterprise
WEF	World Economic Forum
WTO	World Trade Organization

Acknowledgements

The chapters in this volume are the product of a series of meetings held under the aegis of *Policy Network*'s working group on the 'European Social Model', convened during the UK Presidency of the EU in June–December 2005. In total, four meetings were held in Rome, Amsterdam, London and Budapest. The seminars – attended by senior policy-makers and experts from the EU and European governments – were chaired by the editors, and we would like to thank all those who attended. These were unique opportunities to debate and share policy ideas, and compare new strategies for social model reform in Europe. We are particularly grateful for the commitment and support of the authors and participants.

We would also like to thank the many people who have helped in the preparation of this book. In the *Policy Network* offices, Matthew Browne and François Lafond have worked tirelessly to organize these meetings, liaising with authors, editing early drafts and coordinating the production of this volume. Without their dedication and professionalism, this book would never have been published. Thanks are also due to Joanne Burton and Johanna Juselius for their whole-hearted support of the project. Jean-François Drolet provided us with excellent research assistance, and was an enormous source of help in editing and amending various drafts of the book. Victor Philip Dadaleh helped to conceive the project, and has been an invaluable source of help and advice. Anne de Sayrah, as always, played an essential part. We would also like to thank Emma Hutchinson and all the staff at Polity Press who have been efficient and helpful throughout.

Anthony Giddens, Patrick Diamond and Roger Liddle

Introduction

Anthony Giddens, Patrick Diamond and Roger Liddle

This book argues for putting the quest for social justice at the heart of a reformed European Union capable of meeting the challenges of the twenty-first century. A new set of policies for promoting social justice is the key to unlocking the reforms that Europe needs to make but has so far found difficult to achieve.

There are many reasons why the 'European social model' (ESM) must reform. Some have very little to do with external pressures. They result, for example, from factors such as increased life expectancy, with its consequences for pensions and social care, or extended life choices for women, with their impact on the sharply differing fortunes of one-earner and two-earner households: these are problems generated from the ESM's own success. Other pressures for change arise from the failure of universalist systems, in education and health in particular, to deliver in practice the equal opportunity and equity that they promise in theory: a reality the social model's defenders often find difficult to recognize. However, the overarching challenge is economic: the question of sustainability in the light of demography, declining growth rates and the challenge of globalization.

In policy circles, arguments like these are more or less universally accepted as justifications for reform. But there are major differences about what reforms are called for. Do such reforms mean discarding the egalitarian and socially protective effects of a social model that its critics always regarded as inefficient and now see the opportunity to weaken? Or is it possible, as we believe, to devise new policies and revise existing ones so that the values of the welfare state can be fulfilled in a manner appropriate to today's world – with the aim of tackling structural inequalities in the interests of the least advantaged?

For the greater part of the post-war era in Europe (with the notable exception of the Thatcher period in the UK), social justice and economic efficiency were seen to march hand in hand. The deterioration in Europe's economic performance has caused this one-time certitude to be questioned. The question is not just one of the affordability of existing social models as a result of low growth rates and adverse demographics. It is whether the functioning of differing social models in itself undermines the possibilities of economic growth and high employment through the limitations they impose on market flexibility. We must be prepared to face the paradox that defence of the existing social models may in crucial respects not serve the cause of social justice, while reforms that superficially challenge traditional conceptions of social justice may actually fulfil the long-term interests of social justice more effectively.

This questioning is made more urgent by the unfolding challenge of globalization and the economic revolution in Asia. For many Europeans, this phenomenon evinces defensiveness, fear and even paranoia. Such reactions are overdone. In many respects, one can interpret current processes of globalization as the latest development in a process of post-war market opening that started in Europe with the Common Market, moving on to the Single Market and EU enlargement, bringing great benefits as a driver of innovation, productivity and higher living standards. The creation of vast new consumer markets in countries once largely mired in poverty presents great economic opportunities for Europe, as well as representing progress towards global social justice.

At the same time, however, globalization means a massive enlargement of the economic competition that Western societies face. It enables mobile capital to tap the potential of a rapidly expanding pool of labour, now becoming part of the world's urbanized workforce, capable for the first time of meeting efficiently global industrial demands, with the ability to join the ranks of the most highly skilled in the next generation.

Globalization is unlikely to be a boon for all sections of European society, particularly those most exposed to cost-efficient competition. Modernizers lose credibility if they present it as such. In reality, the forces of globalization, simply left to work their way through our societies, will increase inequalities and diminish life-chances for the low skilled and disadvantaged. These effects are already visible today. Maybe Europe's citizens instinctively grasp this fact better than their leaders, which is why, politically, reform has proved so difficult. It is too often perceived as being about forcing people to accommodate to a harsher, more competitive world, rather than equipping each and everyone (and not just those with the natural advantages that will help them prosper in this new world) with the up-to-date tools to cope with it.

Commentators often blame Europe's slow progress in achieving reforms, particularly in the core member states of the Eurozone, on the fact that the European social model is inherently protectionist and corporatist and in the hands of vested interests and 'veto players'. We draw a different conclusion. The reason reform has proved so difficult is because such groups have been able to present themselves as defenders of the general interest in resisting any diminution of social rights: indeed, they genuinely have believed this themselves. Advocates of reform have found this opposition difficult to overcome because a convincing social justice case for reform policies has not yet been made.

The contributors to this book argue that to compete, Europe need not adopt neoliberal orthodoxy, though no one should delude themselves that open markets and liberalization are not an essential part of the overall reform package. Europe's common goal should be a developmental, empowering welfare state that tackles the inequalities globalization exacerbates and equips our citizens for the knowledge-based economy.

This is a political challenge first and foremost for the EU's member states. Although some have performed markedly better than others, none can bask in complacency. Also, member states differ in their social and political preferences for redistribution and the weight to be given to the relative roles of state action, individual responsibility and voluntary initiative.

It is generally accepted that there is no such thing as the 'European social model'. It is more accurate, given the range of national diversity, to speak of Europe's social models. Nonetheless, there is sufficient commonality in the values that underpin the social models of the EU countries to label discussion of shared problems as about the 'future of the European social model'. This proposition applies as much to the new member states as the EU(15). The reality in most of the new member states is that they are not low-tax nirvanas, but have expensive, poorly designed welfare states badly in need of radical reform.

Moreover, the member states of the EU share a common economic and political space and are highly interdependent. Eurosceptics may not care to recognize this, but interdependence is a reality. That is why, despite this diversity of national situations and political preferences, the contributors to this book make the case for a stronger EU role than is played at present. While national welfare systems have developed their own dynamic, which in turn has led to their own distinctive problems and reform agendas, the main challenges for the future – demography, technological change, and globalization – are largely common ones. Recent years have seen a growing convergence of approaches in meeting them. Europe's social models should be redesigned on common principles to meet these challenges, while leaving plenty of scope for the exercise of national political preferences.

Most commentators have explained the failure of reform in terms of implementation – problems of political capacity and will. However, we take the view that there are major problems of definition and justification as well. There are different interpretations of 'reform' even among those who accept that it is crucial for the 'supply-side agenda' to be addressed. The present weakness of Europe stems in part from the pursuit of reform from the wrong direction. Belt-tightening in EU member states has been concerned with making welfare systems affordable given lower economic growth – instead of the approach that we favour – economic reforms and market liberalization that make higher levels of welfare and social protection affordable.

For many on the political left, social and economic reforms in Europe became a euphemism for labour market flexibility, wage restraint and reductions in social 'rights' for the working majority. This association with unpalatable 'Thatcherite' remedies has led 'reform' to be characterized as a British 'neoliberal' agenda. We three editors may be British, but this is not the reform agenda we have in mind.

The benefits of the reform medicine of Thatcherism in the UK were at best partial and largely confined to some privatizations and the creation of a service economy (but with too much low pay and too few 'quality' jobs). In the labour market, the powerful were curbed, but the weak were left unprotected. In other areas, the Thatcher governments did active harm to the British economy, weakening its industrial base (beyond the inevitable restructuring of traditional industries and sectors), while under-investing in human capital and infrastructure. A new agenda for Europe should certainly not replicate these failures.

The debate about Europe's future social and economic direction is as relevant to Britain as to other member states. For us reform is not uniquely British, but European; and not 'neoliberal', but progressive. In previous eras of European history – such as the Brandt period in 1970s West Germany and Sweden under Olaf Palme – reform meant more jobs, more welfare and more pensions, thus conferring new social rights on less privileged groups. The badge of reform needs to be reclaimed by progressive modernizers in Europe, as we have set out to do in this book.

In the first chapter of this volume, Anthony Giddens offers an overview of the current state of the debate about the ESM. He looks at the lessons to be learned from the present debate: it is right to put employment first; it is not the case that only low-tax economies can prosper in a world of intensifying competition; labour market flexibility is essential, but it does not mean American-style 'hire and fire'; the knowledge economy is not an empty term – investment in education, university expansion and the diffusion of ICT are crucial elements of welfare state modernization; an ecological perspective needs to be integrated into the debate; the ageing society should be seen as an opportunity; the impact of immigration cannot be ignored; reform of the state and the decentralization and diversification of public services are seen as crucial issues across Europe. On this basis, Giddens draws up a template for reform: a move from passive to active welfare; an emphasis on incentives as well as benefits, obligations as well as rights; a new view of risk; a refashioning, not an abandonment, of the contributory principle; the need to integrate environmental sustainability into a concept of 'positive welfare' and the importance of de-bureaucratized provision.

Most of the core difficulties facing the ESM are not confined to any one particular country, but are structural. Indeed, many of the problems confronting the welfare state – increasingly ageing populations combined with rising expectations of public services – are the product of post-war security and affluence promoted by welfare policy. This is not to say that globalization does not present a formidable challenge.

Chapters 2–6 go on to explore in more depth the context of the current social model debate. John Sutton deconstructs the argument that globalization makes the ESM inoperable. It is not so much low wage competition that poses the biggest challenge to Europe, but the rapid attainment of competitive 'capabilities' by Asian firms that combine high productivity with products that cross a perceived threshold of quality. Their impact was first felt in low-tech labour-intensive sectors like textiles and clothing, and will next affect 'middle-ground' sectors like the motor industry, where high-quality standards are easiest to replicate. But Europe retains an advantage in industries like machine tools, which depend on know-how. Such firms contain specialized in-house capabilities that are difficult to replicate. Their innate strength is their ability to innovate and adapt. Competitive success will, however, increasingly require the flexibility to reallocate resources swiftly and develop new products. Tight employment protection laws can impede this aim. Their impact is felt not so much on the overall level of employment, but by discouraging the job destruction and job creation that an effective European response to globalization makes necessary. The requirement for flexibility does not imply the end of the tax-financed welfare state, only that industrial policies have to be designed to foster capabilities and the flexibility for new companies to grow. Redistributive social policies have to ensure that they do not create disincentives for work and employment creation.

Katinka Barysch debunks a whole series of popular myths about Polish plumbers, the spectre of flat taxes undermining the possibilities of social democratic government, and the export of industrial jobs from the EU(15) to the new member states. There is no evidence of delocalization of jobs on a massive scale: where jobs have moved, it has tended to be within an integrated supply chain and the impact has strengthened the overall competitiveness of European companies. Fears of tax competition attracting jobs from West to East are largely misplaced: corporate taxes in the new member states are low, but the overall tax burden is not, due to high taxes on labour. To regard the new members as exemplars of a low-tax nirvana is quite false: their problems of low labour market inactivity and expensive welfare burdens are in many cases more severe than in the older EU states. However, the fact that employers can threaten to move jobs to the East may well have strengthened their hand in restraining wages and pushing through corporate restructuring. In addition, the free movement of labour when fully permissible in 2011 may cause problems in member states with less flexible labour markets.

Simon Commander, Axel Heitmueller and Laura Tyson examine the evidence on the impact of immigration and offshoring, making use primarily of US research. In the States there is little evidence that immigration has led to the displacement of jobs previously held by native workers, though it has had some small impact in depressing wage levels. This impact on wages is felt across the whole occupational structure, even when one considers solely the impact of migrant professionals. Offshoring is not a new phenomenon, but the practice has spread from manufacturing to business services, where some studies suggest that the potential cost savings are huge, cutting costs by an average of 30 per cent. This situation offers clear benefits to the global competitiveness of American and European firms: it may, but not necessarily, strengthen the possibilities of generating a virtuous circle of higher profits and investment in the home location. But these benefits go proportionately more to shareholders than to workers.

The degree to which workers suffer losses as a result of outsourcing is conditioned by the ability with which displaced workers can get new jobs quickly at equivalent rates of pay. In the US, the evidence suggests that more than a third do not do so: in Europe, with less flexible labour markets, the figure is likely to be higher. The chapter discusses a range of public policies that could mitigate these adverse social impacts.

René Cuperus paints a vivid and controversial picture of the current social discontents that led to the Dutch 'no' to the Constitutional Treaty. He sets out four principal explanations: disenchantment with the post-war idea of emancipation that each succeeding generation will enjoy a better life; alienation from the European project, which is now seen as a threat to national identities; problems of integration in increasingly multi-ethnic societies; and loss of confidence in our political system. The European elite's discourse on reform, which Cuperus graphically labels 'the machismo of change', is alienating large sections of the European electorate. This is why, in his view, the German Federal elections in September 2005 produced an impasse between adaptation and conservation, unease and change; and an inability on the part of the parties to recognize, or at least acknowledge, that the Rhineland model is dead. Similarly, in France the division over the Constitution was between those who welcome the changes now happening and those who fear them. Cuperus rejects the view that the nation-state is dead; rather, the future of the social model in Europe depends on a reassertion of the values of solidarity at nation-state level based on an open, hospitable, non-xenophobic definition of national identity – what he calls 'a greater Us'.

Cuperus's chapter is a powerful reminder yet again that the challenges facing the welfare states of Europe not only come from without – international competition limiting the redistributive scope and decommodifying power of national welfare states. As Anton Hemerijck outlines, existing systems of social protection are being overstretched, with labour markets and household structures weakened as the traditional providers of welfare. The ability of politicians and policymakers to recast welfare states is also constrained by nationally negotiated social policy commitments in areas such as unemployment and pensions. Welfare reform is a political process that involves the framing of policy problems and solutions by *national* political actors. Reforms are not the product of irresistible global forces, but the result of a lengthy process of negotiation between politicians, governments and the social partners. The European social model will mainly be transformed through processes that are *internal* to the nation-state, though the EU can provide incentives for reform.

Chapters 7–12 address the question, 'What direction should reform of the European social model now take?' It is clear that no one country can be taken as a model for others. In the last 15 years, Germany, Japan and America have all at different periods been held up as models for EU member states to emulate, until major flaws subsequently emerged.

The contributors to this book argue for hybrid social models. Karl Aiginger and Alois Guger compare the successes and failures of the US and European welfare systems. Their work clearly indicates that the Nordic countries have proved to be the most successful in adapting to changing conditions over the years and that there are important lessons to be learned from them. They have preserved the main elements of the welfare state while implementing reforms aimed at increasing efficiency and flexibility, as well as improving incentives and keeping private costs in line with productivity and public expenditure. Aiginger and Guger examine the factors that have created economic dynamism in the last decade and demonstrate that the Nordics have matched the US in performance in key areas such as investment in research and the diffusion of ICT, and outclassed the United States and other European countries on indicators of social inclusion such as employment rates, child poverty and inequality. They do not argue that every EU country should aim for convergence with Scandinavia. National circumstances, history and political choice still matter a good deal in determining new welfare state architecture, but there are common principles that might be widely applicable, such as the adoption of a life-course 'social investment' model.

As Jane Jenson argues, a life-course approach is essential to achieving greater gender equality in the European welfare state. This process requires new social policy instruments. According to Jenson, ensuring income security means confronting a rapidly changing labour market: more attention must be paid to the design of childcare services and parental leave provisions, so that work and family can be better reconciled. Both the EU and its member states must also commit themselves to fighting discrimination and labour force segregation. Discussion of fertility rates in Europe needs to acknowledge parental concerns about economic security, since adequate earnings are as important as the provision of childcare or housing. Finally, as social care becomes more prominent in ageing societies, steps be taken to ensure that household services provide quality jobs for the women who will in the main fill them.

Patrick Diamond argues that traditional welfare states focused on measures to rectify damage to individuals and vulnerable groups. This focus on aftercare needs to be revised today. An active welfare state should adopt preventative measures targeted at women, younger families and children to promote their future opportunities, rather than offer only compensation for past disadvantage. Such measures could include an EU childcare guarantee to lighten the burden of unpaid care and attack the roots of child poverty; learning accounts, transitional job insurance and preventative basic skills training to guard against long-term unemployment; and tax deductions that lighten the load of raising a family. These priorities stem from a refashioned conception of social justice as Diamond terms it, strengthening the individual's capacity for autonomy and self-esteem over the life-course.

Luc Soete suggests that European policy-makers have paid insufficient attention to the nature of knowledge accumulation and knowledge economy labour markets. These offer the prospect of increasing returns, in contrast to labour and capital inputs which in classical economic models are both subject to diminishing returns. Policy-makers have failed to analyse how processes of knowledge accumulation have changed in the last generation from the industrial R&D model of the post-war era to a more endogenous process. With knowledge globally available, ICT as a ready means of codifying it and the increased potential for companies to be successful innovators without conducting their own original research, the nature of knowledge production has changed. This causes Soete to question the logic of traditional EU-level technology programmes and their emphasis on intellectual property protection. The European policy approach should be less Eurocentric and more supportive of open access to knowledge in fields like energy, sustainability, health and security. The EU's 3 per cent R&D target is not a sensible one, because achieving it largely depends on the private sector: rather, Europe should set a broader target for national public expenditures on 'knowledge'. Soete also argues that the spread of knowledge work requires a rethinking of traditional social protection where public policy explicitly acknowledges a difference between those for whom work is oppressive and those for whom it is a pleasure. For the latter section of the labour market, the premium that European social protection places on 'security' puts the EU at an unnecessary competitive disadvantage.

Måns Lönnroth reviews the evidence on the relationship between a strong environmental policy and economic growth. In his view Europe has developed a distinctive environmental model which is a product of the Single Market, based on the universalization through regulation of best available technologies. This model is less subject to economic cost-benefit analysis than in the more contested regulatory environment of the United States. Nevertheless there is little evidence that European environmental policy has damaged competitiveness and some research suggests it may even have helped it. However, the challenge of climate change is a different matter. If Europe continues to offer a global lead, a tightening-up of the emissions-trading regime in future would lead to some form of industrial crunch. In these circumstances a backward-looking social model that could not embrace environmental restructuring could be a major problem. At present, there is lack of bold and original integrative thinking connecting the economic, social and environmental dimensions of devlopment.

Patrick Weil points to Europe's need to be more accepting of large-scale immigration if Europe's population is not to suffer a sharp decline over the next half century. On present demographic trends, France would need an additional 5.5 million immigrants to maintain its present population in 2050, Germany more than 25 million and Italy 19.5 million. The issue for Europe therefore should not be framed in terms of how best to control immigration, but how to regulate it. Common policies will be needed even though, as the above figures demonstrate, national circumstances and the ability successfully to absorb migrants will vary between member states. Weil's policy recommendations focus on the principle of recirculation. A more liberal regime of visas and work permits should enable migrants to move to and fro between their home country and Europe. This would be both pro-development and reduce illegal immigration. For example, immigration policies at present make it difficult for overseas graduates trained in Europe to have permanent rights to work in Europe. But as part of a development programme, health services could offer flexible contracts enabling trained personnel to return home for fixed periods and help the cause of development in their own country, without losing their opportunity to work again in the EU.

In his contribution, Loukas Tsoukalis poses the question, 'Can Europe deliver?' in the context of the enlargement to 25 member states. Whereas past enlargements led to a consolidation of the European social model, the present enlargement may prove more difficult. Previous enlargements were aided by generous structural funds. The current new member states are poorer, and there is widespread evidence of reform fatigue after the efforts of post-Communist transition. This situation may lead to populism, a turning away from European integration and a rejection of further reforms. To stabilize Europe's periphery, the EU needs a centre that functions. At present, that centre is something of a battleground between old-style integrationists and new-style protectionists, on the one hand, and globalization missionaries and market fundamentalists, on the other. A balance has to be struck – but how and where is unclear. The EU must serve as a catalyst and facilitator, but all too often national politicians undermine its potential by treating it as a scapegoat.

Maurizio Ferrera contrasts the logic of 'opening' of European integration, geared towards the expansion of individual options and choices, with the logic of 'closure' which underpins national systems of solidarities and redistribution. For a long time these two logics did not interfere with one another. But the last decade has witnessed the emergence of increasing strains: competition rules have extended their reach into public services and the four freedoms have prompted a legal restructuring of social rights (for example, in the areas of equal pay and discrimination at work, or the entitlement to reimbursable health treatment in any member state). The 'separate tracks' solution can no longer be sustained and a new balance must be found between the 'opening' agenda (economic reforms, more market integration and liberalization) and traditional welfare state objectives. In Ferrera's view these developments all imply the creation of a new regulatory space at EU level that systematically addresses social issues.

Roger Liddle calls for a common social justice policy for Europe. Globalization does not require Europe to dilute social justice, but it will increase inequalities and thereby force a Europe serious about its social justice commitments to make radical reforms. There are successful examples of highly developed social models in Europe which, through a combination of social investment, market openness and activating welfare, have shown a capacity to reform. Proponents of social justice must not allow themselves to become backward-looking defenders of an untenable status quo: they should be reformers determined to create developmental empowering welfare states for the new era. While responsibility for reforms is primarily national, the EU should play an important enabling role. A social justice roadmap should be defined at EU level for member states to follow and, as part of a strengthened process of coordination (building on the national reform programmes that are part of the relaunched Lisbon strategy), the Commission should produce authoritative assessments of member state progress. The roadmap should include benchmarks for improving the 'quality' of national public spending. At the same time the Commission's review of the EU budget, planned for 2008, should look at the feasibility of incentives for reform and the potential for new emblematic EU programmes in key fields such as childcare, scholarships to widen access to higher education, and retraining and adjustment allowances for workers affected by restructuring in mid-life.

Since 1989, much in the European Union has changed, including the very definition of 'Europe' itself. The divisions between East and West have dissolved. The EU has responded actively to these changes, not only by carrying through an ambitious programme of enlargement, but also in pushing ahead with the Single Market and the single currency. Many assumed these projects would usher in a new era of economic dynamism: they would enable 'old' Europe to recover the spectacular economic success it enjoyed in the third quarter of the twentieth century which saw the creation of mass consumer societies and highly developed welfare states. Instead, in 'core' Europe particularly, growth has languished and unemployment has remained persistently high. Perhaps as a result, in their impact on public opinion, enlargement, the Euro and the Single Market, instead of justifying themselves by the fact that they delivered on prosperity, have in some member states become symbols of an increasingly remote and unaccountable Europe.

Those who voted 'no' in the constitutional referenda in France and the Netherlands in May and June 2005 were registering deep worries about Europe's economic and social future – about their own jobs, living standards and security in retirement. Some feared the loss of national sovereignty and had become disillusioned with the capacity of electoral politics to make a difference. Others feared a Brussels-driven market-based agenda, which in their eyes had become the enemy of ordinary people's aspirations.

For the previous decade the 'future of Europe' debate had focused – with tunnel vision – on the efficiency, legitimacy and accountability of EU decision-making. How should EU institutions be reformed in response to the looming reality of enlargement, the deepening of the Single Market, the coming of the Euro, the ambition for a stronger EU foreign policy externally, and an area of 'freedom, justice and security' internally? Three times, intergovernmental conferences – at Amsterdam, Nice and then the Constitutional Treaty – had sought to settle these institutional debates, and three times the results ended in failure. The shock to the EU's leaders has been profound and has forced a consideration of its 'context': the economic and social direction of Europe. In a welcome break with the past decade, these issues are now seen as central to the 'future of Europe' debate.

For all the differences in national starting points, the contributions in this book point towards a convergent agenda of social and economic reform in the European Union, in response to the common internal and external challenges that all Europe faces. Some European countries are well on the way to developing this agenda: in others, they are to a greater or lesser extent feeling their way towards it.

Because the EU countries are undergoing significant policy convergence, it makes sense to incentivize and deepen the spread of best practice at the national level. This book aims to analyse the issues that this agenda must address, help give it concrete shape and substance, and show how the European Union that might speed the implementation of reforms by member states. Global Europe can be a social Europe.

I

A Social Model for Europe?

Anthony Giddens

Europe's welfare system is often regarded as the jewel in the crown – perhaps the main feature that gives the European societies their special quality. In May 2003 two of Europe's most distinguished intellectuals, Jürgen Habermas and Jacques Derrida, wrote a public letter about the future of European identity in the wake of the Iraq war. The welfare state's 'guarantees of social security', 'Europeans' trust in the civilizing power of the state' and its capacity to 'correct "market failures"' rang true.[1] Most other observers sympathetic to the European Union project today would agree. The 'European social model' (ESM) is, or has become, a fundamental part of what Europe stands for.

Cue in 'ESM' in Google and 11,200,000 items come up! Such profusion perhaps reflects the fact that the ESM, like so much else about the EU, is essentially a contested notion. In spite of the fact that it is so central, the idea is somewhat elusive when we try to pin it down with any precision. Moreover, what is said to be so specifically European turns out to be shared by other non-European states.

The ESM, it has been said, is not only European, not wholly social and not a model.[2] If it means having effective welfare institutions and limiting inequality, then some other industrial countries are more European than some states in Europe. For instance, Australia and Canada surpass Portugal and Greece, not to mention most of the new EU member states after enlargement. The ESM is not purely social, since, however it is defined, it depends fundamentally upon economic prosperity and redistribution. It is not a single model, because there are big divergences between European countries in terms of their welfare systems, levels of inequality and so forth.

Hence there are many different definitions of the ESM around, although they all home in on the welfare state. Daniel Vaughan-Whitehead, for example, lists no fewer than 15 components of the ESM.[3] We should probably conclude that the ESM is not a unitary concept, but a mixture of values, accomplishments and aspirations, varying in form and degree of realization among European states. My list would be:

- a developed and interventionist state, as measured in terms of level of GDP taken up by taxation;
- free and compulsory education up to final secondary school level;
- a robust welfare system that provides effective social protection to some considerable degree for all citizens, but especially for those most in need;
- the limitation, or containment, of economic and other forms of inequality.

A key role in sustaining these institutions is played by the 'social partners', the unions and other agencies promoting workers' rights. Each trait has to go along with expanding overall economic prosperity and job creation.

Underlying the ESM is a general set of values: sharing risk widely across society; containing the inequalities that might threaten social solidarity; protecting the most vulnerable through active social intervention; cultivating consultation rather than confrontation in industry; and providing a rich framework of social and economic citizenship rights for the population as a whole.

The past and the future

It is agreed by more or less everyone, supporters and opponents alike, that the ESM is currently under great strain, or even failing. We should begin, however, by putting this situation into context. Some speak of the 1960s and 1970s as a 'Golden Age' of the welfare state, when there was good economic growth, low unemployment, social protection for all – and when citizens were able to feel much more secure than they do today. From this perspective, the ESM has been 'attacked' by external forces, particularly those associated with liberalization, and progressively weakened or partly dismantled.

The reality is more complex. For member states such as Spain, Portugal, Greece and most later entrants to the European Union, there was no Golden Age at all, since welfare provisions were weak and inadequate. Even in those nations with advanced welfare systems, everything was far from golden in the Golden Age. The era was dominated by mass production and bureaucratic hierarchies, where management styles were often autocratic and many workers were in assembly-line jobs. At that period few women were able to work if they wanted to. Only a tiny proportion of young people entered further or higher education. The range of health services offered was far below those available now. Older people were put out to pasture by a rigid retirement age. The state generally treated its clients as passive subjects rather than as active citizens. Some of the changes in welfare systems over the past 30 years have been aimed at correcting these deficiencies and hence have been both progressive and necessary.

The world, of course, has shifted massively since the 'Golden Age'. The ESM, and the EU itself, were in some large part products of a bipolar world. The 'mixed economy' and the Keynesian welfare state served to distinguish between Western Europe and American market liberalism on the one hand and state-centred Soviet Communism on the other. The fall of the Berlin Wall – Europe's 9/11[4] – more or less completely changed the nature of the EU, giving rise to identity problems that still remain unresolved – and indeed were reflected in the refusal of the proposed EU constitution by the people of France and the Netherlands.

The demise of Keynesianism in the West, and the collapse of Soviet Communism, were brought about by much the same trends – intensifying globalization, the rise of a worldwide information order, the shrinking of manufacture (and its transfer to less developed countries), coupled to the rise of new forms of individualism and consumer power. These are not changes that came and went; their impact continues today.

The term 'European social model' is in fact not long-standing. It started to be used only from about the early 1980s onwards, although 'social Europe' is older. It was introduced precisely at the time when free-market thinking came into the ascendant. The concept of the ESM was part of an attempt to redefine the distinctiveness of the 'European approach' in contrast to these new orthodoxies.

Fundamental though the trends mentioned above are, it is essential to recognize that the problems of the ESM today don't just stem from changes happening in the global environment. Some of the core difficulties are internal, or at most only loosely connected with wider transformations in the wider world. They include primarily demographic changes, especially the ageing population, the associated issue of pensions and the sharp decline in birth rates; changes in family structure, with many more one-parent families than before, and more women and children living in poverty; and high levels of unemployment coming in some part from unreformed labour markets.

A few commentators tend to underplay the difficulties faced by Europe, especially when the EU(15) is compared with the United States.[5] Europeans, they say, have made a lifestyle choice: they have traded in a certain level of possible growth for more leisure than is enjoyed by most Americans; productivity in some EU countries rivals that of the US; precisely because of Europe's stronger welfare systems, there are fewer working poor in the EU states than in the US. But these ideas are not convincing, as recent work has demonstrated.[6] Average growth in the EU(15) has declined in relative terms year on year since the 1980s. GDP per head has not risen beyond 70 per cent of the US level over that period. Not only has the US had higher growth, it has also had greater macroeconomic stability over that time. About a third of the contrast in per capita GDP with the US comes from lower average productivity of labour, a third from shorter working hours and a third from a lower employment rate. However, none of these comes purely from choice, and all affect the sustainability of the ESM. There are 20 million unemployed and 93 million economically inactive people in the EU, a far higher rate than in the US. The employment rate of older workers (over 55) is 40 per cent in the EU, compared to 60 per cent in the US and 62 per cent in Japan.

Some of these differences certainly do come from a 'preference for leisure' in Europe, and a better balance between home and work than is found in the US. But there are very many in Europe, including many young people – and over 55s – who want to work but can't. This comment also applies to immigrants. The US has done a much better job of integrating immigrants into its labour market than have the EU countries. The jobless rate of non-nationals in the EU in 2002 was more than twice the rate for nationals. In the US the two rates are almost the same. Enlargement has brought with it a series of issues that are very remote from a 'preference for leisure'. It has increased the EU population by 20 per cent, but GDP by only 5 per cent. Problems of inequality and cohesion are heightened, both across the EU as a whole and within the member states.

There is therefore good reason to support the conclusion that over recent years 'the sustainability of the "European Model" has become more and more questionable'.[7] Achieving higher average levels of economic growth and of job creation must be placed at the forefront, since the current combination of low growth and higher public expenditure cannot continue.

European variations

Some EU states, however, have fared considerably better than others. A minority of nations, especially the Nordic countries (including the non-EU nations Norway and Iceland), the Netherlands, Austria and the UK, have performed relatively well. Apart from UK, they are all small, suggesting that small countries find it easier to change than larger ones – although in point of fact in none of them has change been straightforward. However that may be, all have sustained their welfare institutions in robust condition. The Nordic countries have simultaneously the most developed form of the ESM and the highest rates of employment. It is significant that the countries that have prospered most have also been the most reformist – in respect to welfare and pensions, education, labour markets and use of ICT. The Nordic countries comfortably outrank the US on quality of life indicators, as well as in terms of ecological modernization.

The picture is different in the Central European and Mediterranean states. Germany and Italy have low growth rates, combined with elevated levels of unemployment and underemployment. France has a better growth record in recent years, but has high unemployment, including much youth and long-term unemployment. In these countries a combination of tight labour market regulation and union influence creates insider/outsider labour markets. Those who have jobs may prosper, but those on the outside do much less well. There are high rates of long-term unemployment and many find refuge in secondary labour markets that escape regulation altogether.

Some apologists for Europe's economic performance have argued that Germany is the EU's fundamental 'problem'. Take Germany out of the economic statistics and the EU does almost as well as the US – and Germany has had to struggle with difficulties of reunification.[8] Germany does indeed face some very difficult issues. In mid-2005 its growth rate was virtually zero. Unemployment stood at over 11 per cent (20 per cent in East Germany). Because it is so large, what happens in the German economy is very important for the rest of Europe. But the argument that Germany's troubles alone explain Europe's wider economic woes is demonstrably incorrect. Not only Germany, but France, Italy and to some extent Spain and Greece (and now some of the new member states) are also where Europe's basic problems of unemployment and low growth are centred.

Karl Aiginger (see chapter 7 in this volume) has made a systematic comparison between best-performing European states over the period from the early 1990s to the present day – Denmark, Finland and

Sweden – and the three 'under-performers', Germany, France and Italy.[9] He also compares both categories with the United States. Welfare benefits are more extensive in the three best-performing countries than in France, Germany or Italy, and far more wide-ranging than in the US. Yet the three leading European states are just as competitive and dynamic as the US. GDP growth over the period has been virtually the same as America's. At over 70 per cent, their average employment ratio is behind that of the US, but massively ahead of the European under-performers (61.9 per cent). Public debt is well below both that of America and the three larger European countries.

It has been observed that 'the ESM is little discussed in the new EU member states'.[10] Most have been struggling to reform the welfare systems inherited from their Communist past. They have found the going hard. Unemployment in Slovakia, for instance, stands at 17 per cent. The proportion of those living under the poverty line has increased sharply and levels of education and health care are low. Unemployment in Poland in 2003 stood at 17.9 per cent. It was no less than 39.5 per cent for those under the age of 25. Ireland itself ranks near the bottom of EU states in terms of its high levels of inequality. Yet the future of the ESM is actually a very relevant question to the new member countries, since they will have to seek to radicalize their reforms, and to build new welfare systems as they become more wealthy. It is in their interest to learn from best practice as much as it is for more mature EU states.[11]

Policy controversies

There is intense debate among policy specialists about how far in European welfare systems there is 'path-dependency', inhibiting mutual learning. Following the work of Gøsta Esping-Andersen, it is widely accepted that there are three or four main types of 'welfare capitalism' in Europe.[12] These are the Nordic type, based upon high taxation and extensive job opportunities provided within the welfare state itself; the Central European type (Germany, France), based mainly on payroll contributions; and the Anglo-Saxon type, which supposedly is a more 'residual' form of welfare system, having a lower taxation base and using more targeted policies. The fourth type, alongside the three Esping-Andersen originally recognized, is the Mediterranean one (Italy, Spain, Portugal, Greece), which also has a fairly low tax base and depends heavily upon provision from the family.[13]

Esping-Andersen has made much of the 'service economy trilemma' – originally formulated by Torben Iversen and Anne Wren[14] – that limits the degree to which policies can be applied across these different types. The idea is that it is impossible, in a modern service economy, simultaneously to have balanced budgets, low levels of income inequality and high levels of employment. Two of these goals can be successfully pursued by governments at any one time, but not all three. The different types of system are distinguished partly because they have chosen varying combinations.

In the Nordic countries, for instance, the welfare state acts as employer, providing an expanding number of public sector service jobs. Taxation has to be very high and puts a continual strain on borrowing levels. The Anglo-Saxon countries, such as the UK, have generated large numbers of private sector jobs, and have maintained fiscal discipline, but are marked by high levels of poverty. In the Central European type, such as Germany or France, by contrast, there is a commitment to limiting inequality and (at least until recently) to budgetary constraint. However, these countries are dogged by low levels of job growth.

But how far in fact does path-dependency operate? Is the 'trilemma' real? Hemerijck and his colleagues have argued persuasively that the empirical evidence for all of this is 'surprisingly shaky'.[15] The recent history of Scandinavia suggests that it is in fact possible to have sound public finances, low inequality and high levels of employment. Per contra, it also seems possible to have only one. Germany, for example, now has high levels of unemployment and a burgeoning public debt. Moreover, the various 'types' are not very clear-cut. The Nordic states differ quite widely from one another, for example. It is not obvious that Germany and France belong to a single type. The UK is supposed to be a 'residual' welfare state, but its net taxation levels are now about the same as Germany's. In the shape of the NHS, it has the most 'socialized' system of medicine in Europe.[16] Hemerijck has concluded that the welfare states that have adapted best to changing conditions have created 'hybrid models', borrowed in some part from elsewhere. It is a case I find convincing, and I shall suggest below that a great deal of mutual learning is possible.

Lisbon and after

Unlike other major achievements of the European Union, such as the Single Market, the single currency and enlargement, the ESM has been only minimally shaped by the EU itself. The welfare state was built by nations, not by international collaboration. Some of the member countries with the most established welfare institutions signed up to the EU only relatively late on. Given the grip that member states have on social policy most real change will have to come from within nations.

We don't lack for reports suggesting what should be done to get the under-performing parts of Europe back on their feet again, and generally to make the EU states more competitive. They stretch back well before the proclamation of the Lisbon Agenda in 2000. There is a good deal of unanimity on policies to be followed. André Sapir's six points would be agreed upon by many: (1) make the Single Market more dynamic; (2) boost investment in knowledge; (3) improve EU macroeconomic policy; (4) reform policies for convergence and restructuring; (5) achieve more efficiency in regulation; (6) reform the EU budget, cutting back on agricultural spending and deploying the resources elsewhere.[17]

The Single Market has certainly benefited Europe. It is estimated that EU GDP in 2002 was 1.8 per cent higher than it would have been without the progress that has been made. However, the Lisbon Agenda has proved much harder to implement, and the ambition of making Europe the most competitive knowledge-based economy in the world by 2010 has come to seem remote indeed. The EU countries are supposed to reach an average employment ratio of 70 per cent by that date, but at the moment the target looks unrealizable. There are still states where the level of employment is below 60 per cent of the available labour force, including Belgium (59.6 per cent), Greece (57.8 per cent), Italy (56 per cent), Hungary 57 per cent and Poland (51.2 per cent).[18]

There are clear tensions between the Single Market and the ESM, as many authors have noted – and which come to be centred upon the Services Directive, which seeks to deregulate and increase competition within services across Europe. The Services Directive is the focus of some of the most bitter controversies about the future direction of Europe. For those in favour, it is an essential part of the drive to cope with the EU's problems of unemployment and underemployment. The Directive will create an estimated 600,000 new net jobs in the EU(15) alone. The number might in fact prove to be much higher. It is usually assumed that only a small proportion of services can be delivered 'at distance'. But, as the development of outsourcing from Asia shows, because of the impact of new technologies this assumption is less valid than it was. Similar processes of outsourcing could happen between the EU countries – probably with positive implications for competition and job creation overall.

For those opposed to, or worried about, the Services Directive, it could have largely harmful consequences. The Commission insists that core public services will be protected, but for critics the guarantees offered are inadequate. To those same critics, the Directive also signals the triumph of a market-based Europe over social Europe. For it is all about deregulation and competition. What has happened to the core European values of equity and solidarity? Won't the Directive simply produce greater inequality and economic insecurity?

Debate about the ESM has a special significance in this context. For it could be argued that although the Lisbon Agenda, Sapir report, Kok report and other similar contributions all talk about the ESM, social exclusion and so forth, they have little to say about them in a direct way. They lack a systematic discussion of how the innovations they propose can be reconciled with social justice. One could even say that this missing dimension is part of the reason why their prescriptions have been so hard to realize.[19]

Lessons to be learned

With these difficulties in mind, let us set out what the experience of the past few years in Europe shows us about combining competitiveness and social justice. We should be cautious about success stories of today – they may turn out to be the failures of tomorrow. But they supply our best guesses for the moment. As given here, the points are schematic – each could be developed in far more detail. And the devil, one should remember, is always in the detail.

Growth and jobs

It is right to put growth and jobs at the forefront. A high level of employment, above a decent minimum wage, is desirable for more than one reason. The greater the proportion of people in jobs, the more money is available – other things being equal – to spend on social investment and social protection. Having a job is also the best route out of poverty. The Lisbon aim of getting an average of 70 per cent or more of the workforce into jobs is not in principle unrealistic. But all depends on the will to reform in those countries where the employment ratio is well below this figure.

Many factors, of course, go into creating more net jobs. However, it cannot be accidental that all the countries that have employment ratios of over 70 per cent in Europe have active labour market policies. Such policies provide training for workers who are unemployed or threatened by unemployment and also try actively to match up workers with job vacancies. They were first of all introduced in Sweden many years ago, but since have spread quite widely. They are not all of a piece. The most effective combine social partnership and universal access to benefits that provide for retraining and resettlement – 'flexicurity'.

The Danish example is widely quoted, even if some have expressed doubts about how far it could be instituted elsewhere.[20] However, many in societies with high unemployment levels are now expressing interest in such policies, including political leaders. Agenda 2010 in Germany is a prime example, although of course it has proved politically extremely difficult to implement.

Taxation and GDP

Those on the right side of the political spectrum argue that only low-tax economies can prosper in a world of intensifying competition. Yet the evidence to the contrary seems unequivocal. There is no direct relationship between taxation as a proportion of GDP and either economic growth or job creation. There probably is an upper limit, as is indicated by the case of Sweden, which has for some while had the highest tax rate among the industrial countries, but saw its level of income per head slip markedly in relative terms. But more important than the size of the state is how effective the state institutions are and the nature of economic and social policies pursued.

Labour market flexibility

Flexibility in labour markets is an essential part of the policy framework of the successful states. It does not mean American-style hire and fire. In an era of accelerating technological change, however, 'employability' – being willing and able to move occupations – becomes of prime importance. 'Moving on', however, sometimes has to happen within the same job, because of the importance of technological change. It has been estimated that in the EU(15) economies, 80 per cent of the technology in use over the period 1995–2005 is less than ten years old. However, 80 per cent of the workforce was trained more than ten years ago.

Flexibility has a bad name, especially among some on the left. For them it means sacrificing the needs of the workforce to the demands of capitalistic competition. But the nature of labour market regulation is at least as important as its extent. Many labour rights can and should remain. They include rights of representation and consultation, the regulation of working conditions, laws against discrimination and so forth. Ireland has enjoyed its phenomenal growth while implementing all relevant EU labour legislation of this sort.[21]

Many employees in fact want flexible working, and part-time work, in order to accommodate to family demands. Flexibility also meshes to a considerable degree with wider trends in everyday life in modern societies. Most citizens are accustomed to a much wider range of lifestyle choices than a generation ago, including, if it is feasible for them, when, where and what work to do.

Lovely jobs and lousy jobs

The much-touted knowledge economy is not just an empty term, an invention of the Lisbon Agenda that lost its relevance when the dot.com bubble collapsed – although it should more accurately be called a knowledge and service economy. Only 17 per cent of the labour force on average in the EU(15) countries now work in manufacturing, and that proportion is still falling. To put it the other way around, over 80 per cent of people have now to get their living from knowledge-based or service jobs.

Full employment is possible in the knowledge economy – it has been attained in some of the better-performing European economies mentioned above.[22] But there is a price to be paid. More than two-thirds of the jobs created in the knowledge economy are skilled. They are so-called 'lovely jobs' – and they are becoming more plentiful. Over the period 1995–2004, the proportion of jobs in the EU(15) needing advanced qualifications went up from 20 to 24 per cent.

Low-skilled jobs – 'lousy jobs' - fell from 34 to 25 per cent. But a lot of people must still work in such jobs – serving in shops, supermarkets, petrol stations or coffee shops. The minimum wage cannot be set so high as to exclude the lousy jobs, or we also lose the lovely jobs that come with them. We have to try to ensure that it is set at the right level so that there are no working poor; and to make sure that as far as possible people don't get stuck in those jobs.

ICT

Investment in education, the expansion of universities, the diffusion of ICT are crucial parts of the modernization of the ESM. Finland is an interesting example of a society in the vanguard of ICT and also with a strong welfare system. As Manuel Castells has pointed out, the country shows that the thesis that a high-tech economy must be modelled after Silicon Valley – in a deregulated environment – is mistaken.[23] Finland has a greater degree of IT penetration than the US. Its growth rate in 1996–2000 was 5.1 per cent. It also ranks near the top of all industrial countries in terms of measures of social justice and has a high tax base. Finland, Castells concludes, offers hope for others. Only three generations ago, Finland was a very poor, heavily rural society.

Social justice

It is often said the 'our societies are becoming more unequal', but in many respects this is not the case. The position of women, gays and the disabled, for instance, has improved almost everywhere over the past 30 years. Income inequality has grown in most industrial countries over that period, but there are signs this process is now levelling off. Some societies have managed to stay remarkably egalitarian, with the Nordic countries once more being in the lead.

We can and must defend values of equality and inclusiveness. We do not all have to become Scandinavians in order to do so, at least if this means having highly elevated tax rates. The superiority of the Nordic countries in terms of their low levels of inequality does not come primarily from redistribution through taxes and transfers.[24] The main explanation is their superior investment in human capital. The distribution of poverty risk directly matches levels of education if we use the fourfold typology of welfare states. The Nordic and Continental welfare states have the largest proportion of the population aged 25–64 with at least upper secondary education (75 per cent and 67 per cent respectively). The Anglo-Saxon and Mediterranean types have the smallest (60 per cent and 39 per cent).

We have to invest heavily in early years education since so many capabilities are laid down then. Investment in early education and childcare is a key element in reducing levels of child poverty.

Ecological modernization

Ecological issues must be brought much more to the forefront than in the past. The best way to do so is through the theme of ecological modernization, originally pioneered by the German Greens in the 1980s. The idea was developed in conscious opposition to the 'limits to growth' arguments coming from an earlier generation of ecological thinking. Ecological modernization means seeking wherever possible to find environmental innovations that are compatible with economic growth. These can involve green technologies and the use of market-based and tax-based incentives for consumers, companies and other agencies to become more environment-friendly in their actions.

However, ecological policy can never be only technological or economic – it also has to be political. Like other types of reform, ecological modernization impinges on the interests of many different groups, including nations. The difficulties involved in producing an international consensus on the Kyoto protocol provides an obvious case in point.

Immigration

Immigration has become one of the hottest of hot topics across Europe, far too complex to discuss in any detail here. As societies become multi-cultural, do they inevitably lose an overall sense of social solidarity? Will the majority be prepared to support policies aimed at helping those who are newcomers and culturally different? Comparative studies seem to suggest a tentative 'yes' to this question, as long as certain conditions are in place.[25] These include ensuring that immigrants cover all skill levels – that they are not predominantly unskilled; that access to full welfare benefits is deferred; and that concrete steps are taken to ensure that immigrants accept overall norms of the host culture.

The term 'immigrant', of course, covers a multitude of differences. There are immigrants from 150 different countries living in the UK, for example. Great variations can exist among those coming from the same country, depending upon differences in socioeconomic background, ethnicity, culture and other factors. Some migrants or minorities fare much better than others. Thus in Britain, first- or second-generation immigrants from Pakistan or Bangladesh on average earn far less than the indigenous population. Indians, by contrast, earn more on average than native-born whites.

Older people

The ageing population should be seen as an opportunity, not just as another 'problem'. We know what has to happen – the difficulties in most countries depend upon mustering the political will to make the changes. We have to invest more in children. We have to persuade younger people to save more. The main cause of the ageing society is not that people on average are living longer – although they are – it is the low birth rate. The state has to provide people with incentives to have more children, and make sure the right type of welfare measures are in place.

No matter what innovations are made to help or force people to save, there is only one main way to solve the issue of unaffordable pensions commitments. We have to persuade or motivate older people to stay in work longer. Such a goal is surely not just a negative one. We have to contest ageism both inside and outside the workplace. If it means people over 55, or over 65, 'old age' is no longer the incapacitating factor it once was.

Public services

Continuing reform of the state itself, and of public services, is just as important to the future of the ESM as any of the factors noted above. Where needed, decentralization and diversification are the order of the day. Plainly there has to be a balance between these and integration. The relations of national states within the EU, with power moving both upwards and downwards, are a core example, but nevertheless only one example, of the inevitability of multilayered governance today. Of course, the issue of the privatization of state services, or putting them more in the hands of not-for-profit agencies, continues to be a matter of widespread controversy. Public services should become just as responsive (in some ways, more responsive) to the needs of those they serve as commercial organizations are.

Some have suggested Keynesian solutions both for reform of the ESM and for job-generation in Europe. François Hollande has proposed a strengthening of economic government in Europe, including persuading the European Central Bank to add job creation to its concern for managing the stability of prices.[26] Business taxes should be standardized across Europe and programmes of 'great works', in transport, communications and energy, should be launched on a European level, financed through borrowing.

But why should an approach that has failed everywhere at a national level suddenly work at a transnational one? Some kinds of new infrastructural projects for Europe may very well be worth considering, particularly in the area of ICT, but not solely or even primarily as a means of creating jobs.

Although there are those who insist otherwise, the future of the ESM does not come down to a choice between a Keynesian Europe and a 'deregulated, Anglo-Saxon' Europe. Some have suggested that there was in fact a 'plan B' for Europe in the event of the rejection of the constitution. It was the 'British plan of liberalization and deregulation' favoured by Tony Blair.[27] But this assertion makes no sense in either political or analytical terms. Blair signed up to the Constitutional Treaty, as did all other European political leaders.

Much more importantly, the future of the ESM does not lie in 'becoming more Anglo-Saxon' – certainly not if this means in some sense taking Britain as a model for the rest of Europe. Other countries can learn from what has been achieved in Britain – after all, the UK has a high rate of employment, is the only EU(15) country to have actively increased its investment in public services over the past few years, and has significantly reduced its poverty rate. However, the standard of public services in the UK still lags well behind continental best practice and levels of economic inequality remain high in spite of progress made.

A template for reform

Previous thinking has been rather dazzled by the 'three/four worlds of welfare capitalism', but while real differences do exist, the EU and its member states should be pushing for convergence here as in other areas. Most of the core difficulties facing the ESM are not specific to any country; they are structural. In a globalizing era, solutions can often, or even normally, in principle be generalized.

A future ESM, to repeat, would not be the British model. It would not be the French model. It would not be the Swedish or Danish one either. What I sketch in below is something of an ideal type – a list of traits that might be adopted in varying ways by specific reforming countries. A template for a revised ESM (RESM) might be guided by the following overall characteristics:[28]

- A move from negative to *positive welfare.* When William Beveridge developed his plan for the post-war welfare state, he thought – as did almost all others – of the welfare state as a corrective device. The point of his innovations was to attack the 'five evils' of ignorance, squalor, want, idleness and disease. We should not forget about any of these, but today we should seek much more to make them positives. In other words, we should be promoting education and learning, prosperity, life choice, active social and economic participation, and healthy lifestyles.

- Such goals presume *incentives* as well as benefits and *obligations* as well as rights, since the active compliance of citizens is required. The connection of welfare with citizenship is not, as T. H. Marshall suggested in his classic formulation, brought about only by the expansion of rights, but by a mixture of rights and obligations.[29] Passive unemployment benefits were defined almost wholly as rights – and proved to be dysfunctional largely for this reason. The introduction of active labour market policies makes it clear that the able-bodied unemployed have an obligation to look for work if they receive state support, and there are sanctions to help ensure their compliance.

- The traditional welfare system sought to *transfer risk* from the individual to the state or community. Security was defined as the absence, or reduction of risk. But risk in fact has many positive aspects to it. People often need to take risks to improve their lives. Moreover, in a fast-moving environment it is important for individuals to be able to adjust to, and if possible actively prosper from, change. This statement is as true of the labour force as it is of entrepreneurs; it is as valid for those affected by divorce or other social transitions as it is for the economic world. The creative use of risk, however, does not imply the absence of security – far from it. Knowing that there is help when things go wrong may often be a condition of entertaining the risk in the first place. I take it this is part of the logic of 'flexicurity' in active labour market policy.

- An RESM has to be, at least in many spheres, *contributory.* Services designed to be free at the point of use may be designed with nobility of purpose, but are prone to essential difficulties. Since they have few mechanisms to contain demand, they become over-crowded and over-used. Two-tier systems tend to develop, in which the affluent simply opt out. Contributions, even if relatively small, can not only help with this issue, but can also promote responsible attitudes to the use of services. The contributory principle – contributions from direct users – is therefore likely to play an increasing role in public services, from pensions and health through to higher education.

- An RESM must be *de-bureaucratized*. The pre-existing welfare state was based almost everywhere upon treating citizens as passive subjects. Collectivism was acceptable in a way it isn't, and shouldn't be, today. De-bureaucratizing means standing up against producer interests, promoting decentralization and local empowerment (for interesting examples, see the changes introduced into health provision and education in Sweden and Denmark in the early 1990s). These endeavours should be sharply distinguished from privatization, which is one among other means of potentially pursuing these goals. Social justice, client responsibility, quality of services offered – these are not inconsistent but in fact interdependent.

In more detailed policy terms, I would propose a 12-point sketch of an RESM:

1 Progressive income tax remains in place, as a means of limiting inequalities. Post-tax income in all industrial states is more egalitarian than pre-tax income. Those countries now making use of flat income taxes should ensure that they have a progressive outcome (on the basis of excluding poorer groups from payment). If they are high, taxes on business should be reduced. There is an overall move from labour to consumption taxes – with progressive elements again introduced as far as possible.

2 Fiscal prudence is a guiding principle of welfare funding, although with flexibility in certain situations. This principle is a long-term one, covering for example the capacity to meet anticipated future pensions commitments. Taxation in relation to GDP is high by international standards, but what matters is not so much the level of taxation but the overall policy mix.

3 Active labour market policies are in play, with an appropriate balance of incentives and obligations. They apply to older age groups as well as to others in the labour force. Flexibility goes along with state involvement in training and retraining. Special attention is given to measures for getting people registered as disabled back into active jobs.

4 Job creation plays a central role both in promoting growth and in containing poverty – the best route out of poverty is to hold down a decent job above a minimum wage.

5 Part-time work is actively encouraged. It forms part of an active adaptation to life transitions and to work–life balance. Part-time work is not stigmatized, but attracts the same benefits, pro rata,

as full-time work. Active attention is given to avoiding the balkanization of women's work.

6 Egalitarianism is a thread running through all policies: the whole point of the RESM is to combine economic dynamism with social justice. Levelling-up is much more important than 'stinging the rich', since the 'rich' is a tiny category, while the 'poor' is a very large one. Child poverty is an especial focus of attention. Societies with low levels of child poverty are likely to be more egalitarian than others in many other respects.

7 Targeted anti-poverty strategies are deployed to cope with embedded forms of poverty and social exclusion. They may include the use of negative income taxes or tax credits. The French *prime à l'emploi*, the labour tax credit in the Netherlands and the Belgian work tax credit, all put in place recently, closely resemble those deployed earlier in the US and UK.

8 Special attention is given to those in low-level service jobs, to ensure that, as far as possible, they have promotion chances. This means not just state provision for training, but collaboration with employers to redesign some sorts of jobs. Life-long learning becomes not just an empty phrase, but a reality, with opportunities for proper accreditation.

9 Targeted policies are also aimed at the greater integration of ethnic minorities and immigrants. These include a mix of rights and obligations given to, and demanded of, such groups. Obligations include language learning and acceptance of overall values of the host society.

10 The relation between benefits and contributions is structured so as to minimize opt-out on the part of the more affluent.

11 The state spends less in relative terms than before on the old, and more on the young, with particular attention given to childcare, early years education and incentives to have children.

12 Investment in science, technology and higher education is the leading influence both in industrial policy and the creation of new jobs.

All policies are looked at in terms of their ecological impact: states treat their Kyoto targets as binding; member nations sign up, and seek to promote, the shorter- and longer-term ecological aims of the Commission. Examples include the 2003 proposals requiring chemical companies to show that their products are non-toxic before putting them on the market; and long-term plans such as the proposal to effect a complete transfer to a hydrogen economy by 2050.

An RESM would differ quite radically from the 'American model':[30]

- Costs may be trimmed, and new contributions introduced, but the welfare system continues to offer wide protection on a range of fronts, in terms of social, economic and health risks. Levels of taxation are high in international terms.
- The scope for active government and the state remains large, although more geared to investment in human capital than in the past. The RESM may aptly be regarded as involving a 'social investment state'.
- Welfare policy is more egalitarian than in the US.
- Solidarity is promoted by ensuring that welfare systems remain attractive to more affluent groups.
- The 'social partners' play a key role in determining wage levels and other conditions of work.
- Environmental goals are central to the agenda.

Theory and practice

It is one thing to call for reform of the ESM. It is quite another to implement it. As I have suggested, we know a good deal about what needs to be done. The problem is to get on and do it. We can learn a lot from Europe's best performers, but reform will have to be a continuous process across all states. With the exception of the UK, those countries that have done well are all small. Small countries arguably can reform more easily than larger ones, but equally their small size may make them more vulnerable.

Radical reform seems almost always to follow crisis situations – it is invariably painful, and may involve incurring short-term social and economic costs in the pursuit of longer-term gains. The Nordic countries may have set the pace, but only after experiencing a series of serious economic crises in the late 1980s and early 1990s. Reform in the UK followed a long period during which the country was the sick man of Europe. It was led by Mrs Thatcher's governments, which were not sympathetic to public services and saw the welfare state as largely dysfunctional. Reforms were made to labour markets and union power contained. But nothing was done to limit the economic inequalities that were Britain's hallmark by the late 1980s and which are still apparent today in spite of the new policies introduced by Labour since its return to power in 1997.

Change in Austria and the Netherlands was achieved in a more consensual way, and without the structural damage wrought by Thatcherism. However, it also came after a lengthy period of relative economic decline, which also eventually approached crisis proportions.

A fundamental question for the near future is 'Has the consciousness of crisis in Germany, France and Italy built up to such a point that the resistance of vested interests can be overcome?' So far, governments neither of the left nor of the right have managed to generate far-reaching reforms. As a consequence, each has a welfare state that is unsustainable, coupled to continuing high rates of unemployment and underemployment. But steam is starting to blow out of the pressure cooker – each might also soon produce more radical, reforming governments.

What can be achieved at the European level? The history of attempts made by the Commission to reform in areas where it has no direct power is not encouraging. The open method of coordination has been at best no more than modestly successful. The basic principles of the Lisbon Strategy are just as relevant today as they were when they were enunciated in 2000. But there has been greater receptivity to them among states already moving in this direction than among others. Some of most influential countries have largely ignored it. Agenda 2010 in Germany, for instance, barely mentions the Lisbon Strategy. Germany and France also asserted their power vis-à-vis the Commission by overriding the restraints embodied in the Stability and Growth Pact (SGP).

What should be done when there is clear evidence that the Lisbon Strategy 'has delivered neither a major thrust towards completing the Single Market nor significant labour market reforms'?[31] Some suggest that the overriding emphasis for the moment should be placed upon completing the Single Market, on the grounds that this process would add to the impetus for labour market and welfare reform in those countries that most need it.[32]

But this suggestion runs up against the conflicts that have arisen around the Services Directive, which is crucial both to the Lisbon Agenda and the completion of the Single Market. In March 2005 the European Council rejected the formulation of the Services Directive produced by the Commission a year earlier. Perhaps the way forward is to seek to break the log-jam over the issue. This is exactly where a European-wide debate about the ESM might be so important, especially if it involves Europe's political leaders in a direct way.

Conclusion: the best of all worlds? (with apologies to countries left out)

A Europe to take on the world would have:

- Finnish levels of ICT penetration;
- German industrial productivity;
- Swedish levels of equality;
- Danish levels of employment;
- Irish economic growth;
- French levels of health care;
- Luxembourg level of GDP per head;
- Norwegian levels of education (although not in the EU);
- British cosmopolitanism;
- Cypriot weather.

I originally meant this as satire: but, with the exception of the Cyprus climate, perhaps we should be aiming this high after all?

Notes

I should like to thank the following who provided helpful comments on earlier drafts: David Held, Neil Kinnock, Shirley Williams, and colleagues working on the project on the European social model.

1 Jürgen Habermas and Jacques Derrida, 'February 15, or, what binds Europeans together', in Daniel Levy, Max Pensky and John Torpey, eds., *Old Europe, New Europe, Core Europe* (London: Verso, 2005).

2 Anna Dianantopolou: 'The European social model – myth or reality?', speech at Labour Party Conference, Bournemouth, 29 September 2003.

3 Daniel Vaughan-Whitehead, *EU Enlargement versus Social Europe?* (London: Elgar, 2003).

4 Thomas Friedman, *The World is Flat* (New York: Allen Lane, 2005).

5 See, for example, Jeremy Rifkin, *The European Dream* (New York: Tarcher Penguin, 2004).

6 See especially André Sapir et al., *An Agenda for a Growing Europe* (Brussels: European Commission, July 2003).

7 Ibid., p. 97.

8 Mark Leonard, *Why Europe Will Run the 21st Century* (London: Fourth Estate, 2005), pp. 71–3.

9 Karl Aiginger, 'Towards a new European model of a reformed welfare state', United Nations Economic Survey of Europe, 2005, No. 1.

10 Birgita Schmognerova, 'The European Social Model', European Economic and Social Committee, Brussels, 14 July 2005.

11 Miguel Glatzer and Dietrich Rueschemeyer, *Globalisation and the Future of the Welfare State* (Pittsburgh: University of Pittsburgh Press, 2005).

12 Gøsta Esping-Andersen, *The Three Worlds of Welfare Capitalism* (Cambridge: Polity, 1989).

13 Maurizio Ferrera seems to have been the first to identify the fourth type, in his 'Le Trappole del Welfare. Bologna', *Il Mulino* (1998).

14 Torben Iversen and Anne Wren, 'Equality, employment and budgetary restraint: the trilemma of the service economy', *World Politics*, 50 (1998).

15 See Anton Hemerijck's contribution to this volume (chapter 6).

16 Katinka Barysch, 'Liberal versus social Europe', *Centre for European Reform Bulletin*, August/September 2005.

17 Sapir et al., *Agenda for a Growing Europe*.

18 Figures are for 1993.

19 In 2005, the Lisbon Agenda was supplemented by a new five-year Social Agenda. See European Commission, *Communication on the Social Agenda* (Brussels, 9 February 2005). For a useful definition of social justice in present-day society, see Wolfgang Merkel, 'A reformed welfare state will tackle new inequalities', in M. Browne and P. Diamond, eds., *Rethinking Social Democracy* (London: Policy Network, 2003).

20 Denmark radically revamped its social security policy in the early 1990s. Workers can be dismissed at short notice. Severance pay is not high. Unemployment benefits, however, are good and paid over four years, with lower-paid workers receiving up to 90 per cent of their working wage. Retraining is obligatory after a certain time. It is provided in a highly decentralized way, with extensive involvement from the unions and civil society agencies. The unemployed are obliged to take up offers of employment or retraining made by local departments of employment.

21 James Wickham, *The End of the European Social Model Before it Began?* (Dublin: Irish Congress of Trade Unions, 2004).

22 However, there are problems with the rising numbers of people claiming disability or sickness benefits. In Sweden in 2004, for example, 6 per cent of people of working age were on sick leave or registered as disabled.

23 Manuel Castells and Pekka Himanen, *The Information Society and the Welfare State* (Oxford: Oxford University Press, 2002).

24 André Sapir: 'Globalisation and the reform of European social models', background document for ECOFIN meeting, Manchester, 9 September 2005. Available at <www.bruegel.org>.

25 Nicola Rossi: 'Managed diversity', in Anthony Giddens, *The Progressive Manifesto* (Cambridge: Polity Press and Policy Network, 2003).

26 François Hollande, 'Editorial: Comprendre pour depasser le "Non"', *Revue Socialiste*, 20 (29 May 2005).

27 See Pierre Moscovici, 'L'Europe dans la tourmente', *Revue Socialiste*, 20 (29 May 2005).

28 A different formulation appears in Aiginger, *Towards a New European Model*. I have learned a great deal from Aiginger's perceptive writings on the future of European welfare.

29 T. H. Marshall, *Citizenship and Social Class* (Cambridge: Cambridge University Press, 1950).

30 See also Aiginger, *Towards a New European Model*, p. 114.

31 Sapir, 'Globalization and the reform of European social models', p. 13.

32 Ibid.

2

Globalization: A European Perspective

John Sutton

Is 'social Europe' a problem? Or does the problem lie elsewhere?

The view set out in what follows is that the preference displayed by many West European economies for generous levels of social provision does not in itself constitute a problem; rather, the problems we face arise because the same political preferences that favour such high levels of social provision often favour, in addition to this, a series of market-unfriendly policy responses to specific issues, most notably in regard to the regulatory regimes in which the corporate section operates and in the impact of this on the entry and restructuring of firms; and in the design of employment protection policies. It is the latter points that are central: for if we have high levels of social provision then this must be paid for by a vibrant corporate sector that will advance its capabilities in step with those of its global competition, thus allowing it to generate the high levels of gross real incomes that support the establishment.

The higher the level of social provision, the more acute is the need to get market-friendly policies in key areas. It is not 'social Europe' per se that is the problem; but there is indeed a problem, and it is one that is likely to become more acute in some of the major European economies over the next decade.

The liberalization of the Chinese and Indian economies since the early 1990s offers tremendous opportunities not only within these countries, but across the global economy. Yet the emphasis in the

European debate has focused not only on the newly opening opportunities for Europe's exporters, but also on the adverse impact on European firms that face challenges from 'low-cost imports'. While Europe's consumers gain, Europe's politicians worry increasingly about job losses blamed on 'outsourcing'. I would like to step back in this chapter from the recent headlines on Chinese clothing imports, and take a look at some trends in the world economy over the past couple of decades. I argue that these 'low-wage competition' questions are not the heart of the issue. By way of background to this, I begin with a few remarks about firms, and about what makes them flourish or flounder in the face of changing circumstances.

Capability, environment and survival

A firm's success and survival depends on three elements, which we may lump together under the label of 'capability'. The first element is its level of productivity, i.e. its effectiveness in transforming materials and labour inputs into final products. The second element relates to the products the firm produces: it comprises all those features, such as design, technical performances, and brand image, which raise buyers' 'willingness-to-pay' for its offerings, relative to those of its rivals: a useful shorthand label for these features is (perceived) 'quality'. These first two elements constitute a firm's 'current' capability; and it is its current capability *relative to the current capabilities of its rivals* that determines its current success in the market, whether we measure this by employment, market share or profitability. For the moment, we can confine attention to these two elements of capability; later in the chapter, I will turn to the third element, which relates to the way the firm's 'current' capability develops over time.

In a globalizing world, the survival and success of a firm is driven both by its capability and by local conditions in the country or region in which it operates. Here, two things matter: the local ('real') wage rate, and the local business environment – i.e., the 'cost of doing business', or, in World Bank terminology, the 'investment climate'.

It is useful to begin with a point of reference, by asking how things work if all firms produce standardized, commodity-type products – so that we can set aside the 'quality' dimensions, and treat differences in capability as reflecting differences in productivity alone. Here, everything works in a familiar and straightforward manner. Under free trade, and flexible labour markets, exchange rates will adjust to distribute economic activity across countries – the classic 'comparative

1973

Non Production Workers

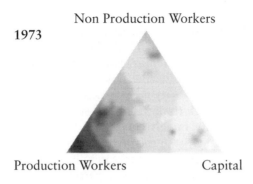

Production Workers   Capital

1983

Non Production Workers

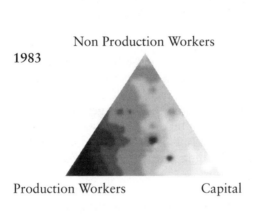

Production Workers   Capital

1993

Non Production Workers

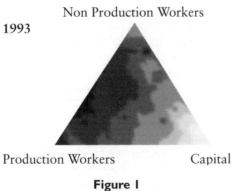

Production Workers   Capital

Figure 1
The Schott–Bernard Study

advantage' scenario: each country ends up producing those products which it is *relatively* good at producing. The key idea is that *low wages can compensate for low productivity*. Low productivity among any country's firms will be reflected in lower wage rates – but the flip side of the coin is that firms can survive, bolstered by these low local wages, even though their productivity is extremely low.

Now let us move back to the 'realistic' setting in which firms differ, not only in productivity, but also in quality. What is new in this setting is a simple but crucial twist in the preceding story about adjustment in the global economy. While low wages can fully offset deficiencies in productivity, they cannot do more than partially offset deficiencies in quality. The reason is straightforward: no matter how low wages fall, there is a lower limit to the price at which a product can be offered, which is set by the cost of the components or raw materials required for its production. Now suppose prices fall to that lowest possible level: given the prices and qualities offered by rival firms and countries on global markets, there will be a quality threshold below which firms from 'low-wage' countries cannot sell at all. In other words, there is a sort of 'quality window' into which they must get, before they can sell at all.

All of this may seem a bit arcane, but we are now at the punch line. The process of industrial development and globalization that has brought India and China into the recent headlines is a process that comprises two phases:

Phase I As newly industrializing countries join the global economy, they first impact relatively 'low-tech', unskilled labour-intensive sectors such as clothing and textiles, where low labour costs confer a major competitive advantage. Much of China's impact on the global economy up to the late 1990s was in areas of this kind. For the developing economy, however, this first phase is accompanied by severe dislocations of other sectors of the economy, as the opening up of trade means that its 'middle ground' industries suffer new competition from countries whose higher wage costs are more than outweighed by their higher-'quality standards'.[1]

Phase II The key challenge faced by all industrializing countries lies in making the transition to exporting products that are technologically more sophisticated, and in which high-quality standards are crucial to success. This demands major efforts from domestic firms in building up their quality standards to internationally competitive levels. Recent events have focused attention on China's impact on the clothing sector, suggesting that the current scenario is one in which China (and perhaps India) are still at the Phase I stage. Such a view would be profoundly misleading; the shift to Phase II has happened over the past decade both in China and India, as I will now show.

Before showing this, however, it is worth asking why the current focus is on Phase I issues. The reason is straightforward: because trade flows of this kind respond so strongly to wage differences, high-income countries have always adopted strong protective measures against them. It is the pent-up pressures released by the ending of the Multi-Fiber Agreement that have led to the present surge in trade flows; the main parties adversely affected by this are low-wage economies in South-East Asia whose quotas have up to now protected their export position vis-à-vis China's even lower wage levels. The adjustment pressures on southern European producers are similar in kind, but levels of social protection and the relative health of other industrial sectors make these pressures much more manageable than is the case in South-East Asia.

But back to the main story: my point of departure for all that follows lies in arguing that the real challenge for the European Union lies in the fact that competition from China and India over the next decade will be driven by a steady advance in quality, as well as productivity, and that the range of sectors affected will cover almost the entire industrial spectrum. To see how far we have already advanced along this road, it is helpful to step back and look at some trends that emerged during the 1990s.

A snapshot of the process

The triangles shown in figure 1 show a profile of the industrial landscape. Each industry is represented by a point in the triangle. The position of the point shows the fraction of costs associated with each of three elements: direct (i.e. 'shop floor') labour, overhead (i.e. technical and managerial) labour and capital equipment. Points closest to the bottom left corner represent the most labour-intensive industries; the most capital-intensive industries lie at the bottom right corner; while the top corner contains those industries that are R&D intensive. Thus, clothing lies at the bottom left; chemicals at the bottom right; and computer software at the top.

The data shown in the figure were computed by Peter Schott of Yale University and Andy Bernard of the University of Pennsylvania; it refers to US manufacturing over the period 1973–93, and it shows the extent to which imports from low-cost countries penetrated different industries over these years.[2] The 'low-cost' countries are defined as those which had a GDP per capita less than 5 per cent of the US level in 1973 (this includes both China and India). The dot representing each industry is shaded to show the degree of import penetration from these countries, and a 'smoothing' of these shadings is used to show the average shading of the dots in each part of the triangle. White shows no penetration,[3] and black, full penetration. If we look at the top triangle, showing the state of play in 1973, we see that import penetration from these low-cost countries is very low, and such penetration as there is confined to the unskilled-labour intensive (bottom left) corner of the triangle.

If we follow the course of events over the next two decades (middle and bottom triangles), we see that, already by 1993, the spread of penetration was extremely broad, except in the most capital-intensive industries (China's big push in chemicals is only now beginning, for example). There is almost total penetration, however, in the relatively high-tech sectors at the top of the triangle – and this is central to what I would like to discuss below. The main lesson I want to draw, however, lies in the final date here: 1993. What the pictures make clear is that the process of capability-building and quality-enhancement was already strongly under way in these countries by the early 1990s. How far, then, have these countries advanced in the intervening decade?

One way to address this question is to turn to detailed benchmarking studies of specific industries. Here, there are huge differences between one industry and another – and the differences reflect, to an important degree, differences in the way capabilities are transferred across firms at a global level. To see what is involved here, it is helpful to look at two industries which represent opposite extremes in this respect.

First, in the car industry, production routines are standardized worldwide, and all international car makers have for more than two decades adhered to similar production processes and procedures, both within the car plants, and – crucially – within those other (direct) component suppliers. In this industry, the transfer of know-how is remarkably effective, and the key channel for this transfer lies in the interaction between the car maker and its suppliers. As car makers have set up new plants in China and India, there has been a remarkably rapid transfer of know-how to domestic firms supplying components and assemblies to these new plants – and this new generation of domestic component suppliers have in turn begun to supply higher quality components at competitive prices to some of the surviving domestic car makers.[4] The result has been that Chinese and Indian car makers are now supplied by a population of component makers who are at, or close to, the frontier of international best practice. This advance in capability occurred almost wholly in a decade, beginning from the early 1990s. The level of quality standards now being achieved in China and India suggests that the next big story in this area will be one of a major export drive into Western markets.

Second, at the other end of the spectrum lie industries such as the machine-tool industry. Here, there is no weaving together of the international industry via 'supply-chains' of the kind we encounter among the car makers. Rather, there remains a very sizeable number of independent producers worldwide, who 'buy in' only computer controls and a few key mechanical elements ('ball screws') from specialist suppliers. The build-up and transfer of capabilities proceeds much more slowly in this setting. Firms in China and India rely to some extent on specific deals with foreign machine-tool makers to license the local production on an existing product; and they also depend to some extent on foreign public sector research institutes for advice. Much of the capability-building, however, is 'in-house', the firms' engineers studying and emulating design principles of leading international suppliers in developing their own products. Here, the speed of capability-building is much slower than in internationally integrated sectors like cars. The Chinese and Indian industries are still grappling with the challenges of holding their domestic market share in the face of intensive competition from imports; and their prospects on export markets remain weak for the present.

These two industries stand at the opposite ends of a spectrum; in between lie the general run of manufacturing industries. As we look across this spectrum, a major difference appears between the Chinese case and that of India. China's speed of advance in terms of building capability in 'middle-ground' industries such as domestic appliances and consumer electronics is now running far ahead of India, where there are very few firms, either domestic or international joint ventures, that appear to have serious prospects for major export successes over the next decade.[5]

That said, the overall picture that will emerge over the next decade is one in which the build-up of high-level capabilities in China, and to a lesser extent in India, will lead to serious challenges for European firms across the entire spectrum of manufacturing industry. The question of interest is: how can Europe's firms and governments best respond?

Some basic lessons

The nature of the challenge to European firms lies not in 'low-wage competition', but rather in the fact that these newly developing countries combine low-wage costs with rapidly advancing quality standards across the general run of manufacturing industries. It is the rising quality levels, and not the low-wage costs per se, that lie at the heart of the issue. But there is a flip side to this: just as low wages cannot compensate for low quality, so too high wages need not be a barrier to success once quality is at the leading edge – indeed, it is the *general* level of capabilities across an economy that determines its general level of real wages; the process of capability-building now in train will steadily narrow the currently huge wage gap between these newly industrializing countries and their Western competitors. The key to success for Western firms lies in underpinning their current wage levels with rising levels of capability across a broad range of industries.

But the central lesson I would like to draw, in this regard, begins from the triangles of figure 1. How, over this 20-year period, did US firms respond to the changing competitive environment? Who failed, and who survived?

It is obvious that high levels of productivity and quality improve survival prospects. But the key finding of the Schott–Bernard study lies in an observation that goes beyond this: what characterizes the 'survivors' among US firms over the period when their industry faced this wave of imports from the low-cost countries was their *flexibility*, as measured by the *changes* they made in the range of products they produced. Survivors are, above all, flexible; they shift from areas where competition becomes intense into new product groups, or adjacent industries – and it is this observation that brings us back once more to the concept of 'capability'.

What underlies, and determines, a firm's level of productivity and quality is, to put it in its simplest terms, the set of elements of 'know-how' jointly possessed by those individuals that comprise the firm. But this set of shared know-how will also determine the effectiveness of the firm in turning to the production of products beyond those which it now makes. The third element of capability, flexibility, measures the firm's ability to broaden, extend or modify its current set of products as conditions change.

Just as the survival of individual firms depends on their flexibility, so too does the performance of the economy as a whole. The needed adjustments are made *within* firms, as they switch their mix of activities, or across firms, as individual employees or groups of employees move between firms or industries, or set up new firms. However it is achieved, this kind of flexibility is a crucial determinant of performance. So how can it be enhanced?

Public policy

Before turning to this question, it will be worth stepping back a little, in order to return to the concept of the 'cost of doing business', which I touched on above. This concept relates to all the costs incurred by a firm apart from its capital equipment, wage costs and materials costs. It is affected by a wide range of influences, from the costs of compliance with public regulations, at one end of the spectrum, to the ease of availability of business services, transportation facilities and power supplies at the other end. In economic terms, a reduction in the 'cost of doing business' amounts to a general fall in average cost for the whole run of firms in the economy; and this in turn translates into a general rise in real wages – hence its central role in current discussions of public policy in developing countries.

For the European Union, too, this area has become one of growing concern. Due in large part to decisions taken by national governments (as opposed to the European Union itself), certain elements in the cost of doing business have been increasing in a worrying way over the past decade. The areas of concern range from the growing regulatory burden, in the case of the UK, to the non-wage costs of employment in Germany, and to the 35-hour week in France. But it is not these elements of the cost of doing business that form my primary concern here. Rather, the point I want to focus on is this: the success of European economies in adjusting to the trade-driven disruptions of the next decade will hinge crucially on the ease with which firms can shift their mix of activities over time – and this in turn depends on the ease with which individuals, and groups of individuals with complementary skills, can move from one business to another. At base, a successful pattern of adjustment requires both separations and hires – and this process is impeded by high 'costs of firing'. Greater employment protection is a double-edged sword.

This point needs to be made with care: it is *not* the impact of such 'unemployment protection' measures on the overall *level* of unemployment that is the issue here. Indeed, both theoretical analyses and empirical evidence suggest that there is no systematic effect of this kind: if we raise the level of employment protection, we slow up both the rate of job losses and the rate of new hires, and the resulting impact on the overall level of employment can go either way. The issue here relates to a different point: what the evidence points to is a systematic effect on the rate of job turnover, i.e. the net rate of movement of employed workers from one firm to another – and this is precisely where these labour market issues tie into the preceding discussion of product markets, i.e. of the adjustment processes that need to occur within and across firms. The cost borne by the economy as a whole takes the form of a reduction in real incomes per capita, driven by the inefficient distribution of individuals across jobs.

At the end of the day, it is not the survival of any individual business that should concern public policy – but rather the putting in place of an institutional environment within which individuals, and clusters of individuals with complementary skills, can both form new companies and restructure old ones, thus allowing the effective deployment of the collective know-how that constitutes the base of firms' capabilities, and so of national wealth.

The discussion of 'globalization pains' within the public press has paid too little attention to this central issue, notwithstanding the discussions of these matters within the OECD, and the European Union's Kok Report of 2003.[6] Instead, attention has been directed to a number of false trails, to which we now turn.

False trails

The issue receiving most attention in the media relates to the 'outsourcing' of component production and of business services to low-wage countries. This has led to the claim that European companies should not outsource, but rather exercise 'social responsibility' by continuing to source locally. Such a policy, if pursued, would be enormously damaging: Europe's producers compete on the international stage with rivals in the US, Japan and elsewhere. The cost of components and services brought in from outside represents a substantial fraction of total costs (one-third to two-thirds over much of manufacturing, for example). To fail to outsource involves a high penalty, equivalent to a major fall in productivity – the short-run gain of a 'buy-in locally' policy would be more than offset by the employment losses among Europe's increasingly uncompetitive final goods producers. Put crudely, if Finland imposed a local sourcing requirement, there would be no Nokia.[7]

A better paradigm for Europe in this regard is provided by the example of Germany's Audi Company. Finding itself in a difficult position in the early 1990s, the company built a new engine plant in Gyor (Hungary). This plant saved the company's fortunes: it reduced costs to the point where it allowed the firm to operate profitably, while at the same time transferring valuable industrial capability to one of the accession economies. This rebalancing of production within the

European Union represents a win–win situation, and offers a better template for future developments.

Sensible industrial policies

So how should European countries frame their industrial policies? The key point here is the least palatable, politically, and is best illustrated by the UK's attempt in 2005 to rescue Rover with Chinese help: negative industrial policies of this kind have consistently proved to be both costly and ineffective.

The first half of a sensible industrial policy lies in a combination of education and training, with programmes of retraining forming part of a package of measures designed to enhance flexibility and reduce the cost of doing business. It is here that the emphasis placed in some recent reports on the importance of 'life-long learning' programmes is relevant.[8] The second half consists of 'active' policies that aid the formation, development and growth of new companies. A key failing of some European economies lies in the fact that firms' adjustment to the changing global environment has been slow and ineffective in comparison to their counterparts in the US, and much of this difference in the effectiveness of their responses can be traced to differences in the institutional environment within which they operate. A recent study by Chris Pissarides has pinpointed the costs and difficulties involved in setting up a new firm as a primary driver of differences in unemployment levels across OECD economies.[9]

Policy lessons

I have identified a number of policies as being of central importance to the adjustment processes that Europe's economies will face in the next decade: these relate to:

- the impact of excessive 'job protection' on the speed of adjustment of firms, and workers, to changing market conditions;
- the need for 'life-long learning' programmes to aid flexibility;
- the importance of minimizing 'setup' costs associated with new firm formation; and
- the value of minimizing inappropriate regulatory burdens on firms.

Beyond these points, here are a number of related policy issues that deserve comment:

1 I have focused here on the need for flexibility in firms' responses, and on the underlying issue of labour market flexibility. But the flip side of this lies in an acceptance that labour markets may either remain restricted and stagnant, to our detriment, or else may become both more flexible, and so more turbulent. If the latter case holds, then the demand for social protection will rise. The design of policy should focus on finding ways of reducing the cost of effective protection, and focusing that protection on the middle-aged; it is Europe's young (unemployed) who stand to gain most from an increase in labour market flexibility.

2 It is taken for granted in much of the public discussion of these issues that Europe retains a great relative advantage in the level of education, skills and training. Yet the figures show that, very worryingly, the position in at least some of the major European economies has been deteriorating relative to that of the US over the past decade. The gap in average years of schooling between the US and Europe has been widening. In some countries, including Germany and Austria, the rate of growth of 'human capital' has been falling for the past decade.[10] This in itself might not be a problem, were it not for the fact that . . .

3 The main 'alternative route' towards laying the foundations for capability-building in Europe's firms lies in attracting highly skilled immigrants both from within and from outside the European Union. Not only is the EU relatively unsuccessful in attracting skilled immigrants, but policy in many EU countries is actively hostile towards 'openness' in this area, hugely beneficial though this can be.[11, 12]

'Social Europe'

The 'costs of social Europe' comprise a number of distinct elements. A central theme relates to each country's choice as to the range and quality of provision of public goods, and the consequent level of general taxation. This basic choice is one about which countries can exercise a wide range of discretion without suffering adverse economic effects.

This point is worth developing, since a casual examination of different countries' experiences suggests that high levels of social provision can coincide with strong economic performance, as has been noted by other contributors. The basic economics underlying the issue can be summarized as follows:

1 The level of capabilities among a country's firms drives the level of gross real incomes. This gross real income can be split into take-home pay and tax-based provision of public goods and services, in a way that reflects the preferences of each society.
2 The effect of labour supply, and on employment, of the choice that is made, depends on two factors:[13]
   (a) According to whether the public sector performs more or less effectively in delivering value for money, individuals may be made better or worse off when this balance between take-home pay and public services is altered. There may be some consequent effect on individuals' labour supply behaviour, but the direction of this response can go either way, and no general claim can be made on this issue.
   (b) A second effect arises insofar as the marginal tax rate on take-home pay diminishes peoples' incentives to work additional hours, or – more importantly – affects their decision to participate in the labour market or to withdraw. Here, the effect of raising social provision is negative, but the size of this impact can be diminished by the appropriate design of tax regimes. The key point here is to avoid the very high marginal rates of tax that have proved damaging at different times in several of the European economies.[14]

These considerations lead into broader issues surrounding specific policy instruments, whose poor design may have seriously adverse consequences. Beyond those already discussed, let me note two issues of this kind that may serve to illustrate the nature of the problems involved.

First, the non-wage cost of employment (associated with employers' social security contributions) is often highly regressive, raising the cost of employing workers at the bottom end of the wage distribution, and generating avoidable unemployment. The point has been made in a series of reports over the past decade, from that of Delors onwards.[15] Second, the structuring of unemployment pay is of crucial importance. By providing high levels of protection over a fixed period, falling to very low levels thereafter, it is possible to offer a high degree of social protection to most workers, with little or no adverse consequences for overall unemployment levels.

What these examples suggest is that the real issues lie in the detailed design of specific policies. It is at this rather modest level of discussion, that the debate on 'social Europe' can be pursued to best effect.

Notes

1 India, having liberalized over a short period in the early 1990s, suffered major dislocations of this kind throughout the decade. The machine-tool industry lost most of its domestic market to imports from Taiwan and elsewhere by the late '90s, and it was only at the end of the decade that a newly-formed producer regained much of the lost ground – see J. Sutton, The Indian Machine-Tool Industry: A Benchmarking Study (World Bank, 2001). In China, where liberalization was a more gradual process, industry-wide shocks of this kind were less evident, but serious regional disparities emerged, with the east and south-east faring well on average, while huge job losses dominated the overall picture as large state-owned enterprises shrank and restructured elsewhere.

2 'Survival of the best fit: exposure to low wage countries and the (uneven) growth of US manufacturing plants', Journal of International Economics, 68 (2006), pp. 219–37. The triangle diagrams appear in the working paper version of this paper, which appeared as NBER Working Paper 9170.

3 Penetration is measured as follows: an 'industry' is defined at the '4-digit' level of the Standard Industrial Classification, i.e. it carries a 4-digit reference number, such as 3811 for 'Engineering and Scientific Instruments'. Each of these industries comprises many 'product groups', referred to by a 5-digit code. Thus, 3811 contains, for example, product group 38111, 'Aeronautical, Nautical and Navigational Instruments, and Automatic Pilots'. The degree of penetration recorded by the colours of the triangle is measured as the fraction of the industry's product groups in which there are recorded imports from the low-cost countries.

4 For a full description of these processes in China and India, see J. Sutton, 'The globalization process: auto-component supply chains in China and India', in F. Bourguignon, B. Pleskovic and André Sapir, eds., Annual World Bank Conference on Development Economics: Europe. Are We on Track to Achieve the Millennium Development Goals? (Washington, DC: World Bank and Oxford University Press, 2005).

5 On the Chinese case, see Loren Brandt, Thomas Rawski and John Sutton, 'China's industrial development', in Loren Brandt and Thomas Rawski, eds., China's Great Transformation, in preparation.

6 See OECD, The OECD Jobs Study: Evidence and Explanations, Part I: Labour Market Trends and Underlying Forces of Change (Paris: OECD, 1994); OECD, Implementing the OECD Jobs Strategy: Assessing Performance and Policy (Paris: OECD, 1999); European Communities, Jobs, Jobs, Jobs: Creating More Employment in Europe, Report of the Employment Taskforce chaired by Wim Kok (November 2003) (Luxembourg: Office for Official Publications of the European Communities, 2004).

7 This is not to say that local sourcing is always detrimental: there is an infant

industry case for local sourcing that is important in (large) developing economies – but even in this context, it is an approach that needs to be used with caution; for a discussion, see Sutton, 'The globalization process'.

8 European Communities, *Jobs, Jobs, Jobs*.

9 C. Pissarides, 'Company start-up costs and unemployment', in P. Aghion, R. Frydman, J. Stiglitz and M. Woodford, eds., *Knowledge, Information and Expectations in Modern Macroeconomics: in Honor of Edmund S. Phelps* (Princeton: Princeton University Press, 2004).

10 These points should not be overstated: one cautionary note relates to indicators of the extent to which education and training is deficient. One such indicator is provided by the wage premium earned by skilled versus unskilled workers, and this premium has *not* been rising in the EU; this is seen by some observers as indicating that no *general* 'skills shortage' is present.

11 The most obvious and easily remedied deficiency in this area lies in the withdrawal of visas from foreign students on completion of their studies.

12 There is some irony in the fact that this widening skills gap, and failure to attract skilled immigrants, should go hand in hand with the EU's determination to subsidize R&D as a route to capability-building. The scarce resource is talent; and subsidies, questionable at best, become futile in the absence of an effective supply of trained and talented individuals to Europe's companies.

13 The impact of demand-side considerations on employment are, in principle, worthy of equal attention, of course, but it is through the supply side that 'social Europe' impinges on these outcomes.

14 A separate series of issues, relating to the real wages–employment link, arises when some form of 'real-wage rigidity', however generated, is present. This has been a focus of attention in the recent German debate, thanks to the contributions of Hans-Werner Sinn; but this is not a feature of 'social Europe' per se, and so I leave it to one side here.

15 See, for example, European Communities, *Jobs, Jobs, Jobs*.

3

East versus West? The European Economic and Social Model after Enlargement

Katinka Barysch

Introduction

The EU's enlargement to the East has been an economic success. Trade between the old and the new members is thriving. Foreign investment by West European companies has helped to create hundreds of thousands of jobs in Central and Eastern Europe, and it has generated multi-billion Euro profits for the investing companies. Workers from Poland, Hungary and elsewhere have plugged skill gaps in those EU countries that have opened their labour markets. Money from the EU budget is flowing into the East's poorest areas. Even East European farmers – previously the region's most ardent Eurosceptics – are much happier now that they can sell their goods to the whole EU, and have at least some access to EU farm subsidies.

Politically, however, the EU has not digested the accession of the ten new members. Voters and some politicians in Germany, Austria and elsewhere believe that enlargement has damaged their economies. Many people in the 'old' EU think that competition in the enlarged Single Market has somehow become 'unfair'. In March 2005, thousands marched in the streets of Brussels to protest against the erosion of the 'European social model' (ESM) after enlargement. In France, opposition to enlargement was one of the reasons why so many people voted against the EU's Constitutional Treaty. Only a minority of people now support further enlargement, not only in France, but also in Austria, Denmark, Finland, Germany, the Netherlands and the UK.

Much of the resentment that has been building up in the old EU is fuelled by false perceptions about cheap Polish plumbers and Latvian builders 'stealing' West European jobs by undercutting local wages and disregarding social standards. Workers in slow-growing Germany and Italy may be jealous of the new members' apparent economic success. But many think that this success has been achieved by luring investment and jobs eastwards with the help of 'unfair' tax competition and 'social dumping'. Some West Europeans worry that enlargement has forced the EU into a 'race to the bottom' in wages, taxes and social standards. The East Europeans, it is said, are 'unfamiliar with the solidarity of the European social model'.[1] Most people in Germany, France and Italy would place the new members firmly into the 'Anglo-Saxon' camp of liberal capitalists – an impression that has been reinforced by Eastern Europe's close political ties with the UK and the US.

The reality, however, is very different. There is no doubt that eastward enlargement is changing the European economy. But much of the impact has already taken place, since economic integration has been going on for well over a decade. Undoubtedly, further changes will be required on both sides as Single Market integration deepens. And some Eurozone countries would be well advised to increase the flexibility of their labour markets before the East Europeans gain the right to apply for jobs across the whole EU in 2011 (and perhaps earlier in some countries).

But the widespread perception that the new members are ultra-liberal, low-tax economies that are damaging Western Europe's social systems is wrong. There are big differences between the individual East European countries. But generally, their levels of taxation and budget spending are only marginally lower than in most West European countries. They tend to have generous social security systems that are under severe strain from persistently high unemployment. Like many 'old' EU countries, the newcomers are struggling to stay competitive in the face of low-cost competition from fast-growing Asia, and are looking for ways to produce more high-tech goods and services and fewer basic manufactured products. For the sake of European harmony, West European politicians should stop spreading stereotypes and instead start a more informed debate on how both old and new members can best benefit from EU enlargement.

The impact of accession

Economically, eastward enlargement is yesterday's news. The EU and the Central and East European countries started to dismantle bilateral trade barriers in the early 1990s, even before they agreed timetables for full liberalization through the 'Europe agreements'. By 2001 there were no more tariffs or quotas for trade in industrial goods, although some restrictions remained for trade in services and, of course, farm goods. The lowering of EU trade barriers – alongside rapid industrial restructuring – fuelled an export boom across Central and Eastern Europe that has been instrumental in the region's recovery. In the ten years before accession, Hungarian exports rose by 380 per cent (in dollar terms) and Czech exports by 280 per cent. By 2000, the big Central European countries were already sending 60–75 per cent of their exports to the EU. In other words, long before membership, they were trading more with the EU than many of the EU countries were trading with each other.

The export boom has been closely related to large-scale inflows of foreign direct investment (FDI). The actual accession to the EU has done little to increase the attractiveness of the Central and East European countries for foreign companies. But the pre-accession process has been important for FDI, for several reasons: First, as the East European countries took over EU rules and policies, their business environments started to resemble those in Western Europe and foreign investors felt more at home. Second, as the EU opened up its markets for goods from Poland, Estonia or Slovakia, these countries became more attractive locations for export-oriented production. And third, the prospect of EU membership acted as an 'external anchor' for economic reforms, guaranteeing a certain amount of stability and insuring investors against policy reversals.

As a result, EU companies have ploughed more than €150 billion into the ten Central and East European accession countries since the early 1990s. For Western Europe, these sums were relatively small: in 2004, the old EU(15) invested eleven times more in each other's economies than in the new member states. But for many of the East European countries, investment inflows from the EU have typically amounted to 5–10 per cent of their GDP. FDI has helped to build up massive new production capacities across Central and Eastern Europe, in particular in the automotive sector, but also in electronics, furniture, pharmaceuticals and other manufacturing sectors. And FDI has been instrumental in creating modern services sectors such as retail, banking, telecoms and transport.

In short, gradual economic integration with the EU has been the key to the new members' economic success. Since the mid-1990s, the Central and East Europeans countries have consistently outgrown most of the old EU. For example, Poland grew by an average of 4.4 per cent a year over the last decade, Hungary by 3.6 per cent and

Table 1   Basic indicators for the new members and the EU(15)

	Population (million)	GDP (€bn) (2003)	GDP per head at PPP EU(25)=100	Read GDP growth % (av. 2000–4)	Inflation % (av. 2000–4)	Current account ($bn)
Czech Rep	10.2	80.3	70	3.1	2.6	−5.6
Estonia	1.3	8.1	51	7.2	3.5	−1.4
Hungary	10.0	72.6	61	3.9	7.1	−8.8
Latvia	2.3	9.9	43	7.5	3.2	−1.7
Lithuania	3.4	16.3	48	6.7	0.5	−1.6
Poland	38.2	185.2	47	3.1	4.3	−3.6
Slovakia	5.4	29.0	52	4.1	7.7	−1.4
Slovenia	2.0	24.9	79	3.4	6.8	−0.3
NMS(10)	73.7	442.1	–	3.6	4.6	−25.4
EU(15)	383.5	9,373.5	109	2.0	2.0	21.8

Figures are for 2004 unless otherwise indicated
Sources: Compiled by the author from various Eurostat and European Commission data

Estonia by 5.4 per cent. By comparison, Germany mustered an average growth rate of 1.3 per cent in 1995–2004 and France of 2.2 per cent. The accession countries also did considerably better than those countries that have not applied for (or been offered the prospect of) membership, for example Russia, Ukraine or Moldova (whose average growth rates in 1995–2004 were, respectively, 2.9 per cent, 1.5 per cent and 1.4 per cent).[2]

Have you got my job?

Some West Europeans suspect that the East's economic success has come at their expense. Have cheap exports from Slovakia and Poland priced Dutch and French goods out of the market? Have the large-scale FDI flows simply transferred jobs from West to East? For most of the EU member states, trade and investment links with the candidate countries have been too small to have a measurable impact. The exceptions are Germany and Austria, which trade a lot with the region and, alongside France and the Netherlands, account for the bulk of foreign investment there. The net impact of economic integration with the East is fiendishly difficult to calculate. Economists at the *Osteuropa-Institut*, a Munich-based research outfit, have looked at the impact of trade and FDI and reached the following tentative conclusions: since Western Europe has traditionally run a trade surplus with Central and Eastern Europe, the impact of trade integration was almost certainly positive for the old EU. According to another study, the EU's trade surplus with the big four Central European candidate countries has created 114,000 jobs in the EU throughout the 1990s.[3]

For FDI, the story is more complicated. Take the case of Germany: German companies have invested some €40 billion in the whole of Eastern Europe since the mid-1990s and German-owned (or co-owned) companies now employ some 900,000 people across the region (80 per cent of whom are in the eight Central and East European countries that joined the EU in 2004). Half of this investment was aimed at profiting from the accession countries' burgeoning consumer markets, for example through building supermarkets or buying local banks, so it has not replaced jobs in Germany. The other half sought to take advantage of low labour costs in the candidate countries, so may potentially have led to job losses in factories back home. To conclude, however, that 400,000 or so jobs have moved from Germany to the East would be wrong. Production in Eastern Europe is much more labour-intensive than in Germany. For each job lost in Germany (or France or Austria), there are usually several created in Poland, Slovakia or Latvia. So the *Osteuropa-Institut* calculates that at most 70,000 German jobs have moved eastward for cost reasons.[4]

This is a sizeable number, but it only accounts for 1.5 per cent of Germany's total unemployment figure of 4.6 million. Such estimates have to be interpreted with caution, not least because they often ignore that outward investment also benefits the country where it originates. Much FDI has come from sectors that are under fierce global competition, for example cars, electronics and chemicals. By shifting parts of their lower value-added production to countries where workers are cheaper, these companies make sure that they stay competitive on a global scale. In other words, FDI in Eastern Europe has helped to preserve jobs in Germany and elsewhere in Western Europe. According to one survey cited by the *Osteuropa-Institut*, 20 per cent of the German companies with investments in Eastern Europe had shifted jobs eastward, while 60 per cent said their investments had helped to preserve or create jobs at home.[5]

The long-term impact

The direct impact of eastward enlargement on the old EU has been marginal. The new members' stronger economic performance may have added a degree of dynamism to the European economy. But since the ten new members account for only 5 per cent of EU GDP (or

10 per cent if measured at purchasing-power parity), they are too small to act as Europe's economic engine. In economic terms, enlargement was the equivalent of adding an economy the size of the Netherlands to a Single Market with 380 million consumers and a GDP worth €10 trillion. But what about the future? Comparing existing trade flows with potential ones (based on factors such as geographical proximity and income levels), most economists assume that trade integration between the old and new members is pretty much complete. Any further trade growth will depend on demand in the big EU markets and developments within the new members. Provided that the new members keep up productivity growth rates (and thus remain competitive), export growth should stay at recent high levels.

Most analysts also expect FDI flows from the old to the new members to remain strong over the medium term. The need to cut costs has been reinforced by sluggish Eurozone growth, a stronger Euro and a ripple effect that is itself the result of outsourcing: as more and more companies transfer production to low-cost locations, the pressure grows on their competitors to follow suit. According to another survey by Rödl & Partner, a consultancy, 80 per cent of German companies polled in 2005 expected to increase their investments in the new member states in the coming years.[6] However, some larger corporations fear that EU membership will push up wages and regulatory costs in the Central and East European countries. As a result, they are moving their production facilities further east or to Asia, while using Prague, Tallinn or Budapest increasingly for the outsourcing of IT and other services. Such investment in services, especially in research and development (R&D), is important for the economic development of the new members. But it is generally less capital-intensive, so it may not show up in the form of higher FDI inflows.[7]

Unfair competition in the EU?

In a poll conducted in early 2004, 73 per cent of Germans said they expected enlargement would threaten their jobs.[8] Germans are particularly sensitive to the issue of migration, not least because some 60 per cent of the million-odd East Europeans who moved to the EU before accession settled in Germany – and that at a time when unemployment continued to rise steadily. Austria has been the second most popular destination, taking perhaps another 5–10 per cent of the East Europeans coming to the old EU before 2004. This is why Germany and Austria have led the campaign for the EU to impose long 'transition periods' on the free movement of workers from the Central and East European countries. Only three EU countries – Ireland, Sweden and the UK – removed restrictions for East European jobseekers in May 2004. In the other 12 old member states, Poles, Hungarians and others still require work permits until at least May 2006, and probably until 2011.

The Polish plumber

Even in those countries where all restrictions were dropped, the number of jobseekers from Eastern Europe has remained limited. In Sweden, only 22,000 people from the new members applied for residency permits between May and December 2004, a rise in the workforce of only 0.07 per cent. Ireland registered an increase of 85,000 in the 12 months following enlargement – the largest relative to its domestic workforce. And Ireland continues actively to recruit East Europeans to alleviate local skill shortages. The UK Office of National Statistics reports that 175,000 people from the new members registered for work between May 2004 and March 2005, of whom perhaps 40 per cent had already been in the country before EU accession. This suggests worker immigration figures of around 10,000 people a month – hardly an uncontrollable flood in a country of 60 million.[9]

Although the absence of restrictions has turned the UK, Ireland and Sweden into popular destinations, many East Europeans still prefer to join the much larger immigrant communities in Germany and Austria. The Polish foreign ministry reports that since accession around 30 per cent of emigrant Poles went to the UK and Ireland in 2004, while around the same proportion moved to Germany despite continued restrictions (comparable figures for the other new members are not available).[10] Many of those going to Germany are thought to be working in the burgeoning black economy. Others have set up small businesses under EU rules for the 'freedom of establishment', which, unlike the free movement of labour, is not subject to transition periods.

A number of East Europeans work in the old EU on the basis of temporary contracts, hired out by service companies from their home countries (under the EU's 'posted workers directive'). The number of East Europeans working on such contracts is small, but they have caused a disproportionate amount of political upheaval in France, Germany, Sweden and elsewhere. The alleged job competition from cheap Polish plumbers fuelled anti-EU sentiment during France's referendum on the EU constitution.[11] In December 2004,

14 Latvian builders were forced to stop working in Sweden for what a local trade union had claimed were 'unfairly' low wages. Similarly, in March 2005 the Danish authorities fined a Polish construction company (owned by a Dane) for undercutting local wages. And Germans were outraged in the autumn of 2004 when about 25,000 abattoir workers lost their jobs to Poles or Czechs willing to work for €5 an hour or less.

Most workers in the old EU countries are not looking forward to the day when restrictions on the free movement of labour are lifted. Migration flows are notoriously difficult to predict but many researchers think that between 100,000 and 400,000 East Europeans will head west every year once they gain the right to apply for jobs in the old EU. Assuming that it will take a decade or two before most of those who want to move have actually done so, they predict that maybe 2–3 million people from the new member states will be living in the old EU by, say, 2020. That sounds a lot, but it only amounts to 0.5–0.8 per cent of the EU's current population.[12]

Fears of the mythical 'Polish plumber' have also fuelled opposition to the Commission's proposal for a further opening of EU services markets through its 'Services Directive'. The Services Directive would make it easier for Polish architects or Slovenian consultants to work across the EU because all member states would have to accept their home country's qualifications. But it would not allow East Europeans generally to undercut West European wages. Local minimum wages and sectoral wage rules would continue to apply for all workers, irrespective of their origin. The reason why German abattoir workers lost their jobs to cheaper competitors was that, unlike the UK, Germany does not have a country-wide minimum wage, only sectoral wage rules.[13]

'Old' Europe is forced to change

Enlargement-related fears go well beyond the impact on slaughter-houses and building sites. West Europeans know they can keep cheap East European workers out of their labour markets, but they cannot prevent their companies going to where labour is cheaper. FDI is usually beneficial for the economies of both the target country and the country of origin. But the benefits are not easy to see. Eastward enlargement took place at a time when many West European countries were (and are) undergoing painful structural reforms, such as the loosening of job protection rules and the reduction in welfare entitlements.

In Germany, company bosses have (successfully) demanded wage restraint in the face of low-cost competition from the East. Scores of companies, from DaimlerChrysler to Siemens, threatened to shift more production eastward unless their workers agreed to work longer hours for the same money or less. Real wages in Germany have been stagnating for years, and unit labour costs are now back where they were in mid-1990s. Germany's belt-tightening, in turn, has increased the pressure on its big West European trading partners. Italy, France and others are now struggling to restore their competitiveness vis-à-vis Germany. As a result, unit labour costs in the entire Eurozone have fallen by an average of 0.5 per cent a year since 2001.

It is impossible to say how far wage restraints and labour market reforms are the direct result of eastward enlargement. It appears that the availability of millions of cheap workers on their doorstep has strengthened the hands of West European company bosses vis-à-vis their workers. But, as pointed out above, the relocation of some production processes or backroom services may also have saved jobs in the face of heightened global competition. Even if Eastern Europe were to disappear from the face of the earth tomorrow, social and demographic trends (ageing, the erosion of traditional family structures), European integration (the Single Market, monetary union) and global competition (from China, India, the US and others) would still force the old EU countries to adjust. However, many people in these countries do not grasp the concept of globalization or tend to deny the changing nature of their own societies. When they fear losing their jobs, they quickly point a finger at Eastern Europe. France's frantic debate about *délocalisation* is mainly aimed at the new member states (and the countries still queuing for membership, such as Bulgaria, Romania and Turkey). Some Germans fear that eastward enlargement is turning their country into a 'bazaar economy' where only a limited number of finished products is assembled, while most of the work is outsourced across the eastern border.

Such fears have gone hand in hand with perceptions that the new members are using 'unfair' means to lure companies eastward, namely low levels of social protection, low taxes and a lack of workers' rights. In short, many people in Western Europe think of the new members as ruthless 'Anglo-Saxon' capitalists whose addition to the EU is undermining the cherished ESM.

The real situation across the new member states is of course much more complex. These states boast relatively flexible labour markets, a feature that they share with the UK, Ireland and, to a certain extent, the Nordic countries. But unlike the latter countries, much of Eastern Europe suffers from very high unemployment rates, higher even than those found in Germany, France or Italy. The new members also resemble the large Eurozone countries in that they have generous social security systems that are funded out of payroll taxes.

Unfair tax competition?

Most of the Central and East European countries lowered their corporate tax rates in the run-up to accession to compensate for the abolition of discriminatory tax breaks, which was required by EU state aid rules. Many countries also introduced 'flat' rates of personal income tax. Slovakia went furthest in its tax reforms by standardizing taxes on profits, income, capital and value added at a low rate of 19 per cent. Tax cuts have spread throughout Central and Eastern Europe and now appear to be extending into the old EU, fuelling fears that there is a 'race to the bottom' in tax rates. Austria cut its corporate tax rate from 34 to 25 per cent in January 2005. Three months later, the German government announced a cut in the federal profit tax rate from 25 to 19 per cent (although the plan was subsequently put on ice). On average, corporate profit tax rates in the EU(15) have fallen by 8 percentage points over the last decade.

It is not clear whether such reforms are the direct consequence of EU enlargement or part of a broader international trend towards lower direct taxation (income and profits) and higher indirect taxes (VAT, property). But it is important to quash the myth that Eastern Europe is a low-tax paradise that flourishes at the expense of its high-tax neighbours. Generally, taxation levels in the new member states are lower than in the EU(15), but not much. In 2003, the ten accession countries collected the equivalent of 36 per cent of their GDP in taxes, compared with just over 40 per cent in the EU(15). Like in the EU, there are big differences between countries. Lithuania's tax level is below that of Ireland's (at 29 per cent of GDP) while Hungary and Slovenia collect as much tax as Germany (around 40 per cent).[14]

It is true that headline corporate tax rates in the new member states are now much lower than in the EU, typically 15–20 per cent compared with 34–38 per cent in Germany, Italy and France. But this does not automatically mean that East European governments are shy to tax local companies. Tax revenue consists of two components: the tax rate and the tax base (on which the tax is levied). West European tax systems tend to be riddled with exemptions and many offer generous depreciation rules to encourage certain investments. So the 'effective' tax rate on corporate profits is often much lower than the headline rate. Estimates of the effective tax rates vary widely. According to some calculations, the effective rate of corporate taxation in Germany is only half the headline rate (38 per cent). Some of the country's largest companies enjoy so many tax breaks that their effective tax rate is zero.[15] Other estimates show that the effective tax rate in the East European members is now a lot lower than in the old EU – for example, around 18 per cent in Poland and Hungary, compared with 35–36 per cent in Germany and France.[16]

Another (albeit similarly flawed way) of gauging the real tax burden is to look at how much money national treasuries actually obtain from companies. According to the European Commission, Germany collected corporate taxes worth only 0.8 per cent of its GDP in 2003, and France 2.2 per cent. Compare that with allegedly low-tax countries such as Ireland and the UK (3.8 per cent and 2.7 per cent of their GDP, respectively) or Slovakia and Hungary (2.8 per cent and 2.2 per cent of GDP, respectively). Even Estonia, which does not tax reinvested profits at all, still managed to collect more than Germany in corporate taxes as a share of its GDP.

But even if one assumes that effective corporate tax rates in Central and Eastern Europe are significantly lower than those found in the old EU, it does not necessarily follow that tax policy is behind Eastern Europe's investment boom. Investor surveys show that tax levels are just one factor among many that companies take into account when they decide where to set up shop. Others, such as economic and political stability, the quality of the labour force, wage and productivity levels, market size or proximity to major markets, usually rank higher.

The East European social model

The perception that Eastern Europe loves low taxes has been reinforced by the fact that four of the new members have introduced 'flat' income tax rates.[17] Estonia started the trend in 1994, and the other Baltic states and Slovakia have since followed. Opposition parties in Hungary, Poland and the Czech Republic are now calling for the introduction of flat taxes and even in more conservative Slovenia the government's economic expert group advises such a move. The rates at which these flat taxes are levied are usually low, ranging from 19 per cent in Slovakia to 33 per cent in Lithuania, and some governments are planning to cut them further.

Such radical tax reforms have captured the imagination of many liberals in Western Europe. They compare Eastern Europe's light and simple income tax regimes to the complicated and cumbersome systems found in their own countries – and call on their governments to copy the East.[18] There are specific reasons why flat taxes were a good idea in Eastern Europe, most notably the weakness of the local tax administration and the pervasiveness of tax evasion. And there are good reasons why West European countries may prefer to stick with their more sophisticated progressive tax systems, for example social fairness (higher tax rates for big earners) and the use of the tax system for specific policy objectives (encouraging pension savings or home ownership). But even if the large EU countries are unlikely to follow the flat tax trend, some of them may go part of the way by simplifying their tax systems and reducing the top rate of income tax rates.

With their low income tax rates and widespread tax evasion, East European countries collect much less money from personal income taxes than West European ones (5 per cent of GDP compared with 10 per cent in the Eurozone in 2003). Instead, governments in the new member countries rely on other ways of taxing wages, namely social security contributions. As a result, payroll taxes in the new members are usually above those found in most of the 'old' member states. In Poland, Hungary and Slovakia, for example, social security contributions add almost 40 per cent to labour costs, more than in Italy or Germany, and twice as much as the UK. On average, the ten new members in 2003 collected 13.3 per cent of their GDP in the form of social security contributions to pay for their health care, pensions and social welfare systems – almost exactly the same as the old EU(15).[19]

Rather than being 'ultra-liberal' and socially minimalist, the Central and East Europeans spend too much on social security, given their rather low level of income and economic development. Most of the new members are working hard to reform their social security systems. They know they need to create social welfare and security systems that are better targeted, and offer better incentives for the unemployed to return to work. In other words, their reform challenges are not that different from those of most West European countries. Like in the West, such changes are politically controversial and often involve big upfront costs, which is tricky given that the new members are keen to join the Euro and so need to reduce their budget deficits.[20] Also in some of the new member states, the social challenges are more daunting than in the old EU: in Hungary one-quarter of the working age population relies on some kind of social transfers as their main source of income. In Poland, one in five people of working age obtains state benefits and less than 2 per cent of all benefits are means-tested.

The truth about East European labour markets

Most people in Western Europe are wholly unaware of the daunting labour market problems that the new members are struggling with (see table 2). Perhaps if they knew more, they would be a little less critical of the East Europeans' desperate attempts to boost growth and attract investment.

The average unemployment rate in the new members stands at around 15 per cent, compared with 8.5 per cent in the old EU(15). The East European average is pushed up by Poland, where more than 17 per cent of workers are looking for a job. Long-term unemployment is also much higher than in the old EU. In countries such as Poland and Slovakia, 10–12 per cent of the labour force appears virtually unemployable. Perhaps even more worrying is the high rate of youth unemployment: almost one-third of the 15–24 year-olds in Central and Eastern Europe are jobless – again, twice the rate of the EU(15). In Poland, youth unemployment stands at more than 40 per cent.[21] That means that millions of young people in Eastern Europe are neither in education nor picking up skills on the job, which does not bode well for their future.

Low employment rates

Unemployment rates in Central and Eastern Europe would be even higher if it was not for the fact that millions of workers dropped out

Table 2   Labour market indicators

	Unemployment rate, % (2005)	Employment rate, % (2004)	Hourly labour costs, € (2003)	Those with at least secondary education, % (2004)	Workers who received training, % (2004)
Czech Rep	7.8	64.2	5.5	91	6
Estonia	7.8	63.0	4.0	82	7
Hungary	6.3	56.8	5.1	83	5
Latvia	9.0	62.3	2.4	77	9
Lithuania	7.8	61.2	3.1	86	7
Poland	17.7	51.7	4.7	90	6
Slovakia	15.4	57.0	4.0	91	5
Slovenia	5.8	65.3	10.5	90	18
EU(15)	7.9	64.7	24.3	74	10

Source: Compiled by the author from various Eurostat and European Commission data

of the labour force altogether during the 1990s. As a result, employment rates in the new members are generally below those found in the old EU, and well below the EU target of 70 per cent by 2010. Currently, only the Czech Republic and Slovenia get anywhere near the average EU employment rate of 64 per cent. In Poland, the region's biggest labour market, only around half of all people of working age actually have a job in the formal economy. At least the downward trend has now been reversed, and most of the new member countries record stable or rising employment rates.

Competitive wage levels

Average wages and income levels in the new member states are much lower than in the old EU. Hourly labour costs in 2003 (the latest date for which comparable data are available) ranged from 12 per cent of the EU(15) average in Latvia to 53 per cent in Slovenia. In the larger countries – Poland, Hungary and the Czech and Slovak Republics – wage levels are 20–30 per cent of the West European level.[22] Productivity levels also tend to be much lower. Most estimates put Eastern Europe's productivity at 35–40 per cent of the EU(15) level, although in export-oriented sectors with lots of foreign investment they are much closer to Western Europe. The new members' dilemma is that to catch up with West European income levels, they need higher wages. High wage growth is only sustainable if backed by high productivity growth, otherwise it leads to a loss of competitiveness. But so far the East Europeans have achieved high productivity growth mainly at the expense of job cuts. In the future, they need to find a way of combining productivity gains with job creation, like Ireland and Spain have done in recent years. This, in turn, requires very high rates of investment, technological progress and rapid skills upgrading.

Solid education systems

On some education indicators, the new members outperform even the old EU countries: they boast very high enrolment rates in secondary education, and very few youngsters drop out of education without a qualification. Eastern Europeans also generally score well on basic educational indicators such as numeracy and literacy. The heavy focus on technical and professional education appears adequate for Eastern

Europe's current specialization in producing cars, consumer electronics and basic manufactured goods. But these skill levels may not be enough to build what the EU likes to refer to as the 'knowledge economy'. For this, the new members need to invest more in tertiary education, refocus curricula towards languages, IT or management, and encourage general skills such as creative thinking and problem solving.

Regional gaps

Most of the new member states suffer from 'dual' labour markets: they have dynamic and tight labour markets in fast-growing urban areas, and stale and stagnant ones in declining industrial heartlands and remote rural areas, where unemployment can reach 30 per cent or more. Inflexible housing markets and inadequate transport make it difficult for workers to move to where job opportunities are better. Regional gaps in skills and the quality of education exacerbate the problem.

Ageing populations

In most Central and East European countries the demographic trends are even more worrying than in Western Europe. While life expectancy is rising, birth rates tend to be extremely low, so societies are ageing even faster than those in the old EU. The UN predicts that the populations of Latvia and Lithuania will shrink by one-third by 2050, while the number of Hungarians and Czechs will fall by more than one-fifth.[23] So rather than being a source of large-scale immigration, the new members will themselves have to admit a larger number of immigrants to help sustain economic growth and patch up national pension systems. But many of these countries are not used to dealing with large numbers of foreign workers. Hungary is currently host to only 50–80,000 foreign workers, mostly from neighbouring Romania. But the country may need as many as two million immigrants over the next five years alone to make up for the fall in its indigenous labour force.

Conclusion

West European concerns about enlargement – from labour migration to low-cost competition – are mostly related to the big income gap that persists between the old and the new members. In principle, therefore, the old member states share the newcomers' objective of rapid income growth. So far, income catch-up has been rather slow, despite rapid productivity growth, because too many people from Estonia to Slovenia are not productively employed. To speed up income convergence, Eastern Europe needs to sort out its labour markets. What could the EU do to help? It is clear what the EU should not do, namely seek to harmonize tax rates and welfare standards across the Union. French and German politicians are calling for the introduction of minimum rates of corporate taxation in the EU to end 'unfair' tax competition from the East. And they accuse the new members of 'stealing' jobs by undercutting West European social standards. As this chapter shows, such accusations are unfounded. The new members' welfare states are already quite extensive, especially given their low levels of incomes and development. And the challenges that the new members struggle with – from ageing workforces to badly targeted welfare systems and under-funded universities – are not very different from those faced by West European countries.

EU benchmarking and peer pressure, in particular the Lisbon process, can help the newcomers with their reform efforts. But for such processes to be constructive, West European politicians need to stop nailing the new members into an ultra-liberal corner. The Central and East European countries are not instinctively liberal. Most of the people in the region grew up with a feeling of entitlement when it comes to jobs and social security, and a strong sense of social fairness and equity. Some researchers think that the East European preference for equality is an 'attitudinal legacy inherited from social-ist times'.[24]

The East Europeans have gone through more than a decade of tur-bulent change to get ready for EU membership. The 'old' EU owes them a welcome. In practical terms, this means that West European politicians should stop exploiting populist resentment of low-wage competition. They should explain to their voters that economic reforms would be necessary even in the absence of enlargement and that, on the whole, the addition of ten new members has been good for the EU economy.

Notes

1 Marjorie Jouen and Catherine Papant, *Social Europe in the Throes of Enlargement*, Policy Paper 15 (Paris: Notre Europe, July 2005), <http://www.notre-europe.asso.fr/>.

2 Data from national statistical offices and the Economist Intelligence Unit.

3 Wolfgang Quaisser, *Kosten und Nutzen der Osterweiterung unter beson-derer Berücksichtigung verteilungspolitischer Probleme*, Working Paper 230 (Munich: Osteuropa-Institut, February 2001).

4 Michael Knogler, *Auswirkungen der EU-Osterweiterung auf die Arbeitsmärkte der neuen Mitgliedstaaten und der EU-15, insbesondere Deutschland*, Working Paper 257 (Munich: Osteuropa-Institut, January 2005).

5 IKB and KfW, *Studie zu den Auslandsaktivitäten deutscher Unternehmen: Beschäftigungseffekte und Folgen für den Standort Deutschland*, prelim-inary version. Cited in Knogler, *Auswirkungen der EU-Osterweiterung*.

6 Rödl and Partner, *Wachstumsschub durch EU-Osterweiterung*. Survey and press release from April 2005, available on <http://www.roedl.de>.

7 Since data on offshoring are scarce, it is difficult to assess how far jobs in Western Europe have been affected by this kind of FDI. So far, West European countries such as Germany still run surpluses in their services trade with the new members.

8 Survey conducted for *Der Spiegel* magazine in April 2004. Cited in Petra Bendel and Jan Jugl, *Osterweiterung und Migration* (Bonn: Bundeszentrale für politische Bildung, July 2005), <http://www.bpb. de/>.

9 All figures cited in Julianna Traser, *Who's Afraid of EU Enlargement? Report on the Movement of Workers in EU-25* (Brussels: European Citizen Action Service, September 2005), <www.ecas.org>.

10 Katinka Barysch, 'Storm in a teacup', *E!sharp* (November 2004).

11 According to *Newsweek* (17 October 2005), only 150 Polish plumbers worked in France in 2005, while the French plumbers association reported 6,000 vacancies. British government statistics show that 75 East European plumbers registered for work in the UK between May 2004 and March 2005.

12 Katinka Barysch, 'Does enlargement matter for the EU economy?' Policy Brief (London: Centre for European Reform, May 2003), <http://www. cer.org.uk>.

13 Milosz Matuschek, *Die geplante Richtlinie ist besser als ihr Ruf* (Munich: Centrum für angewandte Politikforschung, April 2005), <http://www. cap.uni-muenchen.de/>.

14 European Commission, *The Structures of the Taxation Systems in the European Union*, 2005 edn (Brussels: European Commission, 2005), <http //europa.eu.int/comm/taxation_customs/resources/documents/tax-ation/ gen_ info/economic_analysis/tax_structures/Structures2005.pdf>.

15 Katinka Barysch, 'Is tax competition bad?', CER Bulletin 37 (London: Centre for European Reform, August/September 2004), <http://www.cer. org.uk>.

16 Zentrum für Europäische Wirtschaftsforschung and Ernst and Young, *Company Taxation in the New EU Member States* (July 2004), <http://www.ey.com/>. Some of the underlying assumptions, such as equal

inflation rates across the whole EU, mean that the authors probably under-estimate effective tax rates in the new members. See James Owen, 'Tax issues in the new EU members', in *Economies in Transition: Regional Overview* (London: The Economist Intelligence Unit, December 2004).

17 Flat income taxes have also been introduced by Romania, Ukraine, Russia, Serbia and Georgia.

18 Among Western Europe's most prominent proponents are Paul Kirchhof in Germany, Angela Merkel's economic adviser during her election campaign; the Conservative Party shadow chancellor, George Osborne, in the UK; the Dutch government's Council of Economic Advisors; and the Greek Finance Minister Giorgios Alogoskoufis.

19 European Commission, *Structures of the Taxation*, 2005 edn.

20 In 2005, the Czech Republic, Hungary, Poland and Slovakia all had budget deficits of 3 per cent or larger, and spending pressures continue to rise, not least because of the costs associated with EU accession.

21 European Commission, *Employment in Europe*, 2005 edn (Brussels: European Commission, September 2005), <http://europa.eu.int/comm/employment_social/employment_analysis/employ_2005_en.htm>.

22 Wage data from Eurostat, <http://epp.eurostat.cec.eu.int/>.

23 United Nations populations forecasts, <http://esa.un.org/unpp/>.

24 Marc Suhrcke, *Preferences for Inequality: East vs West*, Innocenti Working Paper No. 89 (Florence: UNICEF Innocenti Research Centre, October 2001), <http://www.unicef-icdc.org/publications/pdf/iwp89.pdf>; and Jan Delhey, *Inequality and Attitudes – Post-communism, Western Capitalism and Beyond* (Berlin: Wissenschaftszentrums Berlin für Sozialforschung, 1999).

4

Migrating Workers and Jobs: A Challenge to the European Social Model?

Simon Commander, Axel Heitmueller and Laura Tyson

Introduction

In both North America and Western Europe there is mounting concern among the population that competition from low-wage emerging market economies is eroding job security and reducing wages. Both the immigration of low-skill workers from such economies and the growing offshoring of both manufacturing production and, more recently, production in IT and business services to such economies have aggravated this concern. The fear of the 'Polish immigrant plumber' taking jobs and wages from his high-wage counterparts was a significant factor behind the 'no' votes against the EU constitution in France and the Netherlands. And German firms have used the threat of offshoring production to lower-cost locations in Central Europe and Asia to win significant compromises on wages and job flexibility from German workers. Overall, there is anxiety among both citizens and their political leaders in the US and throughout Europe that both the immigration of low-wage workers and the out-migration of jobs to low-wage locations will force a 'race to the bottom' in terms of wages, job security and social welfare policy. But are such concerns warranted? And if so, how should the basic features of the European social model be adjusted to address the new challenges posed by increasing globalization?

In order to answer these questions, it is important to move from perception to evidence, because many of the fears about globalization are not empirically grounded. For example, both the US and the UK have been and continue to be major recipients of jobs offshored from elsewhere in the world. And a 2005 report from the UK Office of National Statistics found that employment growth in occupations widely considered susceptible to offshoring has actually been very strong. While job turnover has also been high in those occupations, the rate of job loss has also tended to decline. The perception that job security has declined as a result of globalization is also not consistent with the facts. For example, according to longitudinal data for individual workers in the UK – the British Household Panel Survey (BHPS) – average job security has actually improved since 1993.[1] Interestingly, associate professionals – the category for which the largest number of work permits are issued to immigrants to come and work in the UK – do *not* feel more insecure than UK workers in other types of jobs. This result suggests that immigrants in the UK have largely been complements to rather than substitutes for native workers. In short, using this UK dataset, it appears that immigration has not eroded job security.[2] By contrast, using the same dataset, offshoring does appear to have a negative effect on some UK workers' perception of job security.[3] For example, the perception of job insecurity is clearly higher for machine operators – a category of work where offshoring has been quite prevalent – than for other categories of workers. Finally, the BHPS data also suggest that offshoring and work permit categories are broadly linked which, if anything, points to a possible two-way process, with migrants coming in and jobs migrating out in the same broad job categories.

This chapter attempts to link the dual challenges from continued immigration of people and emigration of jobs. While the two are not strictly linked – at least in a causal sense – they have a number of overlapping features in both policy and economic terms. In particular, the chapter has two goals: first, to put the wider discussion of job displacement and wage changes resulting from immigration and offshoring on a firmer empirical foundation; and second, based on the evidence, to recommend changes in the European social model that will allow the European economies to adjust to the challenges – and respond to the opportunities – resulting from increasing globalization. The basic conclusion is that globalization, like technological change, requires active labour market and education policies to enhance the flexibility and skill levels of European workers – to provide them with what the ILO (International Labour Organization) has termed 'flexicurity' – so that they have productivity advantages with which to compete effectively in the global economy. Policy adjustments are also warranted to help citizens who are dislocated or harmed by globalization to cope with a variety of dislocation costs. The purpose of such adjustments is not to save particular jobs but to save individuals from bearing the cost of beneficial economy-wide changes triggered by immigration, offshoring or other forms of global competition.

Migration of workers and job displacement

Immigration has been a contentious issue on both sides of the Atlantic for many decades. In the US, the steady – and often illegal – flow of Mexican immigrants has fuelled anxiety about the economic consequences for American citizens. In Europe, the extension of the European Union towards its southern and eastern perimeters has raised policy concerns about immigration. For example, around 23 per cent of the British population see immigration and race relations as the most pressing political issue and hence immigration constitutes by far the single most important item of public concern.[4]

The pace and extent of immigration has varied across Europe over time. There have been substantial differences in net migration rates and in the origin of immigrants across OECD and EU countries.[5] While in several European countries the immigrant population has remained stable, by contrast, there has been a pronounced jump in the US and Britain. In the latter, the fear that the accession of eastern countries would lead to a further jump in migration appears to have been exaggerated. Since 1 May 2004, only around 176,000 East Europeans have registered under the new scheme, of whom up to a third might already have been in the UK before this date.[6]

There is a large gap between public opinion and academic evidence on the impact of immigration. Public opinion and the media have traditionally worried about the adverse effects of immigration. A commonly held perception is that foreigners take jobs away from native workers, claim benefits for which they do not pay taxes, and jeopardize social cohesion.[7] By contrast, economic theory predicts that immigration, like trade, creates overall economic benefits for the host economy. These benefits are the result of greater efficiency resulting from enhanced specialization. According to this view, immigrants and natives are not interchangeable but, rather, complement one another. However, if immigrants are very similar to native workers in terms of skill and experience, then native workers may experience job displacement as migrant workers compete for jobs and exercise downward pressure on wages. Yet the increased competitiveness of sectors that employ immigrants may also lead to the creation of new, higher-wage, higher-productivity jobs for native workers in other sectors. Furthermore, if the skill and experience of immigrants differ from those of natives, the wages of the latter may increase as they specialize in high-wage, high-productivity jobs and as skill gaps hindering growth in the host economy are closed.[8]

Immigration policy, and hence immigration itself, can be either demand- or supply-driven. Demand-driven immigration tends to be complementary because to obtain the necessary work permits for migrant workers, employers are usually required to provide evidence that home workers are not available. In contrast, supply-driven immigration can bring both substitutes and complements to the native labour force. In reality, the relative magnitudes of different immigration types will depend on a variety of factors that include immigration policy, but also economic performance in both sending and receiving countries. For example, in common economic markets such as the EU, supply-driven immigration may outweigh demand-driven immigration because of the relatively free movement of labour among union members. In short, the overall impact of migration on the labour market is less clear – not surprisingly – than the popular discussion suggests.

A growing number of empirical studies try to establish the impact of immigration on labour market outcomes in host countries. The majority of these studies examine the US experience between 1980 and 2000, a period during which immigration increased the male labour supply in the US by about 11 per cent.[9] There is also a smaller body of work focusing on European countries such as Germany,[10] France,[11] Austria,[12] and, more recently, the UK.[13] Most of these studies fail to find negative employment effects on the domestic workforce from immigration in either the US or Europe. The majority of evidence provides no support for the view that immigrants displace native workers from their jobs.[14] By contrast, the evidence on the effects of immigration on the wages of native workers reaches more ambiguous conclusions, but effects (both negative and positive) are generally rather small.[15]

According to some studies, even the substantial immigration of low-skill workers into the US has had only minor effects on the wages of low-skilled American workers. But more recent work by Borjas documents a stronger effect.[16] He concludes that a 10 per cent increase in the number of migrants reduces earnings of comparable native workers by up to 4 per cent. And in a yet more recent study,[17] he also finds that a 10 per cent increase in the supply of doctorates in a particular field at a particular time as a result of immigration reduces the earnings of that cohort of doctorates by 3 per cent. But such immigration also reduced the relative wages of unskilled workers – those with less than a high-school education – by about 3 per cent, or about one-third of the 10 per cent decline in their relative wages that occurred during the 1980s. This result suggests that when supply-driven immigration of low-wage labour is large enough over a sustained period of time, it can put downward pressure on the wages of native workers with similar skills levels.

Europeans also worry that because a comparatively large percentage of immigrants will draw heavily on the social welfare system, any gains from immigration will be more than offset by the costs imposed on native taxpayers. But the evidence on the fiscal consequences of immigration is far from unambiguous and varies across countries.[18] As to the net positions of migrants with respect to the benefits system, much depends on the age, skill and family profile of migrants, the types of benefits available and the associated conditions of access. For example, research and government studies in the UK have shown that migrants make significant and often large fiscal contributions to the economy.[19]

Finally, inadequate attention has been paid to the consequences of different types of migration policy and to the important distinction between supply- and demand-driven immigration. It is possible that the mix of supply- and demand-driven immigration is responsible for the small effects of immigration on wages and employment of native workers found in existing empirical studies on the European economies. Clearly, this is an area that warrants further research.

Offshoring and the migration of jobs

According to consultancy reports, millions of jobs are likely to be offshored from Europe and the US to the emerging market countries in the coming years. One widely quoted study suggested that the number of jobs offshored from the US will climb from 400,000 in 2004 to 3.3 million in 2015.[20] This translates into about 250,000 lay-offs a year or 2 per cent of all American job losses every year over the next decade. The same consultancy firm projects that up to one million jobs, or 2 per cent of jobs, in the EU(15) are at risk from going offshore over the next ten years, with a high share of the total going from the UK because of the language.[21] According to recent numbers, about 4 per cent of total jobs lost in France between 2002 and 2004 can be attributed to offshoring. And a recent survey in Germany found that up to 130,000 jobs in the IT sector are at risk of being offshored by 2009.[22]

Some observers believe that predictions about the number of jobs that will be lost as a result of this trend over the next decade in both the US and Europe are too low and that offshoring will increase in size and scope much more quickly than anticipated. According to IBM, less than 8 per cent of the $19 trillion spent each year on sales, general and administrative expenses has been outsourced, and many US and European companies project that they can outsource half or more of this work to foreign locations.[23] However, another survey among 500 top European firms shows that only about 40 per cent have relocated services abroad in the past, and that almost 50 per cent are not planning to offshore services in the future. This survey also reveals that over 50 per cent of service offshoring by European firms is occurring *within* Europe. And within Europe, some countries like Ireland are significant net importers of jobs from other European countries.[24]

The prospect of a large and rapid outsourcing of jobs has caused considerable unease among workers and politicians in both Europe and the US. Some companies have undoubtedly aggravated this concern by using the threat of offshoring to win concessions from their domestic workers. In Germany, for example, Siemens, Daimler-Chrysler and Volkswagen have recently confronted their workforce with a choice between accepting lower earnings or seeing parts of the production being moved offshore.

Offshoring is not a new phenomenon. The recent debate triggered by the growing offshoring of business services is very similar to the debate sparked by the offshoring of manufacturing jobs in the 1980s. Today, there is broad agreement among economists that the offshoring of manufacturing jobs has created net benefits for both host and home countries. Nonetheless, there is also agreement that the offshoring of manufacturing production from the US and Europe to low-wage locations in emerging market economies has imposed dislocation costs on individual workers who have lost their jobs and wages.

Like other forms of skill-biased technological change in production processes triggered by the IT revolution, offshoring has reduced the demand for low-skilled workers while increasing the demand for high-skilled workers in high-wage economies. These effects have been most pronounced in the US because American multinationals have relied on offshoring in manufacturing to a greater extent than their European counterparts. It has also been argued that the US tax code has encouraged multinationals to offshore because the corporate tax system permits them to defer taxation on their foreign earnings.[25] The result has been a decline in both the absolute and the relative wages of low-skilled workers compared to the wages of workers with a college education, as well as growing wage inequality. One view is that about a quarter of the wage inequality in the US over the last 25 years is the result of low-wage competition from immigration, imports of labour-intensive products and the offshoring of manufacturing production, all of which has resulted in sustained downward pressure on the wages of unskilled workers.[26]

The current wave of offshoring is no longer confined to blue-collar manufacturing jobs.[27] Increasingly, relatively high-skill, high-wage, white-collar service jobs that have traditionally been 'non-tradable' are being moved to low-wage locations.[28] Several factors are behind these trends. First, recent advancements in digital technology have made it possible to store and share information more easily. Second, there has been a rapid increase in available infrastructure for sending digital information around the globe at very low (and declining) marginal cost. Third, developing countries such as India and China have growing skilled workforces, with labour costs a fraction of those in the OECD countries. Finally, the business environment has improved considerably in the major emerging markets over the recent past, making them far more attractive as investment and production locations.

In terms of motivation, cost considerations have been the single most important driver of offshoring. Labour costs in many of the countries that attract offshore activities are 70–90 per cent lower than in the advanced market economies. For example, the wages of Indian software engineers are about 25 per cent of the wages of comparably skilled US software engineers (as measured between the late 1990s and 2003).[29] Offshoring service production in the presence of such large wage differentials can create substantial costs savings for firms, allowing them to reduce their prices and strengthen their competitive positions in global markets. Overall, average cost savings achieved through service offshoring in recent years have generally been around 30 per cent.[30]

Although cost considerations are usually the most important factor, other considerations – including the quality of services and of infrastructure, language skills requirements (particularly for the growing number of call centres), higher education, staff turnover, time zones and cultural affinity – affect offshoring decisions.[31] However, some of these *soft* factors, such as quality improvements, may be *ex post* rationalizations for offshoring rather than its initial motive. Further, there has been significant variation in the type of service jobs susceptible to outsourcing. In particular, those services that require no face-to-face contact, have low set-up barriers, low social networking requirements, high cross-border wage differentials, high digitization and high information content have been the most exposed.[32]

Will the offshoring of service jobs by firms in the US, Europe and other high-wage countries create net economic benefits for them and enhance the overall economic well-being of their citizens, even if some of them suffer job losses and wage erosion in the process? Economic logic suggests an affirmative answer to this question. Offshoring the production of intermediate business services to low-cost locations should enhance the productivity and competitiveness of American and European companies, allowing them to reduce their prices and earn higher profits. Higher profits in turn can finance more investment to improve existing products or produce new ones. Lower prices can stimulate greater demand, resulting in higher levels of production and employment. And more competition and increases in demand can spark innovation, resulting in new jobs to replace those that have been outsourced. A recent influential study by the US Institute for International Economics documents this 'virtuous cycle of benefits from offshoring' for the IT sector. This study finds that the significant offshoring of component parts by American computer and telecommunications companies in the 1990s reduced the prices of computers and communications equipment by between 10 and 30 per cent. Lower prices in turn stimulated the investment boom in IT and boosted productivity in industries using IT hardware, adding 0.3 percentage points to US economic growth and fuelling the rapid expansion of IT jobs for American workers.[33]

Economic logic also suggests that the offshoring of software products and business services will have similar beneficial effects on economic growth and job creation in the companies and in the countries from which jobs are offshored. And countries like India and China that attract offshored jobs will also benefit from more jobs, higher incomes and faster growth, allowing them to increase their demand for exports from the offshoring nations. In short, offshoring, like other forms of trade, should be beneficial for both exporting and importing countries.

But this conclusion rests on a critically important condition – namely, that the workers whose jobs are offshored in high-wage exporting countries find new jobs at comparable wages. Whether this condition is satisfied depends on both the flexibility of labour markets in these countries and the level of aggregate demand for their products. Moreover, even in a flexible labour market environment, like that in the US, offshoring may foster economic benefits for the nation while imposing substantial 'dislocation' costs on workers who lose their jobs and are compelled to search for others.

Recent studies by the management consulting firm McKinsey & Company document both the importance of labour market flexibility to the potential benefits from offshoring and the uneven distribution of these benefits. In one study, it was estimated that every $1 of business services production offshored to India by US companies creates $1.14 of economic benefits for the home economy and $.33 for the Indian economy. The gains in the US are primarily the result of cost savings for customers and investors, and the cost savings mostly come from substituting cheaper labour abroad for more expensive labour at home. Although the overall economy benefits, there are significant distribution effects. Shareholders get up to 62 cents of the total benefits, while displaced US workers who find other jobs get only 47 cents. And overall nominal labour income falls compared to what it would have been in the absence of offshoring.

A closer look at the McKinsey logic reveals that the aggregate benefits to the US depend on two critical assumptions: first, the redeployment assumption – or what percentage of workers who lose their jobs are able to find new jobs; and, second, the assumption of what percentage of the wages paid to workers in the jobs they lose to offshoring are recaptured by the wages they receive in their new jobs. Using the historical trends of the US economy between 1979 and 1999, the McKinsey estimate is that 69 per cent of American workers who lose their jobs to offshoring to India find a new job within one year and that, on average, these workers earn 96 per cent of their former wages. Yet, even in the flexible US labour market, nearly one-third of workers displaced by offshoring will not find a job within a year and of those who do, more than half will take a job with lower pay. Older, unskilled and less-educated workers are most at risk of suffering long-term or even permanent job and wage loss as a result of offshoring.

In several continental European countries, where employment practices are more rigid than in the US, the redeployment rate for displaced workers is likely to be much lower. If low enough, offshoring could result in an increase in the overall unemployment rate and a decrease in overall income in the offshoring country. Some McKinsey studies conclude that the German economy may lose about €0.25 for every €1 of offshoring of business services[34] and the French economy may lose €0.15 for every €1 of offshoring of business services.[35] These results reflect the low redeployment rates for German and French workers who lose their jobs as a result of offshoring.[36]

The UK is clearly the leader in offshoring in Europe, with the great majority of deals occurring in financial services.[37] However, despite the higher level of service relocation compared to other European countries, a 2004 academic study has shown that the export of services by far exceeds the import of services in the UK.[38] Further-more, around 50 per cent of job growth in the UK over the past two decades has taken place in business services, a category that accounts for only £1 in £20 of imports and just over £1 in £6 of exports. Yet, there is still little empirical evidence on how offshoring will affect the type, number, regional distribution and skill content of jobs in the UK in the future. One consultancy report estimates that offshoring activities in the UK will displace just 3 per cent of employees over 10–15 years, which amounts to around 6 per cent of all job losses in 2004.[39]

Compared to both Germany and France, labour markets in the UK are more flexible, and offshoring is likely to generate both company-level and economy-wide gains, as in the US. But, again like the US, any such benefits are likely to result in significant dislocation costs – in the form of lost wages and lost jobs – on individual workers.

Implications for policy

There is growing concern among European citizens that the immigra-tion of labour from low-wage countries and the offshoring of pro-duction to such countries will mean fewer jobs, lower wages and lower living standards. Yet as the preceding discussion indicates, neither eco-nomic logic nor the available empirical evidence justifies this concern, as long as European labour markets are sufficiently flexible to take advantage of the efficiency- and competition-enhancing effects of immigration and offshoring while easing the dislocation costs they impose on individual workers. The remainder of this chapter focuses on policies to realize this goal.

Policies to manage migration

The empirical evidence suggests that immigration has not had a sig-nificant effect on job displacement among native workers. But this finding may reflect the fact that most OECD countries are already managing immigration flows. It is therefore conceivable that any further opening of borders may result in some negative transitional or even long-term employment effects on native workers, especially if future migrants are similar to them in skill and experience. Hence, the question arises as to whether there should be targeted policies to address displacement effects on native workers from immigration or whether existing general policies to help those who suffer job loss for any reason are sufficient. Given the strong preference across European countries to restrict immigration, this is rather a theoretical question, with little empirical evidence to direct policy-makers. Whether there should be targeted and specific policies to help native workers displaced by immigration depends on whether they suffer disproportionately or are special in any other sense. It also seems plausible that any adverse employment effects that result from immigration will occur more slowly than similar effects caused by technological change or offshoring. On balance, it is hard to see a justification for policies specifically targeted to help native workers who suffer displacement or wage loss as a result of immigration. Effective policies to assist all displaced workers regardless of the cause of their displacement should be adequate.

There is a strong preference in most developed countries for a managed immigration system that will bring them the benefits of demand-driven immigration while minimizing the downside risks – and forgoing any potential upside benefits – of supply-driven immigration. The main policy issue with such an approach is how best to design targeted demand-driven immigration schemes (e.g., the H1B visa programme in the US and the High Skill Migrant programmes in the UK and Germany). The consensus seems to be around a 'points'-based system (e.g., Canada or Australia as models), with the points positively correlated with the skills, experience and income potential of potential migrants and the sectoral needs of the economy.

However, economic consequences are only part of the controversy over immigration. In many European countries public opinion is often more concerned with the social implications of immigration. In response to concerns about the assimilation and integration of immigrants into broader society, a growing number of European countries now require immigrants to attend language and culture courses and civic education. Failure to comply with such requirements can trigger significant penalties, such as lower unemployment benefits or reduced chances of obtaining resident permits.[40]

Policies for offshoring

Whether a country benefits from offshoring depends significantly on whether workers who lose their jobs as a result are willing and able to move to other jobs that pay equal or higher wages. And this in turn depends on the flexibility of that country's labour market. To some, labour market flexibility means the absence of policies to help workers cope with job loss, and the US example comes quickly to mind. But as Denmark and the Scandinavian countries have demonstrated, labour market flexibility can be enhanced by 'active' policies that allow firms to dismiss workers at short notice while helping workers find new jobs through job relocation and training schemes. All the countries in continental Europe that have employment ratios of over 70 per cent have such active labour market policies. For example, in Denmark workers can be dismissed at short notice, and severance pay requirements are not high. Unemployment benefits, however, are generous and are available over four years, with the most generous benefits available to lower-paid workers who are eligible to receive up to 90 per cent of the wages they received in their previous job. Retraining is obligatory after a certain period of time, and unemployed workers are required to accept offers of employment or retraining in order to remain eligible for unemployment benefits. The Danish example suggests that successful active labour market policies combine an appropriate balance of incentives, obligations and benefits that focus on the 'employability' of workers rather than on the number of jobs in a particular company or sector. A key challenge in the design of active labour market policies is how to provide income support for jobseekers while at the same time increasing their incentive to find and accept jobs. As a result, such policies usually involve both 'activation measures' to encourage individuals to become more active in seeking new jobs and income support measures. The UK Jobseeker Allowance is an example of policy that has both features. Germany has also recently introduced some active labour market reforms – the so-called Hartz reforms.

Even though the British and German systems are very similar in some respects, they confront different problems in terms of both the numbers and the characteristics of the unemployed. The UK has the lowest unemployment rate in Europe, and Germany has the highest. The UK has been trying to improve the employability of specific groups such as the disabled and single parents, while Germany has been trying to reduce high unemployment rates across all categories with particularly high levels in the east. As such, the German experience may provide a test of whether the British scheme can be scaled up to work effectively during a recession. However, the fact that German and UK unemployment levels remain persistently different reinforces the broader point that differences in labour market institutions explain much of the difference in labour market outcomes.[41] To that extent, lower employment protection, fewer restrictions on the hiring and dismissal of workers and, until recently, more restrictive and less generous benefits in the UK compared to those in Germany and other continental European countries have contributed to the UK's superior performance in terms of employment levels and unemployment rates.

Distributional consequences of offshoring

While there is general agreement that offshoring can benefit the economy as a whole, the gains are likely to be spread unevenly across the population.[42] In particular, displaced workers are at risk of losing out, as discussed above. European governments offset some of the negative effects of job loss and unemployment by providing *income supplements* for unemployed workers, particularly low-income workers. However, it is important to design the tax and benefit system in such a way that accepting a new job makes economic sense for an individual worker. This is not the case in many European countries because such a worker may face a very high marginal effective tax rate – as much as 80 per cent – if he accepts a new job at his previous wage level.[43] And the marginal tax rate can be even higher if the wage a worker receives in a new job is lower than the wage paid in his previous job.

One approach currently being implemented in the US, Canada and Switzerland – and to some degree also in Germany (only to workers aged 50 or older) and France (only to workers who lose their jobs in 'mass lay-offs') – is that of wage insurance. The basic features of the approach are illustrated by the US scheme. The programme was introduced in 2002 and provides wage insurance for manufacturing workers aged 50 or older who can prove that trade is a 'major cause' of their job loss. The scheme pays eligible workers half the earnings that have been lost if they take a new job with a ceiling of $10,000.[44] The goal of the programme is to encourage displaced workers to accept new jobs quickly to avoid the depreciation of their skills and experience. As noted earlier, older workers are much more likely to face long-term or even permanent job loss as a result of import competition or offshoring unless they are willing to accept new jobs at lower wages than what they earned in their previous jobs. Implementation of the wage insurance programme in the US has been very limited so far, and only a small number of people have actually been beneficiaries. Recently, it has been argued that service workers displaced by offshoring should have wage insurance extended to them. The proposed extension would include permanently displaced full-time workers with at least two years of tenure in their previous job.

The evidence on whether wage insurance has significant benefits is very limited. A controlled experiment in Canada provides evidence of modest employment effects from wage insurance but also finds no impact on the amount or duration of unemployment benefits.[45] Although wage insurance may be helpful in addressing the political fallout from offshoring, such an approach amounts to a wage subsidy programme that, like any other wage subsidy scheme, will distort prices in the labour market. For example, a firm may offer a lower wage to a worker eligible for wage insurance or a firm may specifically hire displaced workers who qualify for wage insurance because they are less expensive than workers who are not eligible. Such possible incentive effects have not yet been analysed in detail. Equally, the fiscal implications of a broad-based wage insurance programme are not fully understood. For example, a recent US study estimated that the proposed extension of wage insurance discussed above would cost up to $4 billion a year.[46]

Role of education, training and R&D

Improving skills and training has long been a major tool to enable displaced workers to find new jobs and shorten their time out of work. There are many challenges confronting European policy-makers in the education arena. These include developing effective job-retraining programmes for such workers and designing educational systems that promote the acquisition of general skills rather than occupation-specific training, which has been the traditional focus for workers in Germany, France and Italy. Recent reforms in the UK have been designed to achieve the latter objective. Wage insurance may also serve as a training subsidy if it encourages displaced workers to take up entry-level jobs providing training on the job while also saving them the opportunity costs of forgone wages during the training period. Policy-makers tend to underestimate the ability of workers to acquire substantially more human capital on the job than in the classroom.

Improving human capital in general may help to reduce potential losses from offshoring. Education and training can have a significant impact on economic growth, particularly through the influence of human capital on the introduction and absorption of new technologies.[47] Furthermore, successful R&D policies can mitigate the effects of offshoring. Although most developed countries distribute only a fraction of their overall expenditure on physical equipment and structure to R&D, evidence suggests that the potential positive externalities to R&D investment are substantial and a major source of long-term economic growth.[48]

Flexible labour markets are important, but their success hinges critically on the ability of an economy to create new jobs. Whether the offshoring of jobs will lead to net employment losses will very much depend on the job creation rate of an economy, and that in turn is closely linked to its productivity performance.

Interplay with immigration policy

Immigration and offshoring are not necessarily distinct phenomena and can happen at the same time and may even depend on one another. For example, immigrants are often prepared to work for significantly lower wages compared to natives for a given skill level, and may therefore ease the cost pressures that encourage a business to send parts of its production offshore to an emerging market location. Hence, policy solutions may benefit from a joint approach given the significant overlap outlined above.

Possible approaches could include selective changes to migration policy (e.g., skill quotas). For example, if offshoring leads to a loss of unskilled jobs in the advanced economies, channels for unskilled migration could be closed off. At a minimum, migration quotas could be used to mitigate job losses in a particular sector as a result of offshoring. In this respect, managed migration schemes can be used (either directly or indirectly) to address the employment effects of offshoring. If offshoring is primarily driven by wage differentials, more open borders could be expected to have an impact on wage levels in advanced economies. However, wage differentials between advanced and developing countries are very large, while a wage floor – often through a legally mandated minimum wage – will obviously limit the degree of wage flexibility.

Looking ahead: concluding remarks

Although there is some evidence from North America that significant immigration at the lower skill end of the labour market can lead to downward pressure on the relative wages of natives, so far the evidence from Europe has been that immigration has had little or no effect on either the wages or the employment levels of native workers.

Based on the evidence, it is reasonable to conclude that while immigration may potentially have an impact on the distribution of wages across skill categories, it is unlikely to have a significant impact on the overall wage level.

Although the out-migration or offshoring of jobs is clearly increasing, evidence about the long-term effects on wages and employment in the advanced industrial countries is still very limited and long-run predictions are fraught with uncertainty. On the one hand, as technological change raises the share of activities that are tradable, and hence shifts the size and composition of the global labour markets in which firms can feasibly operate, it is conceivable that these trends could unleash major and permanent relocations of work across borders, with associated shifts in relative wages. If this is indeed a plausible conjecture, then the obvious challenge for policy will be to address the consequences for the employment and wage prospects of those skill groups for whom the out-migration of jobs may have a significant adverse impact.

In Europe, the migration of jobs through offshoring is in its relative infancy and as yet has had no significant impact on the wages or employment rates of European workers. While the evidence from North America suggests that there will be an impact in the future, there are also reasons for being quite cautious about the size of these effects. For a start, offshoring has mostly been for functions – back office and the like – that are not generally deemed core to companies. Yet many functions within firms remain ill-suited to offshoring for organizational and technical reasons, as well as because of coordination and other costs.[49] There is, of course, a large literature on firm organization – stretching from the managerial to transactions costs – that provides reasons for why this has been and, in many cases, is likely to remain the case. Further, with plausible assumptions concerning labour supply elasticities, the cost advantage of offshore locations will steadily decline over time as labour and capital costs rise in such locations. Indeed, there is already evidence of labour supply constraints beginning to operate in both India and China for certain kinds of skills and in certain locations.[50] Hence, neither the demand- nor supply-side arguments necessarily support the notion that offshoring must accelerate radically in the years ahead. According to a recent analysis by McKinsey and Company, only about 11 per cent of the world's service-sector jobs can be performed at remote locations. Most services, including those associated with homes and with health, must by their very nature be provided by workers in the same location as consumers.

What is clear, however, is that the impact of offshoring on European labour markets and the distribution of skills and income will depend mainly on the institutional context. In this regard, there are already important differences within Europe. The balance between job protection and benefits like unemployment insurance varies among European countries, as does the extent to which active labour market policies are used to strengthen employability. Nonetheless, despite these differences, there is widespread agreement across Europe that policies to provide better incentives for job creation – including reducing the tax rate on labour – and to provide greater skill acquisition will be important to mitigating any adverse effects on the employment and wages of European workers from the out-migration of jobs to lower-cost locations in emerging markets.

Fears among European and American workers about the effects of immigration and offshoring on their jobs and wages are usually dismissed by economists and business leaders. And the evidence reviewed in this chapter shows that at least to date these effects have been insignificant and the fears unwarranted. But such fears have a sound analytical foundation. As Richard Freeman,[51] a respected labour economist at Harvard University, has recently pointed out, the global labour force has more than doubled over the last 15 years as a result of the entrance of China, India and the former Soviet Union into the global system of production and trade. These new workers have brought little physical capital with them. As a result, their arrival has cut the global capital/labour ratio in half and this ratio is the primary determinant of worker productivity and pay. A lower capital/labour ratio also means that the distribution of income – the balance of negotiating power – has shifted in favour of the owners of capital and against labour. Overall, the doubling of the global labour force will mean that over the next several years average real wages are likely to grow more slowly in the advanced industrial countries and that many workers, especially those at the lower end of the skill distribution, are likely to face painful job dislocation and stagnant or falling real wages. So the challenges confronting European governments will be how to adjust their policies to take advantage of the efficiency gains from globalization – the lower prices, greater competition and growing markets – associated with the rise of China, India and other emerging markets, while at the same time making sure that these gains are shared among their populations in accordance with their notions of equity and fairness.

Notes

This chapter does not necessarily reflect the views of the Prime Minister's Strategy Unit.

1 Ordered logit with base year of 1993 with age, tenure, time and regional dummies and occupational classification.

2 C. Dustmann and I. Preston, *Is Immigration Good or Bad for the Economy? Analysis of Attitudinal Responses*, CReAM Discussion Paper No. 06/04 (London: University College, Centre for Research and Analysis of Migration, 2004) argue that the fiscal implications of immigration are more important.

3 Significant when using a Spearman test.

4 MORI, *MORI Political Monitor February: Topline Results* (MORI 2005), <www.mori.com/polls/2005/mpm050221.shtml>.

5 For a comprehensive review of statistics see OECD, *Trends in International Migration* (Paris: OECD, 2005).

6 Home Office, *Accession Monitoring Report* (May 2005), <http://www.ind.homeoffice.gov.uk/ind/en/home/0/reports/accession_monitoring. Maincontent.0012.file.tmp/AM.pdf>.

7 See, e.g., Dustmann and Preston, *Is Immigration Good?*

8 For a comprehensive discussion on the economic effects of migration and a review of the most important studies, see, e.g., G. Borjas, 'The economic analysis of immigration', in O. Ashenfelter and D. Card, eds., *Handbook of Labor Economics*, vol. 3A (Amsterdam: North-Holland, 1999), pp. 1697–760.

9 See Borjas, 'Economic analysis of immigration'.

10 J.-S. Pischke and J. Velling, 'Employment effects of immigration to Germany: an analysis based on local labor markets', *Review of Economics and Statistics*, 79, 4 (1997), pp. 594–604; DeNew and Zimmermann, 'Native Wage Impacts of Foreign Labour: A Random Effects Panel Analysis', *Journal of Population Economics*, 7 (1994), pp. 177–192.

11 J. Hunt, 'The impact of the 1962 repatriates from Algeria on the French labor market', *Industrial and Labor Relations Review*, 45, 3 (1992), pp. 556–72.

12 R. Winter-Ebmer and J. Zweimueller, 'Do Immigrants displace young native workers? The Austrian experience', *Journal of Population Economics*, 12, 2 (1999), pp. 327–40.

13 C. Dustmann, F. Fabbri and I. Preston, *The Local Market Effects of Immigration in the UK*, Working Paper (Department of Economics, University College of London, 2003); S. Glover, C. Gott, A. Loizillon, J. Portes, R. Price, S. Spencer, V. Srinivasan and C. Willis, *Migration: An Economic and Social Analysis*, RDS Occasional Paper No. 67, (Home Office, HMSO: London, 2001); J. Portes and S. French, *The Impact of Freer Movement of Workers from Central and Eastern Europe on the UK Labour Market: Early Evidence*, Working Paper No. 18 (Department for Work and Pensions, HMSO: London, 2005).

14 Exceptions are J. Angrist and A. Kugler, 'Protective or counter-productive? Labour market institutions and the effect of immigration on

EU natives', *Economic Journal*, 113, (2002), pp. 302–28, who find negative but mostly insignificant effects for some European countries.

15 For a summary of studies. see H. Bruecker, J. R. Frick and G. G. Wagner, 'Economic consequences of immigration in Europe', (Mimeo 2004), <http://www.lisproject.org/immigration/papers/wagner.pdf>.

16 G. Borjas, 'The labour demand curve *is* downward sloping: re-examining the impact of immigration on the labor market', *Quarterly Journal of Economics*, 118, 4 (2003), pp. 1335–74.

17 G. Borjas, *The Labour Market Impact of High-Skill Immigration*, NBER Working Paper 11217, (2005).

18 For example, in Austria, Belgium, France and Holland the dependence of immigrants on welfare has generally been higher than that of locals, while the opposite has obtained in other European states, such as Germany, Greece, Portugal, Spain and the UK.

19 Home Office, *The Migrant Population in the UK: Fiscal Effects*, Development and Statistics Directorate Occasional Paper No. 77 (2002), <www.homeoffice.gov.uk/rds/pdfs/occ77migrant.pdf>; IPPR, 'Paying their way in: the fiscal contribution of immigrants in the UK' (2005), <http://www.ippr.org/ecomm/files/Paying per cent20Their per cent20 Way.pdf>.

20 J. C. McCarthy, with A. Dash, H. Liddell, C. Ferrusi Ross and B. D. Temkin, '3.3 million US services jobs to go offshore', Forrester Research (11 November 2002), <http://www.forrester.com>.

21 A. Parker, with D. Metcalfe and S. Takahashi, 'Two-speed Europe: why 1 million jobs will move offshore', *Trends* (18 August 2004), <http://www.forrester.com>; J. F. Kirkegaard, *Outsourcing and Offshoring: Pushing the European Model over the Hill, rather than off the Cliff!*, Working Paper Series WP 05-1 (Washington, DC: Institute for International Economics, 2005).

22 A. T. Kearney, 'Offshoring bedroht 130.000 deutsche IT-Arbeitsplätze', *News Release* (Frankfurt, 18 February 2004).

23 *The Economist*, 'Germany's Surprising Economy' (20 August 2005).

24 UNCTAD and Roland Berger Strategy Consultants, *Service Offshoring* (Geneva: United Nations, June 2004).

25 L. Brainard and R. E. Litan, *'Offshoring' Service Jobs: Bane or Boon – And What To Do?*, Policy Brief No. 132 (Washington DC: The Brookings Institution, 2004).

26 Martin Wolf, *Why Globalization Works* (London: Yale University Press, 2004).

27 L. Tyson, *'Outsourcing: who's safe anymore?'* Economic Viewpoint, *Business Week* (23 February 2004).

28 F. Levy, F. and A. Goelman, 'Offshoring and radiology', paper prepared for the Brookings Trade Forum, 12–13 May 2005, Washington DC.

29 S. Commander, M. Kangasniemi and A. Winters, 'The economics of the brain drain', in R. Baldwin and L. A. Winters, eds., *Challenges to Globalization* (Chicago: NBER and University of Chicago Press, 2004).

30 UNCTAD and Roland Berger Strategy Consultants, *Service Offshoring*, 2004.

31 UNCTAD, *World Investment Report 2004: The Shift Towards Services* (New York and Geneva: United Nations, 2004).

32 A. D. Bardhan and C. Kroll, *The New Wave of Outsourcing*, Fisher Center Research Reports No. 1103 (Berkeley: Fisher Center for Real Estate & Urban Economics, University of California, 2003).

33 C. L. Mann, *Globalization of IT Services and White-Collar Jobs: The Next Wave of Productivity Growth*, Policy Brief 03–11 (Washington, DC: Institute for International Economics Policy Briefs, 2003).

34 McKinsey & Company, *Can Germany Win from Offshoring*, McKinsey Global Institute (July 2004).

35 McKinsey & Company, *How Offshoring of Services Could Benefit France*, McKinsey Global Institute (June 2005).

36 See also D. Farrell, 'Offshoring: value creation through economic change', *Journal of Management Studies*, 42, 3 (2005), pp. 675–83.

37 See UNCTAD, *Investment Report 2004*, and European Monitoring Centre on Change, *European Restructuring Monitor Statistics* (2005), <http://emcc.eurofound.eu.int/erm>.

38 L. Abramovsky, R. Griffin and M. Sako, *Offshoring of Business Services and its Impact on the UK Economy*, Research Briefing Note (London: Advanced Institute of Management, November 2004).

39 Forrester Research, *Two-Speed Europe*.

40 For an overview, see OECD, *Trends in Immigration* (Paris: OECD, 2004).

41 See S. Nickell and L. Nunziata, 'Unemployment in the OECD since the 1960s. What do we know?' *Economic Journal*, 115 (2005), pp. 1–27.

42 L. Tyson, 'Offshoring: the pros and cons for Europe', Economic Viewpoint, *Business Week* (6 December 2004).

43 OECD, *From Unemployment to Work*, OECD Policy Brief (Paris: OECD, June 2005).

44 Brainard and Litan, '*Offshoring*' *Service Jobs*; L. G. Kletzer, 'Trade-related job loss and wage insurance: a synthetic review', *Review of International Economics*, 12, 5 (2004), pp. 724–48; L. Brainard, R. E. Litan and N. Warren, *Insuring America's Workers in a New Era of Offshoring*, Policy Brief No. 143 (Washington DC: The Brookings Institution, 2005).

45 Kletzer, 'Trade-related job loss'.

46 Brainard and Litan, '*Offshoring*' *Service Jobs*.

47 J. Benhabib, and M. Spiegel, 'The role of human capital in economic development: evidence from aggregate cross-country data', *Journal of Monetary Economics*, 34, 2 (1994), pp. 143–73; D. Frantzen, 'R&D, human capital and international technology spillovers: a cross-country

analysis', *Scandinavian Journal of Economics*, 102, 1 (2000), pp. 57–75; S. Dowrick and M. Rogers, 'Classical and technological convergence: beyond the Solow-Swan growth model', *Oxford Economic Papers*, 54, 3 (2002), pp. 369–85.

48 S. Dowrick, *Investing in the Knowledge Economy: Implications for Australian Economic Growth*, Working paper (Canberra: Australian National University, 2002).

49 UNCTAD, Investment Report.

50 A number of the major Indian offshore firms have begun to look towards China to try and ensure adequate supply of skills, as in the case of both Infosys and TCS. However, McKinsey and Company, *Addressing China's Looming Talent Shortage* (McKinsey Global Institute, October 2005), has recently warned about skill shortages in China itself.

51 Richard Freeman, 'What really ails Europe (and America): the doubling of the global workforce', *Globalist* (3 June 2005), <www.theglobalist.com>.

5

The Vulnerability of the European Project

René Cuperus

These are perilous times we live in. History teaches us that acceleration in a modernization process is often accompanied by counter
movements, not infrequently of a very dangerous nature. The process
of modernization is a story of trends and countertrends, movement
and countermovement. To give a major example, the Industrial
Revolution and the evolution of modern liberal society both ultimately produced democracy and prosperity, but also totalitarian
pathologies such as Communism and National Socialism.

It looks as if we are once again in a period of hypermodernization.
All the signals are set for change, for transition and transformation.
Let us list the rather worn-out clichés: globalization, technological
acceleration, the post-industrial knowledge economy, immigration
and the rise of multi-ethnic societies, individualization and social frag-
mentation, environmental degradation, a commercial entertainment
revolt in the media, geopolitical power shifts at the global level, international terrorism linked to political Islam.

These trends all point to a world in flux. Society, the economy and
politics have entered an unprecedented, accelerated phase. Traditional
institutions and attitudes are under great pressure. Such a process of
change produces both optimism and pessimism: fear and unease
alongside a sense of adventure and a spirit of enterprise. Those ready
to welcome the future stand alongside those who fear it. A fairly harsh
division is appearing between winners and losers, a demarcation
line between countries and within countries. China and India versus
Japan, the Arab world and Africa. Ireland, Poland, Finland and
the United Kingdom against France, Germany and Italy. And within

countries: young educated double-earners in the 'exposed' private sector against older, less well-educated industrial *Facharbeiter* and immigrants who are discriminated against on the labour market. New inequalities and polarizations are being produced. The transformation is particularly strong in questions of national, cultural and ethnic identity.

This chapter attempts to defuse the stereotypical dispute between the Anglo-Saxon liberal model and the continental European social model.[1] The economic necessity of reform and modernization of outdated policy systems of social security, care and pensions is not denied. The worldwide trends in globalization, technology, immigration and demography require far-reaching adjustments. There is no doubt that modernization and innovation are needed in order to make the European model economically *and* socially competitive in accordance with the new global rules of the game. But the procyclic modernization of policy systems in response to modernization is not without political and social risks. Indeed, we live in perilous times.

This chapter focuses on the widening gap between the political and policy elites and large groups – if not the majority – of the population of the European welfare states. There is a high level of unease in many Western countries; trust in institutions and politics is at a record low; there is a crisis of confidence and a malaise of political representation.[2] The disturbing thing is that this great distrust and unease is encountered not only in countries that have 'manic depression' as a result of reform postponement (the German and French disease), but also in countries that have actually carried through welfare state reform programmes, such as Denmark, Austria or the Netherlands. The pan-European presence of extreme-right, right-wing or postmodern populist movements remains an alarming and grim reminder of the general unease in the population and the crisis of confidence which besets the established political scene. In the process of transformation and reform, there has been a fundamental breakdown of communication between elites and parts of the population. The populist counter reaction may be considered a 'silent' revolt of the relatively low-educated segments of the middle classes.[3]

The erosion of the post-war 'protection shield'

The unease felt by many people in many countries in the face of a world adrift – especially in Europe where the post-war period produced such a socioeconomic and democratic cultural crescendo – seems to be rooted in the awareness that the basics of the post-war consensus are over.

There is in the first place disenchantment with the ideal of the emancipated middle-class society. The concept of the European welfare state, originally conceived as a socio-preventative protection against fascism and communism, is under fire. Instead of the certainty that the new generation will have a better life than their predecessors, there is growing polarization, insecurity and pressure on the middle classes themselves.[4] The idea was that through education and the spread of culture we could guarantee forever the 'decolonization' and emancipation of the citizen. But despite all the successes achieved in this area (especially in terms of the emancipation of women), social mobility is still subject to hard boundaries; moreover, a new underclass of immigrants has appeared – the story of emancipation has to start all over again.

Then, secondly, there is Europe. For a long time, the French, the Dutch, the Germans, the British and the Italians were all convinced that Europe would turn out just like them: Europe as an extension or projection of themselves. Instead, the EU became, through 'integration by stealth', an amorphous, enlarged labyrinthine polity, without charm or charisma. Following the 'Non' and 'Nee' votes in France and the Netherlands (and the concealed support for that position in a lot of member states), Europe is now experiencing a great sobering up. The idea of 'an ever closer Union' is called into question on existential grounds. The apparently endless expansion, the 'ultraliberal' currency union and stability pact, the regulatory passion of Brussels and spill-over effects of the internal market have created feelings of alienation from the European project. Despite all the rhetoric about Europe as a new superpower, which, as a global player, could compete economically and geopolitically with China, India and the US, the giant with feet of clay is looking pretty shaky. The time-honoured federal ideal is further away than ever; everything points to a certain reassessment of the nation-state, as a basis to regain trust between elites and population and for solving existential identity problems.

In the third place, there is the multi-ethnic society. For a long time, shame about the colonial past and the memory of the Holocaust guaranteed a high level of obligation and tolerance in dealings with migrants and ethnic minorities. The ideal of a multicultural society was alive and kicking: a non-racial, rainbow community in which the tone was set by mutual respect between people and population groups, irrespective of ethnic background, race or faith.

This situation was rudely destroyed by the rise of extreme-right racist parties in many European member states propagating hatred of foreigners. The established democratic parties reacted to this with a *cordon sanitaire*. Migrants were perceived as victims of racism and discrimination. Then came increasing worries about segregation and 'parallel communities', the difficulties of integrating immigrants in education and on the labour market, high unemployment and crime rates: these were ultimately destroying the politically correct concept of the multicultural society. Issues of integration and acculturation are high on the political-social agenda in nearly all European member states.[5]

In the fourth place, the confidence in our political system has been eroded. Following the horrors of national socialism, liberal democracy had arisen as a new religion of freedom, also in contrast to the communist enemy during the Cold War: a representative democracy with a solidly entrenched rule of law and with people's parties as channels for the masses in the democracy. Now many feel repelled by the political system, and there is increasing distrust of institutions and the rules of the democratic game. The representative elite democracy stands suddenly accused by a plebiscitary populism in many European countries, alongside experimental ideas for internet democracy.

What is at stake here is the heritage of the European Civil War in the twentieth century. It is as if the magic of the post-war period, the 'anti-war vaccination' which European society received under the motto 'never again', has worn off, has lost its effect; as if the moral impact of the memory of the barbarism, the scars of the twentieth century, was increasingly fading away. It is as if we have broken out of the 'protective cocoon' of the post-war era.

The risky response of the international policy-making community

What is the response of the political and policy elites to this tricky complex of problems and popular distrust and unease? The core fact is that we can see a dominant reaction all over the world, a reaction which is fairly insensitive to the unease and the insecurity generated in the current period of hypermodernization. This is the procyclic discourse of change, modernization, innovation and adaptation to the new global trends; the dominant international master-narrative of politicians, policy-makers, consultants, the international financial institutions, the business schools, *The Economist*. The story goes that we have to continue to modernize through the transition. We have to make all policy systems fit for the future. We have to make the people fit for the future; to empower and facilitate people for the 'new world'. We have to open up to the new world in terms of free trade, free traffic of persons, goods, thoughts and challenges. We have to give (back) to the citizens the qualities of autonomy, personal responsibility and individual freedom of choice; we have to organize society on the basis of successful emancipation, with the middle-class ability to cope on one's own as a role model.

It is also the story of cosmopolitan global citizenship and a cosmopolitan Europe, or, in other words, of self-dissolution of nation-states. Or as Mark Leonard puts it: 'The twentieth century was the century of the nation-state. The future belongs to strong regional alliances which are needed in order to create prosperity.'[6] This scenario of openness, change and increasing flexibility has good credentials. It has the charm of infectious enthusiasm, hands-on pragmatism, 'the optimism of the will', forward-looking vision. Embrace the future. Let's make things better.

This 'machismo of change' discourse, however, goes hand in hand with a powerful debunking and combating of other responses to the world's turbulences. The forces of fear and unease tend to be ridiculed and demonized. Continental Europe, for instance, is portrayed as the dope or the lame duck, as the great deviant with respect to the global liberal model with an assured future *à la* America and Asia. The entire continental model – Rhineland, socially protective – is supposedly failing to understand the writing on the wall and has turned its back on the future. This model is consigned to the wastebin in the international master-narrative of politicians, policy-makers and consultants. American-British-Asian self-confidence forms the background to a radical modernization discourse and an 'everything is possible if you really want it' storyline. It is the story of the winners of globalization, the discourse of the winning mood. Future-oriented hyperactivity set against timidity in the face of innovation. Optimism set against gloom. Infectious enthusiasm set against unfashionable conservatism (with a small 'c'). Fear and unease set against self-assurance and faith in the future.

Postponed reform: the German disease

The radical procyclic modernization discourse becomes particularly visible in its hard clash with the alleged 'innovation-shy' countries such as France and Germany. In terms of crude caricature, continental European passivity here faces Anglo-Saxon hyperactivity. The political and social climate in Germany has become the classic case of confrontation between fear and change, modernization and unease.

Report after report has offered the German political scene timetables for adjustment and change, but the political system has remained in the grip of *Reformstau*. The great old-fashioned giant is wheezing and creaking its way through the modern age. Let there be no doubt: Germany has to *abspecken*. The policy performance of successive governments with regard to the labour market and unemployment has been, to put it mildly, a disaster. But the integration of the old GDR into the Federal Republic can be cited as a very substantial, and internationally still too much neglected, excuse.

But behind the existential hesitation of the *blockierte Gesellschaft* lies a story more tragic than the one which all those 20-year-old economic analysts of the business news TV channels are able to comprehend and comment on. For Germany, its social market economy and welfare state have played a vital role in its *Vergangenheitsbewältigung* – i.e. its coming to terms with the collective war trauma. *Wirtschaftswunder, Wohlstandsstaat* and a social market economy with harmonious labour relations were Germany's road to normality and the creation of a new, positive self-image, a new civil religion on the mental and material ruins of post-war Germany.[7] The socioeconomic success also had to serve as surrogate for a totally clouded, absent national identity. Germany had to reinvent its national identity without relying on the foundations of its recent history: the prosperous German welfare state was the anchor of this process.

But there is more. Germany, being a deep-rooted industrial society and culture, is wrestling – like all of Europe – with a way out of the dilemma between American-style globalization and retention of its own mental and cultural essence. From the perspective of many economists, German society is conducting a bitter and drawn-out rearguard action. All the statistics put over the same message: the Rhineland model is dead. But things are different for the major political parties in Germany: they must ultimately aim, in a certain sense, to redefine the social order in globalizing world. But what perspectives are available? So far, organizational experts, politicians and employers have not been able to paint a credible and attractive perspective for everyone in the industrial sector. For the political community, this is the tough and so far insoluble core of the problem: reforms are required to make the welfare state sustainable in the future, but what form should this society soon be taking? Will something of the Rhineland model remain or will the country simply slide towards hard-hearted individualism? To what extent can a state continue to lead in such a situation? Are all the fine words and ideas actually nothing more than a roundabout way of saying that it's all going to get harder? Everyone understands that something has to be done, but as long as the country is not a poorhouse and there is no attractive and credible alternative perspective on offer, inhibiting and delaying change still provide more security in the short term than going along with reforms.[8]

And thus the result of the Federal elections on 18 September 2005, which had promised to provide a *Politikwechsel*, were in line with the dominant climate: an impasse between adaptation and conservation, unease and change. The demarcation line of change versus retention, of liberalization versus social protection, still runs right through Germany, right through the SPD, right through the German trade union movement, right through the bureaucratic elites and the majority of the population.

A new social faultline?

There are some who like to dismiss the German electorate, or the Dutch and French 'no' voters in the constitution referendums, as xenophobic nationalists, as frightened enemies of the open society, as people who turn their back on the future, as deniers of globalization and immigration. But these critics are off the mark. There may be great danger involved when a cosmopolitan postnational elite carelessly argues away the nation-state and national identity, just at the moment that the nation-state is for many a last straw of identification to cling to, a beacon of trust in a world in flux.

A casual cosmopolitan reaction forcefully denies the strong polarizing currents to which society is currently subjected and which can have very different results for different groups. It denies the extremely weak sociocultural and political climate in Europe, which is reflected by the pan-European rise of the populist right (and to a less strong extent, left-wing protectionism). There are many signs of a worrying gulf between political elites and significant parts of the population. This came to the surface in the results of the French and Dutch referendums on the European constitution. But it is also alarmingly reflected in the pan-European presence of the populist (extreme) right – from Le Pen to Carl Hagen, from Vlaams Belang to Pia Kjaersgaard. Now populist left or protectionist left parties are also entering the arena, such as the German 'Linkspartei' of Lafontaine and Gysi or the Dutch Socialist Party (SP).

Sociopolitical research in the Netherlands, Flanders or Austria reveals the great distrust (major social unease combined with lack of

confidence in politicians and institutions) among large parts of the
population and a great divergence of opinion between the 'political
and social elite' and the general population.[9] The issue is thus the crisis
of political representation for traditional parties and the new socio-
logical faultline in today's European society, a faultline which we have
just encountered so clearly yet again in voter behaviour on the
European constitution, both in the Netherlands and in France: *la
France d'en haut* versus *la France d'en bas*, a division between the
less educated and the highly educated, the well-off against those
who struggle to keep up with modern developments. We could even
speak of two groups, those who 'embrace the future' versus those who
'fear the future', people who are convinced that the new world has
nothing good in store for them and who feel betrayed by 'the political
elite'. This represents an existential problem, especially for social
democracy, as the dividing line between these groups cuts straight
through the middle of the social-democratic electorate.[10]

Again, the great question is how the present dominant master-
narrative of policy-makers, politicians and decision-makers – a radical
discourse of change in response to radical change; 'policy flux' in
response to a world in flux – relates to the crises of confidence and representation in the current political and social system.

Welfare state reform and national identity

The previously described problem cluster of social unease and distrust
regarding European integration and the reform of the welfare state, as
well as the demarcation line between future optimists and future pes-
simists, can to an important extent be assigned to the problem of (perceived) threatened identity.

As I have argued in the case of Germany, the welfare state is, especially on the continent, a strong identity issue in itself. Around the
concept of the welfare state an enlightened view of national identity
did arise after the Second World War in many European countries.
This sentiment may be described as 'welfare chauvinism', to be defined
as a 'civil religion' of communitarianism and egalitarianism institutionalized through the national solidarity of welfare state arrangements in countries like Sweden, Denmark, the Netherlands, Belgium,
Finland and Germany.

Europeans for decades thought that the European social model (the
sum of national social welfare states) presented something resembling
Francis Fukuyama's 'end of history' thesis: the apogee of human

civilization, social paradise on a human scale, the final theoretical stage of social politics. This self-assurance is suffering a nasty hangover, since the welfare state stays under permanent serious pressure (from within and without).[11] This is not just a question of slimming-down, but also involves its very foundations, its sustainability and thus its continued existence. The self-image has been shaken so strongly that even the contrast with the American capitalist model is no longer proudly and unanimously supported any more. This is causing identity problems. The consequences of globalization, modernization, Europeanization and mass immigration for the well-being of the welfare state have repercussions at the level of national identity and societal self-image. For this reason alone we cannot afford to ignore feelings of national identity in the debate on the 'European social model'. Only in this way can we understand the unease which is spreading around Europe and resulting in a political and mental blockade to reforms, be they necessary or not. This unease can be both a pre-reform and a post-reform phenomenon, to be found both in a country such as Germany – a notorious case of postponed welfare state reform – and in the Netherlands, a case of reform fatigue or welfare state blues.[12]

In general, it does not seem wise or advisable for progressives to deny the 'lived reality' of national identities and thus to allow this issue to become the monopoly of the right.[13] In fact it is the task of progressives to develop an open, hospitable, non-xenophobic definition of national identity: *a greater Us*. There is a tension between the concept of a 'greater us' and the ongoing internationalization, for the purposes of this argument understood as a dual process: the process of European unification and the creation of multi-ethnic societies, the cultural and ethnic differentiation of European society. Both can lead to a felt loss of identity, according to an official advisory body of the Dutch government that was commissioned by the government to study this subject.[14] A double 'integration issue' results from the process of internationalization: the integration of the nation-states in the European Union; and the integration of immigrants in the nation-state. In the rest of this chapter, I will concentrate on the first integration question, i.e. European affairs.

European integration: the revenge of national identity

In recent years, the European Union, and this is the real crux of the matter, has become for many people more of a threat than an inspired solution. It is where we encounter what I will call the 'nationalism paradox' of European unification. European cooperation was originally begun as a way of transcending the aggressive nationalism of the nineteenth century, which in the following century resulted so catastrophically in European civil war. But with current developments (the expansion, the neoliberal currency union, a super-state constitution, technocratic centralization and regulatory spill-over), the EU would seem to have reached a critical boundary. Europe generates strong national counterforces and, like a magician's apprentice, now produces the nationalism which it actually aimed to transcend.

The process of European unification has led to a substantial reduction in the policy freedom of the nation-state. The process of delegation of authority to European institutions has progressed further than many are aware. This can be called 'integration by stealth' – a process that may be either intentional or unconscious. All things considered, the EU is a slim project of the elite. Per country, the European dossier has been 'delegated' to a 'Europe cartel' comprising a handful of European politicians and specialists, set alongside a population which is quite uninvolved – this is what the analysis of the constitutional referendums indicates for Spain, France and the Netherlands.[15]

One has to ask what the European process of unification will ultimately mean for the future position of the nation-states and above all for national identity (even though it is clear that different loyalties and identities are not mutually exclusive, in the same way that ethnic-cultural identity and national identity can also coexist). The Treaty of Maastricht formally states that the European Union must respect the national identity of its member states, but this issue is crucial to the process of federation or confederation formation. One might have expected this question, certainly in view of the enormous cultural diversity of Europe, to have been a permanent focus of attention. The tragic aspect of the European unification is that neither the functionalistic method of Monnet nor the 'prosperity method' of the internal market have really dealt seriously with this existential question. In the end, Europe is an economic-materialistic project: culture, identity and tradition are the poor cousins of integration. To some extent this is the bitter harvest revealed by the constitution referendums: the revenge of cultural history, the revenge of national identities and traditions.

And it also proves that someone like Larry Siedentop is right: there has been insufficient high-quality debate about the vital relationship between the historic nation-states of Europe and the EU, certainly when one compares the American process of federation formation in the late eighteenth century. Why are there no European counterparts to Madison, Hamilton and Jay? As Siedentop puts it: 'Why is there nothing which has seized the imagination of European peoples about the direction of their own development, about their own fates? And what does the absence of a grand debate suggest about the condition of Europe?'[16] There has been no debate about checks and balances against 'bureaucratic despotism'; instead, there is 'integration by stealth', or – again and again right now – a careless apolitical analysis of the economic and geopolitical inevitability (failure signifying ruin: unite or die!) of a Great European Empire, which is able to compete with competitor global players like the US, China and India more by virtue of unity than diversity.

It is this unrealistic and laconic self-abolition of the nation-state and the total avoidance of issues of national identity, cultural diversity and political pluriformity which are generating the new 'euro-distrust', the 'inside-nationalism' against and within the EU. It is entirely legitimate and understandable for people to harbour distrust, rooted in concerns about democracy and human rights and feelings of 'nationalism', towards a budding empire embracing at least 450 million people. The burden of proof when claiming that the formation of a *sui generis* super-state hyperconstruction such as the European Union represents historical progress in terms of democracy, rule of law and effective government still lies with those who advocate a larger, more powerful Europe.

The new Euroscepticism in the Old Europe[17] is not necessarily scepticism about the EU as a whole. Most people are still in favour of forms of European integration and cooperation. They support the European model of welfare policies, of human rights, but they are worried about the transformation of Europe in the last period: the Big Bang expansion, the non-deliverance of the EMU in terms of growth and jobs, the irresponsible accession of corrupt Romania, the over-balanced neoliberal market approach, the early promises to Turkey, etc. And they are worried about the lack of respect in Brussels directories or Luxemburg jurisprudence for national cultures and traditions (German beer, Dutch social housing, Swedish pharmacies, French cheese). In this perception, the European adventure has recently been the victim of imperial overstretch: the seemingly endless expansion, Europe as the heavy-handed transmitter or accelerator of globalization and liberalization, Europe as the shears used to keep the member states uniformly trimmed.

The Eurocratic narrative on the future of Europe focuses consciously or unconsciously on a European super state: the nation-states have apparently become too weak. They are unable to survive on their own in this new world order. So we must form a strong European bloc, a European *puissance* that is able to compete with the economic and geopolitical power of America, China and India. This master-narrative about a strong and firmly welded Europe is precisely what is causing so much concern to the people who worry about the lack of respect for national and cultural diversity in European discourse – particularly in view of the deterministic way in which this European vista is presented as being the only practicable path. Thatcher intimidation at a European level; TINA, There Is No Alternative for European scaling-up; *Unite or Die! Reform or Perish*: 'Europe is faced with a fundamental choice. One way we sink into economic decline, losing the means to pay for our preferred way of life. The other way, we press ahead with painful economic reforms that can make us competitive once again in world markets.'[18] But what is the price of a more powerful centralized Europe, speaking with one voice, and who is supposed to pay? How realistic in the end is this future scenario of a powerful European unity? How social will this new polity be and how democratic?[19]

Concluding observations

This chapter has examined European unease, an unstable undercurrent in European society at odds with modern global trends and at odds with the dominant response by policy-makers and decision-makers, with particular reference to the issue of threatened national identity. In dealing with the theme of national identity, I ventured into tricky terrain, certainly for centre-left progressives who mostly prefer to sing a postnational cosmopolitan and laconic multiculturalist melody. National identity, however, can be understood in a enlightened sense. It seems typically European that it is precisely the social model of the post-war welfare state and the social market economy, which form a substantial part of the positive self-image of various European populations. The unease is to be found in the perception of threat and undermining of national characteristics through processes of internationalization: on the one hand, the globalization of production of goods and services as well as capital markets and the apparently boundless European unification, and, on the other, a seemingly uncontrollable immigration and the development of multi-ethnic societies with problems of integration, segregation and multicultural 'confusion'.

Contrary to the gospel of the modernizing pundits who advocate the self-abolition of the nation-state in favour of new regional power centres, unstable and dislocating undercurrents in European society require some prudence in further modernization, integration and innovation. It may also require the rehabilitation of the nation-state as a forum for restoration of trust, as an anchor in uncertain times, as a renewed test case for socioeconomic performance, as a source of social cohesion between the less and the better educated, between immigrants and the autochthonous population. There is, at least, a need for a balanced redirection of the European integration process, for a more realistic and fair division of labour between Brussels and the member states in terms of subsidiarity and democratic account-ability. There is also a need for reflection on the limits of the European project, in terms of geography, the span of control of democratic pol-itics and common values. The key notion is that the ambitions and aspirations for further European integration and cooperation must be tempered by the recognition that the European project by its very nature is a vulnerable project. This is even more so when, at national level, traditional patterns of political representation have been weak-ened and undermined. Only a more modest EU will guarantee a stronger popular support for the Union.

A restoration of trust between politicians and citizens will have to take place mainly at the national level, as will the creation of a har-monious multi-ethnic society. Europe must facilitate this process, and not obstruct it. In other words, the future of the EU, the European social model and harmonious multi-ethnic societies lies, first of all, with the nation-state. The motto for the coming period of transition is therefore (freely rendered from Alan Milward[20]): *How the nation-states must rescue the European Union . . .*

Notes

1 Katinka Barysch, 'Liberal versus social Europe', *Centre for European Reform Bulletin*, 43 (August/September, 2005), p. 1.

2 M. Elchardus and Wendy Smits, *Anatomie en oorzaken van het wantrouwen* (VUBpress 2002); Sociaal en Cultureel Planbureau (SCP), *De sociale staat van Nederland 2005. 21minuten.nl*, Report of McKinsey and Company, 2005.

3 On the causes and backgrounds of the populist revolt, see René Cuperus, 'Roots of European populism: the case of Pim Fortuyn's populist revolt in the Netherlands', in Xavier Casals, ed., *Political Survival on the Extreme Right. European Movements between the inherited past and the need to adapt to the future* (Barcelona: Institut de Cicncies Polítiques I Socials (ICPS), Universitat Autònoma de Barcelona, 2005), pp. 147–68; René Cuperus, 'The fate of European populism', *Dissent* (Spring 2004), pp. 17–20; René Cuperus, 'The populist deficiency of European social democracy: the Dutch experience', in Matt Browne and Patrick

Diamond, eds., *Rethinking Social Democracy* (London: Policy Network, 2003), pp. 29–41.

4 Saskia Sassen, 'De grote stad: snijpunt van mondialisering en lokaliteit', in *Rotterdam, Het vijfentwintigste jaarboek voor het democratisch socialisme* (Mets & Schilt/Wiardi Beckman Stichting, 2004); A. van der Zwan, *De uitdaging van het populisme* (Meulenhoff/WBS, 2003).

5 See the fascinating comparative study on Belgium, Denmark, France, the Netherlands, Austria and Sweden: Rinke van den Brink, *In de greep van de angst. De Europese sociaal-democratie en het rechtspopulisme* (Antwerpen/Amsterdam: Houtekiet) 2005.

6 Mark Leonard, 'Why Europe will run the 21st century'; Quote from interview in *NRC Handelsblad*, 17 September 2005.

7 René Cuperus, 'Wie die Kollision von Zivilgesellschaft und Gerechtigkeit eine rechts-populistische Revolte in Europa produziert', in Thomas Meyer and Udo Vorholt, eds., *Zivilgesellschaft und Gerechtigkeit. Dortmunder politisch-philosophische Diskurse* (Projektverlag: 2004) pp. 90–102.

8 Ben Knapen, 'De malaise van Duitsland is de malaise van Europa', *NRC Handelsblad*, 17 September 2005.

9 Elchardus and Smits, *Anatomie en oorzaken*; Sociaal en Cultureel Planbureau (SCP), *De sociale staat van Nederland 2005*.

10 Kees van Kersbergen and André Krouwel, 'De buitenlanderskwestie in de politiek in Europa', in Huib Pellikaan and Margo Trappenburg, eds., *Politiek in de multiculturele samenleving* (Beleid en Maatschappij Jaarboek/Boom, 2003), pp. 195–6.

11 Anton Hemerijck, 'Waarom we een nieuwe verzorgingsstaat nodig hebben', *Socialisme & Democratie*, 10, 11 (2003), pp. 42–53; G. Esping-Andersen, D. Gallie, A. Hemerijck and J. Myles, *Why We Need a New Welfare State* (Oxford: Oxford University Press, 2002).

12 This is the title of the contribution of Frans Becker and myself to Vivien Schmidt et al.'s *Public Discourse and Welfare State Reform* (Berlin: Karl Renner Institut, 2005).

13 Here I follow the line of thought and argumentation of the Dutch Council for Social Development (RMO) in its report *Nationale identiteit in Nederland. Internationalisering en nationale identiteit*, advies 9, September 1999. S.W. Couwenberg, ed., *Nationale identiteit. Van Nederlands probleem tot Nederlandse uitdaging* (Civis Mundi jaarboek 2001), p. 9.

14 RMO-report. Koen Koch and Paul Scheffer, eds., *Het nut van Nederland. Opstellen over soevereiniteit en identiteit* (1996).

15 Europese tijden, *De publieke opinie over Europa. Europese Verkenning 3*, bijlage bij de staat van de Europese Unie 2006, Centraal Planbureau & Sociaal en Cultureel Planbureau', final conclusions, p. 38.

16 Larry Siedentop, *Democracy in Europe* (London: Penguin Books, 2001), p. xi.

17 René Cuperus, 'Why the Dutch voted No. An anatomy of the new Euroscepticism in Old Europe', *Progressive Politics*, 4, 2 (Summer 2005), pp. 92–101.
18 Peter Mandelson, 'More than a squabble: this goes to the heart of Europe. The EU faces a stark choice – painful reforms, or economic decline', *Guardian* (20 June 2005), <htttp://europa.eu.int/comm/commission>.
19 *Europese tijden*, 'De publieke opinie over Europa'.
20 Alan S. Milward, *The European Rescue of the Nation-State* (London: Routledge, 1992).

6

Social Change and Welfare Reform

Anton Hemerijck

The welfare state as an evolutionary system

The striking intensity and the comprehensive character of welfare reform across the majority of the member states of the European Union since the 1990s is very much at odds with the prevalent image of a 'frozen welfare landscape' in the academic literature. Most important, the substantive extent of welfare redirection adds up to a momentum of system change which goes far beyond the popular concepts of 'retrenchment', 'roll-back', 'retreat' and 'demise'. To say that European welfare states are far from sclerotic is not to say that they are in good shape. With 20 million citizens out of work and 90 million people otherwise inactive, there certainly is no room for complacency.

Welfare reform is surely not a smooth process. Corrective measures are difficult, but in the face of protracted policy failures they are enacted and implemented through the competitive political process. While reform experience over the past two decades was primarily built on processes of domestic (crisis-induced) lesson-drawing, more recently, cross-national social learning in the context of the EU is being taken up. In short, welfare reform is a highly reflexive and knowledge-intensive political process. And, as a consequence, the welfare state is best considered as an imperfect 'evolutionary' system, whose goals, aims, functions and institutions change over time, albeit slowly.

Today, an increasing number of academic observers advocate a new welfare repertoire, based on consistent normative principles, coherent causal understandings, (re-)distributive concerns and institutional practices, comparable in generality to that of the male breadwinner Keynesian welfare state of the post-1945 decades. They all prioritize high levels of employment for both men and women as the key policy objective, while combining elements of flexibility and security, facilitating men and especially women to accommodate work and family life, managed by new forms of governance and based on subtle combinations of public, private and individual efforts and resources.[1] There is a growing recognition that the current imperative of recasting the welfare state is rooted in the incongruence between new 'post-industrial' social risks and diverse family and labour market needs, on the one hand, and institutional resilience of male breadwinner social policy provisions, on the other. The Keynesian welfare state emerged as a response to the risks of the industrial economy within the framework of the nation-state and well-functioning male breadwinner labour markets and stable families. By adopting a life-course perspective, the advocates of the 'new' welfare state are able to identify the interconnectedness of social risks and needs over time on the basis of which they are able to draft a 'social investment' policy agenda. Hereby, the Keynesian emphasis on 'effective demand' management seems to give way to an emphasis on 'effective supply', with the implication of taking out social barriers for labour market entry, discouraging early exit, making labour market transitions less precarious and providing gender equality and equality of opportunity throughout the life-cycle in response to the drastic changes of the world of work and welfare.[2]

My argument is built up as follows. First, I will qualify the under-specified use of the concepts of the alleged 'European social model' in the face of the three-pronged challenge of economic internationalization, post-industrial differentiation, and permanent austerity. Next, I present an inventory of a number of substantive changes in the make-up of Europe's mature welfare states over the final quarter of the twentieth century. The next section tries to articulate core elements of the 'social investment centred' welfare agenda of the twenty-first century. In conclusion, I address the political constraints and opportunities for such an 'investment centred' strategy. It is my contention that with a little more policy creativity, we should be able to turn the current tide of inward-looking pessimism about the sustainability of the 'European social model' into a renewed political effort in forward- and outward-looking 'social pragmatism'.

Caveats and challenges to the 'European social model'

In the heated debate over the future of the EU, the expression of a distinctly 'European social model' (ESM) is increasingly used in policy discussions and political debate. Although European welfare states share a number of features that set them apart from other geopolitical regions in the world, like North America and South-East Asia, it is important at the outset to make a number of qualifying remarks about the underspecified use of the notion of an ESM. My most important caveat is that the notion of a European social 'model' concept is inherently *static*. While the architects of the post-war welfare state, John Maynard Keynes and William Beveridge, could assume the existence of stable male breadwinner families and expanding industrial labour markets, this picture of the economy and society no longer holds. Since the late 1970s, consecutive changes in the world economy, labour markets and family structures have disturbed the once sovereign and stable welfare equilibriums of employment-friendly macroeconomic policy, collective wage-bargaining, progressive taxation, broad social security coverage and protective labour market regulation.

As a consequence, all the developed welfare states of the European Union have been recasting the basic policy mix upon which their national systems of social protection were built after 1945.[3] Moreover, couching policy discussions in terms of competing 'models' easily triggers ideological strife, a battle between warring alternatives, separating antagonistic advocacy coalitions. A casual glance at the French referendum campaign in 2005 over the Constitutional Treaty clearly reveals the contestation between two polarized positions. The French version of the ESM was pitted against a false stereotype of the 'Anglo-Saxon' model of capitalism, allegedly a 'free market without a safety net'. In addition, the notion of a distinct European model suggests a large degree of *uniformity* transcending national boundaries, which surely cannot be sustained empirically in a union of 25 member states. There are immense differences in development, policy design, eligibility criteria, modes of financing and institutional make-up across Europe.[4] Finally, the notion of a distinctly European social model suggests a lot of *virtu* on the part of rational policymakers, which also gives the impression that best practices can easily be transported from one member state to the next. Many social reform initiatives taken in recent years across Europe were expedient responses to impending economic crises and political conditions. Also, before they start to pay off in terms of growth and jobs, the incubation periods of reforms are extremely long. Usually, it is incoming governments that reap the benefits of painful reforms enacted by their predecessors. In short, there are no models of eternal bliss to copy, if only because of the intensified dynamism in our economies and societies.

Today, despite the enormous strides made by different countries, three sets of challenge confront policy-makers in their efforts to redirect the welfare state, to redesign institutions and to elaborate on new principles of social justice. First, *from without*, international competition challenges the redistributive scope and decommodifying power of the national welfare state. Many academic observers believe that the increase in cross-border competition in the markets for money, goods and services has substantially reduced the room for manoeuvre of national welfare states.[5] Economic internationalization constrains countercyclical macroeconomic management, while increased openness exposes generous welfare states to trade competition and permits capital to move to the lowest-cost producer countries. Finally, there is the danger that tax competition could result in an under-provision of public goods. Second, *from within*, ageing populations, declining birth rates, changing gender roles in households as a result of the mass entry of women into the labour market, the shift from an industrial to a service economy and new technologies in the organization of work all engender sub-optimal employment levels, new inequalities and skill-biased patterns of social exclusion. According to Gøsta Esping-Andersen, the most important reason why the existing systems of social care have become overstretched stems from the weakening of labour markets and family households as traditional providers of welfare.[6] In addition, new sources of immigration and segregation, also in the housing market in metropolitan areas, pose a challenge to social cohesion. And, third, while policy-makers must find new ways to manage the adverse consequences of economic internationalization and post-industrial differentiation, their endeavour to recast the welfare state is severely constrained by long-standing social policy commitments in the areas of unemployment and pensions, which have ushered in a period of *permanent austerity*.[7] The maturation of welfare commitments, policies put in place to cater for the social risks associated with the post-war industrial era, now seem to crowd out and overload the available policy space for effective policy responses, especially in public services under conditions of low economic growth. This spectre of permanent austerity is likely to intensify in the face of population ageing. As an intervening variable in the process, EU economic and political integration has, since the mid-1980s, become ever more involved in domestic issues of work and welfare. It is fair to say that in the EU we have entered an era of *semi-sovereign welfare states.*[8] European (economic) integration is fundamentally recasting the boundaries of national systems of social protection, both constraining the autonomy for domestic policy options but also opening opportunities for EU-led multilevel policy coordination.[9]

The adaptive capacity of the welfare state

The welfare state, in the shape and form in which it developed in Western Europe in the second half of the twentieth century, represents a unique historical achievement. Never before in history, as Fritz Scharpf puts it, 'has democratic politics been so effectively used to promote civil liberty, economic growth, social solidarity and public well-being'.[10] Towards the late 1970s, the celebration of the welfare state gave way to doubts. The oil crises of the 1970s, together with the changing character of international competition, deindustrialization and the eroding effectiveness of domestic Keynesian demand management, led to a massive surge in unemployment not seen since the 1930s. In the 1980s, the 'prospects for survival' of the welfare state were recognized as poor. Economists singled out the accumulation of perverse labour-market rigidities produced by the welfare state, impeding flexible adjustment, blocking technological innovation and hampering employment and economic growth in an integrating world economy.[11] But despite the obvious 'irresistible forces' urging for reform, the European welfare state proved to be, as one leading scholar put it, an 'unmovable object'.[12]

A finer-grained comparative analysis of long-term developments, however, shows that the empirical foundations of economic stagnation welfare inertia are fairly shaky. On the contrary: over the final quarter of the twentieth century, developed welfare states of the European Union have been recasting the basic social compact upon which their national welfare states were built after 1945. If we interpret the welfare state more broadly than social protection narrowly understood, it is possible to paint a broad, cumulatively transformative process of policy change across a number of intimately related policy areas.

Up to the late 1970s, Keynesian macroeconomic policy priorities, geared towards full employment as a principal goal of economic management, prevailed. In the face of stagflation – i.e. the combination of high inflation and rising unemployment – the Keynesian order gave way to a stricter macroeconomic policy framework centred on economic stability, hard currencies, low inflation, sound budgets and debt reduction. Persistently, high public deficits and inflation rates are undesirable in themselves and incompatible with global financial markets. The current framework of EMU and the stability pact, however, does not provide for an adequate macroeconomic regime. The key problem today is that EMU and the SGP (Stability and Growth Pact) do not do justice to the differences in economic circumstances across the member states. The European Central Bank (ECB) set interest rates in accordance with European-wide averages and development in the trade cycle, rather than nation-specific shocks. Although fiscal discipline is in the self-interest of member states, once a recession hits it is already too late to tinker with employment regulation and social protection. Moreover, inconsiderate and bold reforms of labour market regulation and social protection in a downturn stifle the market and are likely to generate economic stagnation and social unrest. Macroeconomic stability is a must, but a little more flexibility is called for.

In the 1980s, the responsibility for employment shifted away from macroeconomic policy towards adjacent areas of social and economic regulation. In the area of wage policy, a reorientation took place from the 1980s onwards in favour of market-based wage restraint in the face of intensified economic internationalization. From the early 1980s, wage restraint resumed importance as a requirement for successful adjustment by facilitating competitiveness, profitability and, as a second-order effect, employment. Strategies of wage moderation have been pursued in many countries through a new generation of social pacts in Europe, linked with wider packages of negotiated reform, including labour market regulation and social protection. The rediscovery of a jobs-intensive growth path in the Netherlands, Ireland and Denmark, by way of social pacts, have also allowed sectoral bargainers to strike decentralized deals over productivity, training and job opportunities for less productive workers. In the 1990s, the EMU entrance exam has played a critical role in the resurgence of national social pacts for hard-currency latecomers, like Italy and Portugal and Greece, stimulating policy-makers and the social partners to rekindle cooperative, positive-sum solutions to the predicament of economic adjustment, i.e. by making taxation and social protection more 'employment friendly'.[13]

In the area of labour market policy, in the 1990s the new objective became to maximize employment rather than induce labour market exit, and this implied new links between employment policy and social security. The greater the number of people participating full and part time in the labour market, the greater the contribution they make towards maintaining the affordability of adequate levels of social protection. This is also the key message of the *Jobs, Jobs, Jobs* report of the Employment Taskforce, established by the European Commission and chaired by the former Dutch Prime Minister Wim Kok.[14] In the process, public employment services (PES) in many countries have lost their placement monopoly. And although private placement agencies have still not gained much market share, they have at least pushed PES towards modernizing service delivery. With respect to labour market regulation, narrowly understood, empirical evidence from Denmark and the Netherlands suggests that the acceptance of flexible labour markets is enhanced if it is matched by strong social guarantees. While systems combining restrictive dismissal protection with meagre unemployment benefits essentially cater to the interests of insiders, 'flexicure' systems based on minimal job protection but offering decent standards of social protection for the unemployed are best able to bridge the gap between insiders and outsiders.

Within the sphere of social security, the changes in macroeconomic management and wage policy have resulted in a shift from passive policy priorities aimed at income maintenance towards a greater emphasis on activation and reintegration of vulnerable groups. In the process, the function of social security changed from the passive compensation of social risks to corrective attempts to change behavioural incentives of claimants and employers together with an emphasis on preventative social investments. This is also captured by the shift from out-of-work benefits to in-work benefits. Different strategies are appropriate to different welfare states. In the UK, where income guarantees and unemployment benefits are modest, individual tax credits to support low-wage workers and their families are very popular. In continental Europe, the main problem is that heavy social contributions price less productive workers out of the market. In the face of the relative weakening of traditional male breadwinner social insurance programmes, policy-makers in these countries have turned towards strengthening minimum income protection functions of the welfare state, coupled with strong activation and reintegration measures. Many European welfare states seem to be evolving towards a dual social protection model, combining both Bismarckian social insurance and Beveridgian minimum income protection tiers. In this respect, the French and Belgian welfare states have increased social assistance protection for the neediest, using targeted benefits instead of universal benefits, financed through taxation and general revenues. In 2005, through the so-called Hartz IV reforms, Germany has followed suit while stepping up job search requirements among the unemployed.

In the area of old-age pensions, the most important trend is the growth of (compulsory) occupational and private pensions. Most welfare states are engaged in developing multi-pillar systems, combining pay-as-you-go and fully funded methods with a tight (actuarial) link between the pension benefits and contributions. Fiscal incentives have been introduced to encourage people to take out private pension insurance. In the 1990s, a number of countries, notably the Netherlands, France, Portugal, Ireland and Belgium, started to build up reserve funds in order to maintain adequate pension provision when the baby-boom generation retires. Also, changes in indexation rules have helped to reduce pension reliabilities. In Spain, restrictions have gone hand in hand with attempts to upgrade minimum pension benefits. Measures to combine work and retirement with tax allowances and partial pension benefits have been introduced in Denmark and Belgium. Finland has developed policy approaches to improve occupational health, work ability and the well-being of ageing workers, in order to keep older workers in the workforce as long as possible.[15]

Social services have experienced something of a comeback lately. Spending on childcare, education, health care and the elderly, next to training and employment services, has increased practically everywhere in Western Europe over the past decade.[16] Ageing and longevity, in particular, make demands on professional care that working families cannot or are no longer able to meet. In Scandinavia, the expansion of services to families began in the 1970s in tandem with the rise in female labour supply. It was in large part this policy of 'defamilialization' of caring responsibilities which was the catalyst to the dual-earner norm. In most other European countries, the expansion of female employment came much later.[17] In Southern Europe it is only during the past decade or so that we have seen a sharp rise. Throughout the EU, holiday arrangements have also been expanded, both in terms of time and in the scope of coverage, to include care for the frail elderly and sick children. Social service delivery organizations have also been given more autonomy to decide how they use resources in the pursuit of agreed outcomes and more incentives to innovate in the search for improvements, while structuring their accountability to service users and central government in new ways.

In terms of the financial architecture of the welfare state, finally, we observe an increase in user financing in the areas of childcare, old-age care and medical care. At the same time, fiscal incentives have been introduced to encourage people to take out private services and insurance, especially in the areas of health and pensions. Management audit systems have been introduced to control and monitor the volume of public expenditures, involving limited annual budgets and delegating financial responsibility and autonomy to schools and hospital in countries like Sweden, Germany and the Netherlands. With respect to taxation, as a result of intensified competition across the EU, many member states started to pursue a combination strategy of lower statutory tax rates and a broadening of the tax base. This implies a shift away from a focus on vertical redistribution between rich and poor citizens, but this is a consequence of a broadening base, not per se at the expense of prevailing welfare commitments.

Over the past two decades, as the above inventory of reform shows, many European welfare states have – with varying success, but also failure – taken measures in order to redirect economic and social restructuring by pushing through adjustments in macroeconomic policy, industrial relations, taxation, social security, labour market policy, employment protection legislation, pensions and social services and welfare financing. Many reforms have been unpopular, but a fair amount occurred with the consent of parties in opposition, trade unions and employer organizations. In the process, we have seen the rise and fall, respectively, of the Swedish macroeconomic management model of the 1970s, the German 1980s Rhineland model of diversified quality production and the Dutch employment miracle of the 1990s. While today, the Celtic Tiger, the Danish Lego-model, the Finnish knowledge economy and revamped New Britain under Tony Blair all figure as model countries to emulate, nothing can guarantee that their welfare systems will prove effective in responding to the next phase of social and economic turmoil.

Towards a social investment strategy

The welfare reform momentum of the 1980s and 1990s was triggered largely by intensified international competition within the context of the internal market in the enlarged EU. Thus far, the endogenous dynamics of the transformation of work, gender, family and demography remained as a subsidiary in the reform agenda, in part due to opposition from the remaining vestiges of male breadwinner welfare provision. There is a real opportunity to take on these post-industrial issues in the next wave of reform in the early twenty-first century. The guiding question of recasting the European welfare state today is: What sort of 'new welfare architecture' is compatible with international competitiveness, fiscal austerity, the revolutionary change in working life, the weakening of traditional family care, demographic ageing and overall expansion of the EU? By adopting a life-course perspective, we are best able to identify the investment character of family policy, education and training, labour market policy and pension policy provision. When reasoning from the policy perspective that social cohesion, health, education, activation and stable industrial relations are *productive* resources, the alleged contradiction or big 'trade-off' between economic competitiveness and social justice surely breaks down.

Family-friendly policy

Thus far, social policy has failed to respond to the revolutionary role change of women as they have become full participants in the labour market. Hence the capabilities of the family to internalize caring responsibilities have been weakened in recent decades. Since the future of welfare states depends on how well we resolve the dilemmas associated with women's new career preferences, it is impossible to imagine a positive equilibrium without an effective reconciliation of women's new career preferences and family functions. Failure to do so will produce either fertility rates below the renewal level or suboptimal levels of employment and income. Female employment is the key to resolving child poverty, which is on the rise in most European countries. Child poverty rates decline by a factor of three or four when mothers work. Labour market participation rates in Southern Europe, especially for the younger female cohorts, are rapidly catching up with North European averages. Among older women (age 55–64) the employment gap is still considerable, with the rate of those employed standing at only 16 per cent in Italy and 23 per cent in the Netherlands, compared to 65 per cent in Sweden. Exit from the labour force at the age of 50, as Esping-Andersen forcefully argues, leads to a major drop in income and lifestyle and probably to inferior pension entitlements for women, and to a loss of government (tax) revenue for the public economy. The standard family-friendly policy package includes a neutral, individual taxation regime, maternity-cum-parental leave with job-security and subsidized childcare.[18]

Since life-chances are so over-determined by what happens in childhood, a comprehensive child investment strategy with a strong emphasis on early childhood development is imperative. Access to affordable quality childcare is sine qua non for any workable future equilibrium. Esping-Andersen maintains that childcare demand cannot be adequately met via commercial care markets. In a purely commercial regime, low-income parents would probably not be able to afford quality care. They may respond by placing children in cheap low-quality care or by withdrawing from the labour market altogether. Also, inaccessible childcare will provoke low fertility, low-quality care is harmful to children and low female employment raises levels of child poverty.[19] It should be emphasized that the stress on early childhood development goes *beyond* the idea that childcare is necessary to allow parents to reconcile work and family life. A 'child-centred social investment strategy' is needed to ensure that children will be life-long learners and strong contributors to their societies. More children, educated to perform in a knowledge economy, are needed to keep the economy going for a retiring baby-boom generation with high caring needs.

Human capital investment push

If Europe wishes to be competitive in the new, knowledge-based society, there is an urgent need to invest in human capital throughout the life-course. The activity rate of those with higher education exceeds 80 per cent practically everywhere in Europe, whereas the corresponding figure in the case of people with only primary education is less than 40 per cent. Considering the looming demographic imbalances we face, we surely cannot afford large skill deficits. High school dropout rates provide a good indicator of the welfare deficit we face (above 30 per cent in Spain, almost 25 per cent in the Netherlands and less than 15 per cent in Denmark and Sweden). While inequalities are widening in the knowledge economy, this also implies that parents' ability to invest in their children's fortunes is becoming more unequal. Everyone's favourite solution is, of course, education. The revitalization of both the Irish and the Finnish economy is in part based on increased investments in education, preventing early departure from formal education and training, and facilitating the transition from school to work, in particular school leavers with low qualifications. Social and employment policies aimed at developing the quality of human resources for the knowledge economy assume the role of social investments.

Flexicure labour markets for all

The interaction between economic performance and the welfare state is largely mediated through the labour market. The majority of

Europe's mature welfare states are confronted with a syndrome of labour market segmentation between 'insiders' and 'outsiders'. While family and gender issues were still of secondary importance in the reform momentum of the 1980s and 1990s, post-industrial social and economic change seem perversely to reinforce an over-accumulation of insurance benefits on the side of 'guaranteed' breadwinner workers with quasi-tenured jobs, alongside inadequate protection for those employed in the weaker sectors of the labour market, particularly youngsters, women, immigrants and older low-skilled workers. Most likely, labour markets will become ever more flexible. While the boundaries between being 'in' and 'out' of work have been blurred by increases in atypical work, low wages, subsidized jobs and training programmes, one job is no longer enough to keep low-income families out of poverty. Post-industrial job growth is highly biased in favour of high-skill jobs. However, increased labour market flexibility, together with the continuous rise in female employment will, in addition, encourage the growth of a sizeable amount of low-skill and semi-skilled jobs in the social sector and in personal services. The policy challenge is how to mitigate the emergence of new forms of labour market segmentation through what could be called 'preventive employability', combining increases in flexibility in labour relations by way of relaxing dismissal protection, while generating a higher level of security for employees in flexible jobs. Flexible working conditions are often part and parcel of family-friendly employment policy provisions. There is a clear relation between the ratio of part-time jobs and female employment growth. But the ability of part-time employment to harmonize careers with family depends very much on employment regulation, whether part-time work is recognized as a regular job with basic social insurance participation, and whether it offers possibilities for career mobility.

Special attention should be given to labour market problems of migrants and non-EU nationals, whose rate of unemployment averages twice that of EU nationals. Skills, cultural and language barriers, together with discrimination, call for a real improvement in integration policies, including access to social citizenship. In our ethnically and culturally diversified societies, the welfare state faces a major challenge of ensuring that immigrants and their children do not fall behind. Recent outbreaks of violence in the *banlieux* of the metropolitan cities of France reveal how economic exclusion and physical concentration reinforce educational underperformance, excessive segregation and self-destructive spirals of marginalization. The overriding policy lesson is that, in the face of demographic ageing and in the light of a declining workforce, nobody can be left inactive (for long)!

Later and flexible retirement

Many of the so-called 'new social risks' – like family formation, divorce, the elderly becoming dependent on care, declining fertility, and accelerating population ageing – fall primarily on young people and young families, signifying a shift in social risks from the elderly to the young. The late entry into the labour market of youngsters and the early exit of older workers, together with higher life expectancy, confront the welfare state with a looming financial deficit. Most European regimes are both inequitable and ineffective, and replete with early exit measures defended by labour market insiders. Age is a challenge, but also blessing, since people live longer in good health. Two trends justify adjustment in retirement regimes: (1) the health status of each elderly cohort is better than that of the last; at present a man aged 65 can look forward to a further ten healthy years. And (2) the skill gap between the elderly and the young is rapidly narrowing. Older people in the future will be much better educated than now to adapt to the knowledge economy with the aid of retraining and life-long learning. Beyond the development of multi-pillar schemes, including both PAYGO (pay-as-you-go) and funded schemes, in the area of pension policy, the challenge lies in how to allocate the additional expenditures that inevitably accompany population ageing.[20] Of crucial importance in terms of equity remain general revenue-financed first-tier pension guarantees, indexed to prices, for when the next generation of flexible labour market cohorts start to retire. Sustainable pensions require that we raise the employment rates of older workers and move the retirement age to 67 years. Later retirement is both effective and equitable. It is efficient because it invokes more revenue intake and less spending at the same time. It is intergenerationally equitable because both retirees and workers contribute in equal proportions. Flexible retirement and the introduction of incentives to postpone retirement could also greatly alleviate the pension burden. Although there has been a slight increase of part-time work among the elderly, it has been shown that part-time work and participation rates among older people are positively related, and that there is still little systematic and comprehensive policy activity to enhance the variable opportunity set for older workers. If older workers remain employed ten years longer than is now the norm in early exit welfare regimes, household incomes would increase substantially, which implies less poverty, less spending on social assistance and greater government revenue.

Minimum income support

We cannot assume that early childhood development, human capital investment, together with high-quality training and activation measures, cultural integration through economic participation, or later and flexible retirement will remedy current and future welfare deficiencies and deficits. Greater flexibility and widespread low-wage employment are likely to increase overall economic insecurity for sizeable groups in the population. An unchecked rise in income inequality will worsen citizens' life-chances and opportunities. As a consequence, it is impossible to avoid some form of (passive) minimum income support. It is therefore necessary to have an even more tightly woven net below the welfare net for the truly needy to meet minimum standard of self-reliance.

Joined-up governance

One of the most distinctive institutional features of the European welfare state has been its public nature. Various developments have been challenging this state-centric edifice in recent years – a challenge often summarized in the emergence of new forms of 'governance' beyond the traditional territorial nation-state. Diversified demand in the face of tight budgets makes it increasingly difficult for governments to apply typical uniform rules and procedures and regulations to welfare servicing. Customization of welfare services to meet more diverse needs with transfers and services goes together with institutional devolution, decentralization, liberalization and privatization. There is an increasing recognition that effective social policy formation and implementation today requires 'joined-up' governance across government departments, public agencies, private sector organizations and community associations, together with more effective forms of policy coordination, including information pooling and feedback, across various functionally differentiated policy areas of activation, social protection, employment activation and family servicing.

The imperative of social pragmatism

Welfare state futures are not preordained. Neither the doomsday scenario of the demise of the European welfare state, predicted by economists in the 1980s, nor the prevalent image of a 'frozen welfare status quo', pictured by comparative scholarship in the 1990s, can be corroborated by the welfare reform experienced in Europe since the late 1970s. In the 1980s welfare provisions became more austere. Since the mid-1990s, we have observed an incipient process of 'contingent convergence' of employment and social policy objectives, the adoption of increasingly similar policy initiatives (encouraged also by the deepening of the EU social agenda), signalling a transition from a corrective and passive welfare state to a more proactive social investment strategy, with much greater attention paid to prevention, activation and social servicing. In hindsight, it seems that in trials of repairing the increasingly dysfunctional policy repertoires of the Golden Age, domestic and EU policy-makers, pressed by intensified economic internationalization and post-industrial differentiation, under conditions of permanent austerity, have turned to combining elements from different welfare regimes. In their different attempts to achieve greater efficiency and equity, we can observe a trend of welfare hybridization, based on policy experimentation and processes of domestic and cross-national social learning. The EU, as an institution that spans national boundaries, provides an additional vital exploratory policy space for cross-national agenda-setting and sharing domestic policy reform experience. Social policy reform, however, remains a domestic enterprise: reforms have to be endorsed by elected governments and national political parties, preferably supported by key organized interests and implemented through domestic administrative structures. By the same token, processes of welfare reform surely do not involve a search for a 'blank slate' new model, a radically novel blueprint to replace existing national social and economic policy repertoires. We live in a world of path-dependent solutions. Reform, even radical policy change, does take place, but it is 'institutionally bounded' change. Any attempt to reform social and economic performance is critically dependent on identifying particular institutional conditions under which it is possible to formulate and implement effective and equitable policies. The interaction between economic performance and welfare policy is far too complex and dynamic to allow for simple remedies and quick fixes. The analysis of social policy as an investment resource thus relies heavily on sophisticated understandings of the modus operandi of the welfare state that are more complex that those supported by neoliberal orthodoxy, which, at best, views social policy as necessary side-payments to groups adversely affected by economic restructuring. But in contrast to the possible adverse effects of social policy on economic performance, the reasoning behind the idea of social policy as an investment occupies a difficult intellectual and political position. Although comprehensive welfare states are surely not economically dysfunctional, there are social policies that do have a negative impact on economic processes, like excessively generous social benefits, not backed by activating labour market policies. We always need to consider the 'fine' structures of the welfare state in conjunction with inside and outside policy pressures. This also makes the political nature of policy prescriptions imminently conditional.

Welfare reform is a political process, which involves the strategic framing of policy problems and solutions by political actors and interests. Reforms are the products of lengthy processes of (re-)negotiation between political parties, governments and often also the social partners. In order to gain political legitimacy for promising new policy formulas, political entrepreneurs wishing to put novel policy alternatives on the political agenda are pressed to elaborate new normative priorities (or, to redefine old ones) and communicate their (novel) cognitive insights of the challenges ahead in a publicly compelling manner so as to convert current anxieties over economic internationalization, post-industrial differentiation and conditions of permanent austerity into a more mobilizing pursuit of policy priorities and political ambitions. The more that reform proposals alter the distributive balance between groups and vested interests, the more important of course it is to put forward and elaborate new normative frameworks and discourses capable of advocating the reform agenda as a 'win-win' project, i.e. justifying reform in terms of underlying 'moral foundations'. Following the logic of Sen's capability approach, the policy priorities listed above concern policy interventions to empower citizens to act as autonomous agents and, especially, to allow for choice between different employment statuses according to shifting preferences and circumstances during the life-course.[21] The normative focus of social policy hereby shifts from *ex post redistribution* towards *preventive* or *ex ante employability*. However, equal opportunity can be achieved only in a society that keeps the scope of inequality at bay. Temporary inequalities, low wages and poor jobs are less problematic than long-term poverty and inactivity traps. They become problematic when they negatively affect opportunities for future life-chances on a structural basis.

Necessary investments in family services, education and training, subsidized employment, integration and labour market for immigrants, decent basic pensions and adequate minimum income protection do come with a price ticket. However, in the medium term, the gains are very likely to outweigh the initial costs of the social investment strategy. Moreover, investments in (public and private) social services also provide job opportunities, especially for women, older workers, the young and immigrants. And while they raise the volume and quality of the workforce, they support economic growth. This, in turn, generates additional government revenue, which ultimately contributes to the long-term sustainability of the European welfare state.

Notes

1 G. Esping-Andersen, D. Gallie, A. Hemerijck and J. Myles, *Why We Need a New Welfare State* (Oxford: Oxford University Press, 2002); G. Esping-Andersen, 'Putting the horse in front of the cart: towards a social model for mid-century Europe', WRR-lecture, The Hague, 8 December 2005; J. Jenson and D. Saint-Martin, 'Building blocks for a new welfare architecture: is LEGO the model for an active society?' Paper prepared for the 4th International Conference on Social Security, Antwerp, Belgium, 4–7 May 2003; P. Taylor-Gooby, ed., *New Risks, New Welfare. The Transformation of the European Welfare State* (Oxford: Oxford University Press, 2004).

2 OECD, *A Caring World: The New Social Policy Agenda* (Paris: OECD, 1999); M. Ferrera, A. Hemerijck and M. Rhodes, *The Future of Social Europe: Recasting Work and Welfare in the New Economy* (Oeiras: Celta Editora, 2000); Esping-Andersen et al., *Why We Need a New Welfare State*; L. Kenworthy, *Egalitarian Capitalism. Jobs, Incomes, and Growth in Affluent Countries* (New York: Russel Sage Foundation, 2004); National Economic Social Council (NESC), *The Developmental Welfare State*, NESC, Dublin no. 113, May 2005.

3 A. Hemerijck and M. Schludi, 'Sequences of policy failures and effective policy responses', in F. W. Scharpf and V. Schmidt, eds., *Welfare and Work in the Open Economy: From Vulnerability to Competitiveness* (Oxford: Oxford University Press, 2000).

4 G. Esping-Andersen, *The Three Worlds of Welfare Capitalism* (Cambridge: Polity, 1990); *Social Foundations of Post-industrial Economies* (Oxford: Oxford University Press, 1999); Ferrera et al., *The Future of Social Europe*.

5 F. W. Scharpf, 'Economic changes, vulnerabilities and institutional capabilities', in F. W. Scharpf and V. Schmidt, *Welfare and Work in the Open Economy: From Vulnerability to Competitiveness*, vol. 1 (Oxford: Oxford University Press, 2000), pp. 21–124.

6 Esping-Andersen et al., *Why We Need a New Welfare State*.

7 P. Pierson, ed., *The New Politics of the Welfare State* (Oxford: Oxford University Press, 2001).

8 S. Leibfried and P. Pierson, 'Social policy', in H. Wallace and W. Wallace, eds., *Policy Making in the European Union*, 4th edn (Oxford: Oxford University Press, 2001), pp. 267–91.

9 M. Ferrera, *The Boundaries of Welfare: European Integration and the New Spatial Politics of Solidarity* (Oxford: Oxford University Press, 2005). See also Ferrera's chapter in this volume (chapter 14).
10 F. W. Scharpf, 'The vitality of the nation-state in 21st century Europe', in WRR, *De Vitaliteit van de Nationale Staat in het Europa van de 21ste Eeuw*, WRR-lectures 2002 (Groningen: Stefert Kroese, 2003), pp. 15–30.
11 OECD, *The OECD Jobs Study*, 2 vols (Paris: OECD, 1994).
12 P. Pierson, 'Irresistible forces, immovable objects: post-industrial welfare states confront permanent austerity', *Journal of European Public Policy*, 5, 4 (1998), pp. 539–60.
13 G. Fajertag and P. Pochet, eds., *Social Pacts in Europe: New Dynamics* (Brussels: ETUI, 2000).
14 W. Kok et al., *Jobs, Jobs, Jobs: Creating More Employment in Europe.* Report of the Employment Taskforce chaired by Wim Kok (Brussels: European Communities, 2003).
15 G. L. Clark and N. Whiteside, eds., *Pension Security in the 21st century* (Oxford: Oxford University Press, 2003).
16 Taylor-Gooby, *New Risks, New Welfare*.
17 M. Daly, 'A fine balance: women's labor market participation in international comparison', in F. W. Scharpf and V. A. Schmidt, eds., *Welfare and Work in the Open Economy*; Vol. II: *Diverse Responses to Common Challenges* (Oxford: Oxford University Press, 2000).
18 Esping-Andersen, 'Putting the horse in front'.
19 Ibid.
20 J. Myles, 'A new social contract for the elderly', in Esping-Andersen et al., *Why We Need a New Welfare State*, pp. 130–72.
21 G. Schmid, 'Sharing risks: on social risk management and the governance of transitional labour markets', Sinzheimer Lecture (Amsterdam: Hugo Sinzheimer Institute, University of Amsterdam, 10 November 2005); A. K. Sen, *Development as Freedom* (New York: Alfred A. Knopf, 2001).

7

The European Socioeconomic Model

Karl Aiginger, Alois Guger

Why the discussion came up

The economic performance of Europe since the beginning of the 1990s is well documented. Economic growth is now lower than it used to be and lower than in the US; Europe did not benefit from the strong growth of the world economy during 2004–6. Unemployment remains high; productivity is falling. There is less consensus, however, as to the reason for the underperformance. Some people claim that it has been the consequence of a neoliberal policy in Europe, blaming the reduction of budget deficits, insufficient wage increases, privatization of firms, the liberalization of markets and the rise in income differences. The opposite view is that Europe is doomed to slow growth and decay because of high taxes, large government, strict regulation, expensive labour and the public provision of services. We assume an intermediate position and argue that a bad mix of economic policies, reform inertia and the 'Paris Consensus'[1] are contributing to low growth rates in Europe. Too many other priorities prevent the enactment of an active, growth-oriented economic policy, as outlined in the Lisbon Strategy or in any textbook or survey on the determinants of long-term growth in an advanced economy.[2]

Two developments since the 1990s have initiated renewed interest in the discussion of social models. The first is the better performance of the two extreme models: namely, the liberal Anglo-Saxon countries and, even more surprising to mainstream economists, the Scandinavian countries, with their comprehensive 'cradle to grave' welfare state. We analyse the performance differences specifically between the Scandinavian countries and the continental economies and put them down to institutional variation.

The chapter is structured as follows. In the next section we define the European model, which in our understanding is not only a 'social model', but also shapes incentives, efficiency and competitiveness, and has an impact on security, leisure time, education and health, as well as on the 'innovation system' of the various countries. We therefore prefer to speak of a model of European society or a socioeconomic model. We will then compare the performances of Europe and the US, and of different types of model, first by examining the dynamics of GDP, productivity and employment and then by investigating a wider set of indicators. A three-tier policy strategy for the most successful countries is outlined (following Aiginger).[3] The next section presents quantitative evidence on the fiscal strategies, social expenditures, regulations, industrial relations and, most importantly, on the differences between countries and models in the level and dynamics of future investments (i.e. research, education and new technologies). The data reveal differences not only between Europe and the US, but also between European models. In the following section, we look at the differences between the traditional European welfare model and the new model now emerging in much of Europe, most specifically in the successful Scandinavian countries. The new European model certainly differs from the old welfare state model and from the US model, even though Anglo-Saxon European countries are trying to combine some elements of both. The final section will summarize the arguments put forward.

Model(s) of European society

Literature on the European social model (ESM) is abundant, but there has nevertheless been no agreement on a common definition; there is a consensus that it is reasonable to distinguish between different types of European socioeconomic model. Even here, opinions differ as to which characteristics constitute a 'model', how many of them exist and which model is applicable to which country. We claim that it makes sense to extend the horizon of the discussion beyond 'social institutions' proper. In our analysis, therefore, we include educational institutions, elements of the 'innovation system' and the 'knowledge-based society', the extent of administrative and economic regulation and the tax rates.

Our definition of the European socioeconomic model is based on terms of responsibility, regulation and redistribution:

- Responsibility: society has a broad responsibility for the welfare of individuals, sheltering them against poverty and providing support in case of illness, disability, unemployment and old age; society encourages, and actively promotes and often provides, education, health and the support of families (the latter through transfers, as well as the provision of care and housing facilities).
- Regulation: labour relations are institutionalized; they are based on social dialogue, labour laws and collective agreements. The business environment is quite regulated and is shaped by social partners (on the branch and firm level). Administrative and economic regulation for product markets exists. Business start-ups depend on permits and partly on the qualifications of owners or managers.
- Redistribution: transfers, financial support and social services are open to all groups; differences in incomes are limited by redistributive financial transfers, taxation, taxes on property and on bequests.

These three basic characteristics (responsibility, regulation and redistribution) reflect the fact that the European model is more than just a social model in the narrow sense. Indeed, it also influences production, employment and productivity and, thus, growth and competitiveness and all other objectives of economic policy. Furthermore, the European model influences social relationships, cultural institutions and behaviour, learning, and the creation and diffusion of knowledge. This is why we prefer to speak about a European socioeconomic model rather than merely a social model.

Nevertheless, the literature on the social model proper is more elaborate and has been standardized. We use this as a basis from which we can differentiate between several versions of the European model (see table 1). It is standard practice to distinguish between a Scandinavian model (often called the Nordic model), a continental model (also known as the corporatist model and sometimes as the Rhineland model) and a liberal model applicable to countries with less market interference, low transfers and underdeveloped public safety nets (the Anglo-Saxon model). We believe it makes sense to differentiate between countries in which low levels of social expenditures are combined with supportive family networks and other characteristics of an agrarian society, and those countries in which less government interference is the result of an explicit policy or ideology, e.g. deregulation following a period of strong government involvement. The Anglo-Saxon model comprises countries aiming for a lower degree of intervention through the implementation of an explicit policy. We ascribe the name 'Mediterranean model' to the southern European countries. A fifth model, not yet elaborated, may emerge in the future, consisting of the new member countries (former socialist countries). Several social institutions have been founded since the transition of these countries, which lack the financial means for a comprehensive welfare system and are determined to catch up with the old member countries. We will therefore call this the 'catching-up model'. Outside Europe, the US model serves as the standard benchmark. The US is grouped together with Canada, Australia and New Zealand as the 'Anglo-Saxon overseas model'. Japan, as well as the other industrialized Asian economies, remains an outsider to this discussion.

The Scandinavian model is the most comprehensive, with a high degree of emphasis on redistribution; social benefits are financed by taxes. The Nordic model relies on institutions working closely together with the government; trade unions are strongly involved in the administration of unemployment insurance and training, and the model is characterized by an active labour market policy and high employment rates. The continental model emphasizes employment as the basis of social transfers. Transfers are financed through the contributions of employers and employees. Social partners play an important role in industrial relations, and wage-bargaining is centralized. Redistribution and the inclusion of outsiders are not high on the agenda. The liberal model emphasizes individual responsibility; its labour market is not regulated and its competition policy is rather ambitious. Social transfers are smaller than in the other models, more targeted and means-tested. Labour relations are decentralized, and bargaining takes place primarily within companies. In the Mediterranean countries, social transfers are small; families still play a significant role in the provision of security and shelter. Trade unions and employer representatives are important to the rather centralized bargaining process for wages and work conditions. Employment rates, specifically those of women, are low.

The Scandinavian model is practised in five countries, namely the three countries with the best (overall) performances over the past 15 years (which Aiginger calls the top three countries)[4] plus Norway and the Netherlands. The inclusion of the Netherlands in this group is the most contentious choice, because the Dutch model is less ambitious, redistributes less and places less emphasis on gender equality (at least up to the 1990s).[5] We pool five countries in the continental model – France, Germany and Italy, which are the three big continental

Table 1 Performance: short and long run growth of GDP; GDP per capita, employment 2005

	1960/1990	1990/2005	GDP per capita at PPP 2005 1,000 €	Employment rate 2005	Unemployment rate 2005
	Annual growth in %				
Scandinavian model	**3.3**	**2.3**	**29.0**	**74.2**	**5.6**
Denmark	2.7	2.2	28.6	77.2	4.6
Finland	3.9	2.0	26.6	68.6	8.4
Netherlands	3.4	2.2	28.7	73.6	5.1
Sweden	2.9	2.0	27.0	73.7	6.8
Norway	3.9	3.2	34.7	77.7	4.0
Continental model	**3.5**	**1.7**	**25.2**	**66.2**	**8.9**
Germany	3.2	1.6	25.0	70.0	9.5
France	3.8	1.9	25.9	63.8	9.6
Italy	3.9	1.3	23.7	62.0	7.7
Belgium	3.4	1.9	27.6	61.8	8.0
Austria	3.5	2.2	28.0	74.8	5.0
Anglo-Saxon model Europe	**2.6**	**2.7**	**27.8**	**71.9**	**4.6**
Ireland	4.1	6.5	31.9	68.6	4.3
United Kingdom	2.5	2.4	27.6	72.1	4.6
Mediterraean model	**4.6**	**2.8**	**21.8**	**63.6**	**9.1**
Greece	4.5	3.0	19.5	55.0	10.4
Portugal	4.8	2.1	17.5	70.5	7.4
Spain	4.6	2.9	23.1	64.1	9.2
Anglo-Saxon model overseas	**3.6**	**3.0**	**35.0**	**72.9**	**5.2**
USA	3.5	3.0	35.8	72.9	5.1
Canada	4.0	2.8	29.5	74.1	6.8
Australia	3.8	3.5	27.6	72.1	5.2
New Zealand	2.4	3.2	22.1	59.6	4.0

EU(15)	*3.4*	*2.0*	*25.3*	*67.2*	*7.9*
Japan	6.1	1.3	26.3	77.2	4.5
Catching-up model	—	*2.5*	*15.7*	*61.2*	*7.5*
Czech Republic	—	1.3	16.7	65.4	7.9
Hungary	—	3.9	14.5	56.2	7.0
EU(15)/USA	0.96	0.65	0.71	0.92	1.55

Source: Eurostat (AMECO). The values for a model class (Scandinavian model, etc.) are calculated as weighted average over the countries included; the value for EU(15) is that reported in the AMECO database.

countries, plus Belgium and Austria, two high-growth countries with top positions in per capita GDP.[6] It is striking that the social model typology groups Germany and France together into one group. When analysed in terms of intervention (high in France, low in Germany), mode of industrial policy (sectoral in France, horizontal in Germany) or the importance of nationalization and competition policy (with France favouring nationalized champions, while in Germany competition policy is seen as the holy grail), these two countries would be ascribed to different models. But the literature is undivided when it comes to the inclusion of France and Germany into the same group of 'social models'. There is a certain amount of disagreement as to whether Italy fits better into this group or into the Mediterranean group. Since we have placed Italy in the continental group, the Mediterranean model comprises Spain, Portugal and Greece. The Anglo-Saxon model is championed in Europe by the United Kingdom. As far as the low degree of regulation and the social system are concerned, Ireland exhibits a certain degree of similarity to the United Kingdom, but policy interventions have been intense, as is typical of a catching-up country: high shares of inward FDI, low taxes for business and a regional policy supporting small and medium-sized firms. In Europe, these strategies are now the paradigm for catching-up economies. Outside Europe, we group Canada, the US, New Zealand and Australia together, under the heading 'Anglo-Saxon overseas' model.

Economic performance: Europe vs the US, according to model type

In Europe, growth has been lagging behind that of the US since the early or mid-1990s. If we take 1995 as the starting point, the US enjoyed annual growth of 3.3 per cent as opposed to 2.1 per cent in the EU(15) (1995–2005). The difference is due to higher growth in productivity per worker, namely 2.1 per cent as opposed to 1.3 per cent and to higher growth in employment, which was 1.4 per cent as opposed to 1.1 per cent. Although Europe chose a more labour-intensive growth path, unemployment decreased only slightly from 10 per cent in 1995 to 8 per cent in 2005. The absolute difference in productivity per worker, which had narrowed throughout most of the post-war period, thus increased from 20 to 35 per cent per worker and from 5 to 9 per cent per hour (see figure 1).

Looking at the growth dynamics in the various types of model, the long-run dynamics are all very similar. Taking 1960–90, for example,

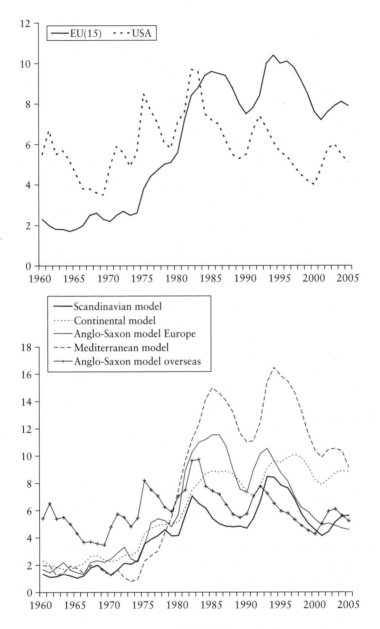

Figure 1
Unemployment
Source: Eurostat (AMECO). The values for a model class (Scandinavian model, etc.)
are calculated as weighted average over the countries included; the value for
EU(15) is that reproted in the AMECO database.

the long-term growth rates range from 2.6 per cent to 3.6 per cent for three European models (Anglo-Saxon, Scandinavian and Continental) and for the Anglo-Saxon overseas group. It is higher only in the Mediterranean model, and there is little variation within models (with lowest growth rates for the United Kingdom and New Zealand; see table 1 above). Performance in the 1990s (1990–2005) diverged. The countries in the Mediterranean model group and those in the Anglo-Saxon European countries came closest to the US, with a growth rate of 2.8 per cent and 2.7 per cent respectively for GDP, partly because the initial starting point was at a relatively low level of GDP per capita.[7] A striking divergence occurred between the Scandinavian group, which enjoyed a growth rate of 2.3 per cent for these 15 years, despite a severe crisis in many countries in the early 1990s, when the growth rates of the countries associated with the continental model plummeted to 1.7 per cent, due to low growth in Germany and Italy. France, Austria and Belgium surpassed the group average, but did not reach the level attained by the Nordic group.

This evidence is supported and expanded elsewhere by Aiginger, who uses a set of 12 indicators on the dynamics of output, productivity and employment, as well as on the level and changes of unemployment and fiscal balances, to derive a more comprehensive 'performance evaluation' of countries since 1995. Apart from the Irish growth experience, Sweden, Finland and Denmark have been the best performers and were therefore designated by Aiginger as the 'top countries'.[8] The three big continental countries, which exhibited low dynamics, inferior employment records and high fiscal deficits, are grouped together at the lower end of the hierarchy.

In his analysis, Aiginger illustrates that the strong performance of the top countries is based upon three pillars, which comprise the foundation of the so-called three-tier strategy. First, these countries contained private and public costs in order to restore profitability and fiscal prudence. Second, they improved incentives by fine-tuning their welfare systems and deregulating part-time work and product markets. And third, they significantly increased investment in future growth, surpassing the investments of larger European economies in research input and output, in education expenditures and quality and in information technology. In contrast, the large continental economies (France, Germany and Italy) underperformed in terms of investment in growth drivers, refrained from labour market reform and constantly ran up fiscal deficits.[9]

The role of government and the importance of investing in the future

Europe has a much larger government sector, higher social expenditures and is more regulated than the US. But these tendencies differ across countries and models, and the data reveal that some important changes have been taking place.

Government revenues as a percentage of GDP are 45.1 per cent in Europe and 30.7 per cent in the US. This difference in taxation widened from 11 to 15 percentage points between 1990 and 2005, since the tax rate[10] increased by 2 per cent in Europe and decreased by 2.5 per cent in the US. Revenues as a percentage of GDP decreased slightly in the Scandinavian countries (where tax rates are still the highest) and increased in the countries associated with the continental model. Tax rates decreased in Ireland and increased marginally in the United Kingdom. They also increased in the Mediterranean countries, narrowing the difference from the lowest to the EU average to less than four percentage points (see table 2). Starting from a level lower than in Europe, the decrease in US government expenditure was somewhat greater than in the EU. However, this trend may soon be reversed, as the US has recently increased its spending. Within Europe, the decline in expenditure has been strongest in Scandinavia (by three percentage points). In the continental countries, the share of government expenditure increased in France and Germany.

The most striking differences are evident in the budget position. Europe's deficit shrank from 4.6 per cent to 2.7 per cent, while it remained at about 4 per cent in the US (with a surplus up to 2000, followed by a rapidly deteriorating balance since then). The Scandinavian countries, which had a deficit of 1 per cent in 1990, now enjoy a surplus of 2.5 per cent. This fiscal prudence is part of the change in strategies implemented by the Scandinavian countries, which have not been known before for budgetary discipline.[11] The continental countries were able to reduce their deficits from 4.5 per cent to 3.5 per cent, but this overall trend was made possible by the large reductions in Italy and Belgium, while Germany and France increased their deficits. The Mediterranean countries managed to reduce their deficits thanks to their successful campaigns for the introduction of the Euro, but deficits here have increased again somewhat since 2000. The United Kingdom enjoyed budgetary surpluses up to 2000, but in 2005 had a deficit in the 3 per cent range.

This chapter is concerned with the crucial institutional elements of the new socioeconomic model of Europe; we do not take short-term

Table 2 National finances and social expenditures

	Public revenues			Public expenditures			Budget deficit			Social expenditures	
	1990	2000	2005	1990	2000	2005	1990	2000	2005	1990	2002
Scandinavian model	*51.5*	*54.2*	*53.3*	*52.8*	*48.6*	*50.8*	*21.0*	*5.6*	*2.5*	*28.5*	*27.8*
Denmark	54.7	56.5	58.0	55.9	53.3	54.4	-1.3	3.2	3.5	27.9	29.1
Finland	53.5	55.9	53.5	48.1	48.8	51.7	5.4	7.1	1.8	24.2	25.6
Netherlands	47.4	45.6	46.4	52.5	43.4	48.2	-5.1	2.1	-1.8	29.6	26.7
Sweden	—	62.4	58.2	—	57.4	57.1	0.0	5.0	1.2	31.6	31.3
Norway	56.2	58.2	56.8	54.0	42.6	43.6	2.2	15.6	13.3	25.6	25.8
Continental model	*44.3*	*47.8*	*46.1*	*48.8*	*47.9*	*49.6*	*-4.5*	*-0.1*	*-3.5*	*24.9*	*28.1*
Germany	42.1	46.4	43.1	44.1	45.1	46.9	-2.0	1.3	-3.8	24.4	29.4
France	47.7	50.4	50.6	49.8	51.8	53.9	-2.1	-1.4	-3.2	26.5	29.0
Italy	42.6	46.2	44.9	54.3	47.0	49.2	-11.8	-0.8	-4.3	23.7	25.1
Belgium	45.5	49.1	49.0	52.2	49.1	49.2	-6.7	0.0	-0.1	25.1	26.2
Austria	49.7	49.8	47.6	52.0	51.4	49.6	-2.4	-1.6	-2.0	25.7	28.3
Anglo-Saxon model Europe	*40.0*	*40.8*	*41.0*	*41.7*	*37.0*	*44.2*	*-1.7*	*3.8*	*-3.2*	*21.6*	*25.9*
Ireland	40.0	35.9	34.9	42.8	31.5	35.3	-2.8	4.4	-0.4	17.6	15.4
United Kingdom	40.0	41.2	41.4	41.6	37.4	44.8	-1.6	3.8	-3.4	21.9	26.6
Mediterranean model	*9.6*	*39.8*	*39.9*	*12.7*	*41.4*	*41.0*	*-3.1*	*-1.6*	*-1.2*	*19.1*	*21.0*
Greece	34.5	47.9	43.7	50.2	52.1	47.4	-15.7	-4.2	-3.6	21.5	25.9
Portugal	33.6	40.1	41.3	39.9	43.0	47.3	-6.3	-2.9	-5.9	14.6	22.9
Spain	0.0	38.1	38.8	0.0	38.9	38.6	0.0	-0.9	0.2	19.4	19.7

Anglo-Saxon model overseas	32.7	34.9	30.9	37.1	33.3	34.6	-4.3	1.6	-3.7	—	—
USA	31.7	34.2	30.7	36.0	32.5	34.6	-4.3	1.6	-3.9	—	—
Canada	43.7	44.3	—	49.6	41.3	—	-5.9	3.1	0.0	—	—
Australia	34.3	36.3	36.6	39.2	38.9	—	-2.7	-0.6	—	—	—
New Zealand	49.2	—	—	53.8	—	—	-4.6	—	—	—	—
EU(15)	42.7	46.2	45.1	48.2	45.3	47.8	-4.6	0.9	-2.7	24.4	26.9
Japan	34.3	32.1	31.5	32.3	39.6	38.0	2.0	-7.5	-6.5	—	—
Catching-up model	—	41.3	42.2	44.7	44.7	46.6	—	3.4	-4.4	—	20.1
Czech Republic	—	38.5	41.2	—	42.1	44.2	—	-3.7	-3.1	—	19.9
Hungary	—	44.7	43.4	—	47.7	49.5	—	-3.1	-6.1	—	20.4
EU(15)/USA	1.35	1.35	1.47	1.34	1.39	1.38	1.08	0.58	0.69	—	—

Source: Eurostat (AMECO). The values for a model class (Scandinavian model, etc.) are calculated as weighted average over the countries included; the value for EU(15) is that reported in the AMECO database.

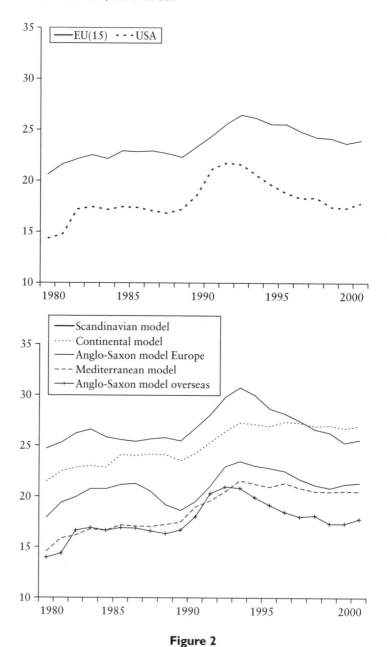

Figure 2
Public social expenditures as a percentage of GDP
Source: Eurostat (AMECO). The values for a model class (Scandinavian model,
etc.) and for the EU(15) are calculated as weighted average over the countries
included.

macroeconomic policies into consideration. Nevertheless, it should be kept in mind that 'even the most successful structural reform in Europe will not generate growth if the macroeconomic conditions are not right. Weakness in aggregate demand can ruin any economic party.'[12]

Regulation of product as well as of labour markets is much higher in Europe than in the US. The differences have existed for a long time (including that period in which productivity increase in Europe surpassed growth in the US); but if anything, the differences are now narrowing.[13] However, differences within European models are quite large too. The empirical data given in figure 2 were collected by OECD and are partly qualitative assessments; they are on a scale from 0 (no regulation) to 6 (highly regulated) and exist for product market regulation between 1998 and 2003 and for labour market regulation between 1990 and 2003 (see table 3).

Product market regulation across the four countries of the Anglo-Saxon overseas model is rated as low (1.3) and is quite similar in all cases, declining between 1998 and 2003 to a value of 1. It was rated as 1.9 in Europe and declined to 1.4 in 2003. The figure for Ireland and the United Kingdom is similar to that of the US – in fact marginally lower. Product market regulation in countries of the Scandinavian model equalled the European average in 1998, but, at least in Denmark and Sweden, they are now as deregulated as in the Anglo-Saxon model. The countries of the continental model started and ended with a marginally higher regulated product market, with Italy and France lagging behind Germany and Austria. The Mediterranean countries have more regulated product markets (see table 3).

As far as labour markets are concerned, the differences between the Anglo-Saxon countries on the one hand and the European countries in general and the continental countries in particular are much larger. The differences between Europe and the US seem to narrow a little bit, but there were some statistical changes in 1998 which create a bias in the apparently low figures for the US and UK. Scandinavian countries have traditionally always had somewhat less regulated labour markets and they have kept this advantage. Specifically, Denmark and Finland now have considerably less regulated labour markets (indices: 1.8 and 2.1 respectively) than France (2.9), Germany or Belgium. An interesting feature is that the Scandinavian countries did not change the regulations for regular contracts (they are marginally more regulated than the continental model countries), but they did so for temporary contracts. Sweden, Denmark and the Netherlands cancelled most administrative limits for temporary contracts (while providing pro rata benefits to them), and temporary contracts are now much less

Table 3 Product and labour market regulation

| | Product market regulation | | Labour market regulation | | | | | |
| | | | Total | | | Temporary contracts | | |
	1998	2003	1990	1998	2003	1990	1998	2003
Scandinavian model	*1.9*	*1.3*	*2.8*	*2.3*	*2.3*	*3.0*	*1.7*	*1.7*
Denmark	1.4	1.1	2.3	1.8	1.8	3.1	1.4	1.4
Finland	2.1	1.3	2.3	2.2	2.1	1.9	1.9	1.9
Netherlands	1.8	1.4	2.7	2.3	2.3	2.4	1.2	1.2
Sweden	1.8	1.1	3.5	2.6	2.6	4.1	1.6	1.6
Norway	2.4	1.4	2.9	2.7	2.6	3.5	3.1	2.9
Continental model	*2.2*	*1.5*	*3.1*	*2.8*	*2.6*	*3.9*	*2.9*	*2.4*
Germany	1.8	1.3	3.2	2.6	2.5	3.8	2.3	1.8
France	2.4	1.6	2.7	2.8	2.9	3.1	3.6	3.6
Italy	2.7	1.8	3.6	3.1	2.4	5.4	3.6	2.1
Belgium	1.9	1.4	3.2	2.5	2.5	4.6	2.6	2.6
Austria	1.8	1.3	2.2	2.4	2.2	1.5	1.5	1.5
Anglo-Saxon model Europe	*1.1*	*0.9*	*0.6*	*1.0*	*1.1*	*0.3*	*0.3*	*0.4*
Ireland	1.4	1.0	0.9	1.2	1.3	0.3	0.3	0.6
United Kingdom	1.1	0.9	0.6	1.0	1.1	0.3	0.3	0.4
Mediterranean model	*2.2*	*1.6*	*3.8*	*3.2*	*3.1*	*3.9*	*3.5*	*3.4*
Greece	2.7	1.7	3.6	3.5	2.9	4.8	4.8	3.3
Portugal	2.2	1.7	4.1	3.7	3.5	3.4	3.0	2.8
Spain	2.1	1.5	3.8	3.0	3.1	3.8	3.3	3.5
Anglo-Saxon model overseas	*1.3*	*1.0*	*0.3*	*0.8*	*0.8*	*0.3*	*0.3*	*0.3*
USA	1.3	1.0	0.2	0.7	0.7	0.3	0.3	0.3
Canada	1.4	1.1	0.8	1.1	1.1	0.3	0.3	0.3
Australia	1.3	0.9	0.9	1.5	1.5	0.9	0.9	0.9
New Zealand	1.5	1.2	1.0	0.8	1.3	0.5	0.4	1.3
EU(15)	*1.9*	*1.4*	*2.8*	*2.5*	*2.4*	*3.0*	*2.2*	*2.0*
Japan	1.9	1.3	2.1	1.9	1.8	1.8	1.6	1.3
Catching-up model	*2.7*	*1.8*	*—*	*1.7*	*1.8*	*—*	*—*	*—*
Czech Republic	2.9	1.6	—	1.9	1.9	—	—	—
Hungary	2.4	2.0	—	1.5	1.7	—	—	—
EU(15)/USA	1.49	1.36	13.82	3.54	3.39	10.12	7.48	6.74

Source: OECD (ECO/CPE/WP1(2004)9/ANN3). The values for a model class (Scandinavian model, etc.) and for the EU(15) are calculated as weighted average over the countries included.
Index between 0 (unregulated) and 6 (regulated).
Note: administrative regulation = licence and permits system, communication and simplification of rules and procedures, administrative burdens for corporations, administrative burdens for sole proprietor firms, sector-specific administrative burdens; economic regulation = scope of public enterprise sector, size of public enterprise sector, direct control over business enterprises, use of command and control regulation, price controls, legal barriers, antitrust exemptions.

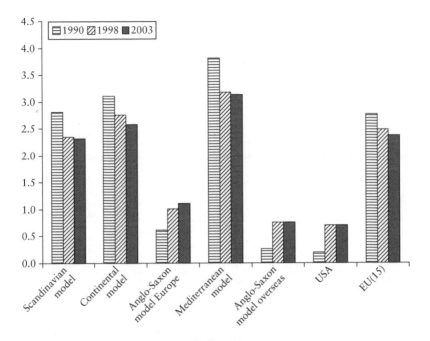

Figure 3
Labour market regulation
Source: OECD (ECO/CPE/WP1(2004)9/ANN3). The values for a model class
(Scandinavian model, etc.) and for the EU(15) are calculated as weighted average
over countries included.
Index between 0 (unregulated) and 6 (regulated); between 1990 and 1998
slightly changed definition: largest difference between old data and new data in
the USA: 1998 old version 0,2; new version 0,7; in the United Kingdom:
1998 old version 0,6; new version 1,0.

regulated than in countries of the continental model (with the exception of Germany and Austria). Regulation is stricter for all contracts in the countries of the Mediterranean model (see figure 3).

Labour relations

Trade union density is low and decreasing in the US, falling from 22 per cent in 1980 to 15 per cent in 1990 and 13 per cent in 2000. Over the same period, it decreased in Europe from 50 to 43 to 39 per cent. A drastic decline occurred in the UK, namely from 51 to 31 per cent, with, however, no deceleration in the 1990s relative to the '80s. Starting from a low level, it has increased slightly in the Mediterranean

Table 4 Labour relations and part-time employment

	Trade union density (%)		Collective bargaining coverage (%)		Part-time employment (as % of full-time equivalent)		Reason for part-time employment (%)	
	1980	2000	1980	2000	1979	2004	No full-time job found	No full-time job wanted
Scandinavian model	*59*	*54*	*75*	*82*	*19.7*	*22.8*	*13.4*	*54.3*
Denmark	79	74	70	80	22.7	17.5	13.6	50.9
Finland	69	76	90	90	6.7	11.3	32.8	25.5
Netherlands	35	23	70	80	16.6	35.0	2.5	68.8
Sweden	80	79	80	90	23.6	14.4	23.2	47.6
Norway	58	54	70	70	27.3	21.1	9.3	55.3
Continental model	*36*	*25*	*81*	*79*	*8.7*	*16.8*	*20.9*	*31.9*
Germany	35	25	80	68	11.4	20.1	11.9	18.3
France	18	10	80	90	8.1	13.4	25.0	62.4
Italy	50	35	80	80	5.3	14.9	33.8	26.3
Belgium	54	56	90	90	6.0	18.3	20.0	8.3
Austria	57	37	95	95	7.6	15.5	10.8	16.7
Anglo-Saxon model Europe	*51*	*31*	*70*	*30*	*15.7*	*23.8*	*9.3*	*19.3*
Ireland	57	38	—	—	5.1	18.7	14.2	63.3
United Kingdom	51	31	70	30	16.4	24.1	9.0	16.4
Mediterranean model	*19*	*18*	*53*	*68*	*7.8*	*8.1*	*24.1*	*14.5*
Greece	39	27	—	—	—	6.0	46.5	31.1
Portugal	61	24	70	80	7.8	9.6	15.9	22.3
Spain	7	15	60	80	—	8.3	21.2	9.7

Anglo-Saxon model overseas	24	14	29	18	16.1	14.1	—	—
USA	22	13	26	14	16.4	13.2	—	—
Canada	35	28	37	32	12.5	18.5	—	—
Australia	48	25	80	80	15.9	27.1	—	—
New Zealand	69	23	60	25	13.9	22.0	—	—
EU(15)	50	39	78	78	11.0	16.1	19.2	34.6
Japan	31	22	25	15	15.4	25.5	—	—
Catching-up model	—	24	—	27	—	3.3	—	—
Czech Republic	—	27	—	25	—	3.1	—	—
Hungary	—	20	—	30	—	3.6	—	—
EU(15)/USA	2.25	2.99	3.00	5.57	0.67	1.22	—	—

Source: ifo (DICE). The values for a model class (Scandinavian model, etc.) and for the EU(15) are calculated as weighted average over the countries included.

countries, surpassing the (low and declining) trade union density in the US. It declined by ten percentage points to 25 per cent in the continental countries, with the exception of Belgium where it is stable. Surprisingly, the very high trade union density has not changed in Scandinavia in general, with an average rate of 59 per cent and rates above 75 per cent in Sweden and Denmark. Collective agreements cover 82 per cent of employees in the Scandinavian countries (and the trend is on the rise), and they cover at least as large a share of employees in the continental countries (the rate is stable at 80 per cent). In the UK, trade union coverage of collective bargaining plunged from 70 per cent in 1980 to 40 per cent in 1990 and 30 per cent in 2000. Conversely, the trend is upward in the Mediterranean countries. Among the countries included in the Anglo-Saxon overseas model, industrial relations vary significantly: the rate is steady at 80 per cent in Australia, but has declined to 14 per cent in the US (see table 4).

Future investments

According to growth theory, the medium-term growth rate of an advanced economy depends on R&D, human capital and the speed of diffusion of new technologies. Here, we summarize expenditures on research, education and information and communication technology (as a proxy for the investments and diffusion of a new technology). Future investment was 13.1 per cent in the US in 1992 and increased to 16.1 per cent in 2002. The same expenditures amounted to 11.6 per cent in Europe and increased to 13.8 per cent. In Scandinavia, the trend mirrors that of the US in level and dynamics, while the level and dynamics of the continental countries are close to that of the EU(15). The Mediterranean countries are catching up and are presently 2.5 percentage points behind the EU average. The continental countries are the least dynamic, recently falling marginally behind the European average. In Scandinavia, expenditures on R&D and information technology have sky rocketed, in both categories exceeding those of the US. Expenditures on education and life-long learning are higher than the EU average, although their share of GDP is not increasing. The OECD PISA ratings of educational performance between countries stress the excellence of education in Scandinavia. Furthermore, other studies confirm the quality of life-long learning in these countries. The continental countries have not raised their R&D ratio, have average expenditures on education, are ranked moderate in the PISA ratings and under-invest in ICT.

Table 5 Investment into the future (growth determinants)

	Investment in the future (as % of GDP)		
	1992	1995	2002
Scandinavian model	*14.2*	*15.2*	*17.3*
Denmark	14.4	15.4	17.8
Finland	13.8	14.8	16.9
Netherlands	13.3	13.7	14.7
Sweden	15.6	17.7	21.1
Norway	—	—	—
Continental model	*11.3*	*11.8*	*13.8*
Germany	11.8	11.8	13.4
France	12.3	13.2	14.2
Italy	8.9	9.9	11.3
Belgium	12.2	12.6	15.1
Austria	11.6	11.8	14.3
Anglo-Saxon model Europe	*13.1*	*14.5*	*15.2*
Ireland	12.7	13.5	11.3
United Kingdom	13.2	14.5	15.5
Mediterranean model	*8.0*	*9.0*	*11.3*
Greece	6.0	7.6	10.2
Portugal	9.8	11.2	13.9
Spain	8.1	8.9	11.1
Anglo-Saxon model overseas	*13.1*	*14.2*	*16.1*
USA	13.1	14.2	16.1
Canada	—	—	—
Australia	—	—	—
New Zealand	—	—	—
EU(15)	*11.6*	*12.2*	*13.8*
Japan	10.4	10.7	14.5
Catching-up model	—	—	—
Czech Republic	—	—	—
Hungary	—	—	—
EU(15)/USA	0.89	0.86	0.86

Source: Eurostat; EITO. The values for a model class (Scandinavian model, etc.) are calculated as weighted average over the countries included; the value for EU(15) is that reported.

Towards a new European model: a tentative sketch of its features

As far as institutional structure and policies are concerned, the strategies of the most successful European countries (Denmark, Finland and Sweden, which all fall into the Scandinavian model) differ greatly

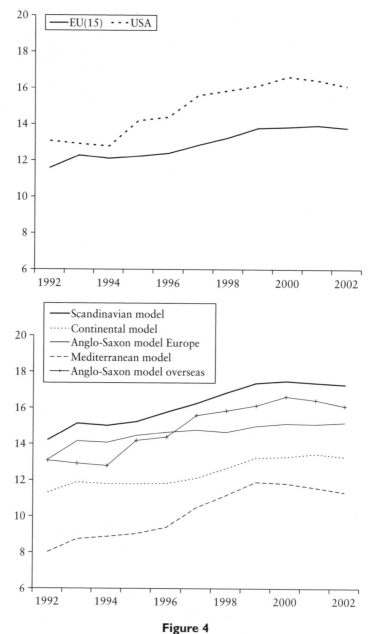

Figure 4
Investment in the future (growth determinants)
Source: Eurostat; EITO. The values for a model class (Scandinavian model, etc.) are
calculated as weighted average over the countries included; the value for EU(15)
is that reported.

from the US system, particularly in terms of welfare and government involvement, and also in their commitments to redistribution and training. Their labour market policy offers a high degree of flexibility for firms (e.g. easy dismissals), but is still a significant source of security for individuals through the prevention of poverty on the one hand and provision of support on the other, when it comes to finding new jobs and upgrading qualifications. This system is therefore called 'flexicurity' and relies on 'active labour market policies'. These countries ascribe high priority to new technologies, efficient production and the competitiveness of firms. In contrast to the US, they rely on proactive industrial policies, with government support for information technology, for agencies promoting research, for regional policies and for clusters.[14] These countries suffered severe financial crises in the late 1980s (Denmark) and in early '90s (Finland, Sweden). Many of the problems which can be expected to arise in a highly developed welfare state surfaced during the crises – e.g. costs increased faster than productivity and government expenditure increased faster than taxes. Then the governments embarked on a new strategy, improving institutions and incentives without abandoning the principles of the welfare state and without giving up their environmental goals. We believe that the specific elements of the political reforms in these northern European countries, together with similar reforms in the Netherlands, the UK and other small countries, suggest that there may be a new kind of reformed European model, which combines welfare and sustainability, on the one hand, and efficiency and economic incentives on the other.[15]

The new reformed model, as represented by successful policy reforms, differs from the old welfare state in the following ways:

- The social system remains inclusive and tight, with the exception that minimum standards on social benefits designed to prevent poverty depend on the input of the individual and transfers may be conditional to certain obligations; replacement rates are lower than they used to be in order to provide stronger incentives to work but are still high by international standards.
- The welfare system is more service-oriented (care facilities for children, the aged and the handicapped) than transfer-oriented, in order to increase equality.
- Taxes are relatively high, but in line with expenditure, aiming at positive balances in the medium term, to cover future pensions and to repay current debt.
- Wages are high, but the position of the individual is not guaranteed, as business conditions vary. The assistance and training

opportunities offered to people who lose their jobs are personalized, less bureaucratic and less centralized. The public services are complemented by private agencies.

- Welfare-to-work elements have been introduced, generally on a decentralized – sometimes even private – basis; conditions vary according to the size and kind of problems, the background philosophy being one of giving help without incriminating the unemployed of being inactive.
- Part-time work and the adaptation of work to life-cycles are encouraged, not prevented. Social benefits are extended pro rata to part-time work, which is valued as a right of the individual and as an instrument of personal choice, rather than a fate preventing gender equality.
- Technology policy and the adoption of new technologies, rather than the subsidization old industries, are a precondition for the survival of the welfare state, and lead to more challenging and interesting work.[16]

Nevertheless, the new European model also differs from the US model in at least the following ways:

- Even where welfare costs are streamlined and incentives improved, the welfare system offers comprehensive insurance against economic and social risks and a broad coverage of health risks.
- Environmental and social goals, as well as the equity of income distribution and the prevention of poverty, remain high on the political agenda.
- Government and public institutions play a proactive role in promoting innovation, efficiency, structural change, higher qualifications and life-long learning. Public institutions also provide the largest share of education and health care, which is open to all residents, of high quality and available at affordable conditions.
- Social partners (institutions representing employers and employees) negotiate wage formation, develop labour laws and co-determine economic policy in general.
- Government is large and taxes are high, even if there are mechanisms to limit increases in spending and goals for achieving a sound fiscal policy ('fiscal rules') in periods of high demand. Firms are partly sheltered from high tax rates; there are high taxes on consumption and specifically on energy.

Summary

Income per capita in the US is 40 per cent higher than in Europe and there is no trend towards convergence. Productivity per worker is 30 per cent higher in the US. Over the course of a long period during the post-war years, Europe was indeed catching up in productivity per worker and came very close in productivity per hour. However, during the past decade, the US once again increased its lead. Income per hour is the most favourable indicator of European performance, revealing a gap of less than 10 per cent, but again the difference has recently been increasing. Employment indicators show that the US created 78 million jobs between 1990 and 2003, while Europe created 42 million. Up to the 1970s, the employment rate in Europe was higher than in the US; now it is 13 percentage points lower (although the gap has recently narrowed slightly). Unemployment is higher in Europe, even excluding the significant number of people on disability or early retirement schemes, which decreases open unemployment. The number of hours worked is lower in Europe, which is partly voluntarily and partly due to the lack of full-time jobs. Leisure takes a higher priority in Europe.

International organizations (e.g. the OECD) often blame higher welfare costs and the stricter regulation of labour and product markets for the lack of dynamics in European economies ('Paris Consensus'). However, an assessment of performance differences across Europe reveals that the countries that perform best (aside from Ireland, which experienced a remarkable process of catching up, and the UK,[17] which has managed to grow faster than the EU average since the 1990s after a long period of low growth) are three Scandinavian welfare states: Denmark, Finland and Sweden. All three countries experienced periods of structural and cyclical crisis, which appeared to confirm some of the bleak predictions for welfare states in general. Over the past decade, however, they have been performing better than other European countries, with growth performances close to those of the US. At the same time, they are successfully combining welfare with higher efficiency. We highlighted the main characteristics of these countries and their reforms, enabling a tentative delineation of a new European model of a reformed welfare state. It provides an alternative model to that of the US in achieving economic efficiency, while maintaining the traditional European concerns for social welfare and environmental quality. The model thus combines security for citizens with efficiency and flexibility for firms.[18]

The fact that welfare states performed well in the 1990s does not imply that costs are irrelevant to performance. After suffering severe crises, the countries comprising the Scandinavian model realized, together with other European countries, that costs needed to be cut and fiscal balances stabilized, that incentives had to be implemented and institutions reformed. But most importantly, they realized that cost-cutting is a short-term strategy, which needs to be complemented by proactive policies to promote research, education and the diffusion of new technologies, including a commitment to use macroeconomic policy for stabilizing demand and to foster growth, in order to restore business and consumer confidence.[19] A successful new European model emphasizes cost-balancing, institutional flexibility and the reorientation of technologies. Firms are more flexible with regard to the use of labour, and workers who are laid off are efficiently assisted in their search for new jobs. Replacement ratios have been reduced and benefits are conditional to the search for employment and training efforts. Thus the new European model of the reformed welfare state has three major elements: social and environmental responsibility, flexibility and technology promotion.

We may carve out three or four stages of development of the European social model. The model was conceived as a reaction to the consequences of industrialization; it was at this stage that European countries began to assume responsibility for the greatest risks encountered by their citizens. In the wake of World War II, the coverage of risks and persons was boosted considerably, above all in response to the poverty of the Great Depression and the desire to avoid a repetition of the economic and social turmoil that had led to war. The third phase dates back to the 1970s and '80s, when the system was completed and expanded, partly as an answer to the problems of the oil crises and rising unemployment rates. A fourth phase appears to have begun during the 1990s, in an effort to counterbalance the financial and fiscal crises confronting a number of countries. This fourth phase builds on the awareness that the welfare state could only be maintained if it is made more flexible and more future-oriented. The vision of this phase of the European socioeconomic model could be the redirection of incentives in such a way that the welfare state is able to shift from a burden (increasing costs and lowering flexibility) to a productive force. It expands the qualifications of its citizens through training programmes, offers various forms of employment, wider choices and new opportunities, supports innovation and the diffusion of technology, thus making countries competitive by relying on the capabilities available to and needed by welfare states.

Notes

1 By 'Paris Consensus', we understand the position as upheld by the OECD, as, for example, in the study on jobs and in many country reports, where it is maintained that liberalization, deregulation and flexibility are necessary and sufficient for boosting economic growth, innovation and full employment. We have to acknowledge that reports on economic growth (OECD, *The OECD Growth Project*, Paris: 2001), as well as recent statements on the monetary policy of the European Central Bank, call for a proactive economic policy, which enhances measures in innovation and macroeconomic policy respectively.

2 For a similar view, see also A. Sapir et al., *An Agenda for a Growing Europe: Sapir Report* (Oxford: Oxford University Press, 2004).

3 K. Aiginger, 'The three tier strategy followed by successful European countries in the 1990s', *International Review of Applied Economics*, 18, 4 (2004), pp. 399–422.

4 Ibid.

5 Some authors classify the Netherlands as a member of the continental model group.

6 It is interesting that at least four of the six founding members of the EU belong to this group. The Netherlands is on the borderline between the continental and the Scandinavian models, and Luxembourg is between the continental and the Anglo-Saxon models.

7 The exception with respect to the starting level is the United Kingdom, which started in 1990 from a medium position as far as per capita income was concerned and then experienced a growth rate of 2.4 per cent, but here growth over the three decades before had been rather low.

8 Aiginger, 'The three tier strategy'.

9 Ibid.

10 Revenues as a percentage of GDP comprise taxes proper, contribution to social security, duties and irregular revenues. The difference between Europe (EU(15); weighted) and the US in the revenue/GDP ratio is 45.0 per cent vs 31.6 per cent.

11 A. Alesina and S. Ardagna define episodes of loose fiscal policies for OECD countries between 1960 and 1994. Finland and Sweden lead the table with ten loose periods, Norway and Denmark have five and six respectively, while the average amounts to three per country. See their 'Tales of fiscal adjustment', *Economic Policy*, 20, 27 (October 1998).

12 M. N. Baily and J. F. Kirkegaard, *A Transformation of the European Economy* (Washington: Institute for International Economics, September 2004), p. 18, available at <http://bookstore.iie.com/merchant.mvc?Screen=PROD&Product_Code=353>. See also Sapir et al., *Agenda for a Growing Europe*; J. P. Fitoussi and F. K. Kostoris Padoa Schioppa, eds., *Report on the State of the European Union*, vol. 1 (Houndsmills: Palgrave Macmillan, 2005).

13 Papers claiming that the differences in regulation explain the underperformance of Europe as opposed to the US have therefore to claim that a given degree of regulation is more detrimental in periods of rapid change (globalization) than in 'calm' periods. In econometric studies this effect is captured by an interaction term (regulation is interacted with export ratios etc.). For an overview, see K. Aiginger, 'Labour market reforms and economic growth: the European experience in the nineties', *Journal of Economic Studies*, 32, 6 (2005), pp. 540–73.

14 Part of the difference between the US and Europe with regard to industrial policies may be in rhetoric only or in the specific instruments chosen: see C. Ketels, 'Industrial policy outside the European Union: United States and Japan', and K. Aiginger, 'Towards a renewed industrial policy in Europe', in European Competitiveness Report, 2005.

15 For earlier suggestions along this line, see Aiginger, 'The three tier strategy', K. Aiginger and M. Landesmann, *Competitive Economic Performance: The European View,* Conference on Transatlantic Perspectives on US–EU Economic Relations: Convergence, Conflict & Cooperation, Harvard University, April 2002, WIFO Working Paper No. 179 (Vienna: WIFO, June 2002); K. Aiginger, *The New European Model of the Reformed Welfare State*, European Forum Working Paper 2/2002, Stanford University (December 2002).

16 The policies pursued by the leading countries have many similarities with the economic policy recommendations of the Steindl-Kalecki tradition, as described in A. Guger, M. Marterbauer and E. Walterskirchen, *Growth Policy in the Spirit of Steindl and Kalecki*, WIFO Working Papers 240 (Vienna: WIFO, 2004).

17 The policy strategy of the UK has some striking similarity to the Scandinavian model (welfare-to-work programmes and a recently high emphasis on improving infrastructures after a period of insufficient investment) but also remarkable differences (lower taxes and regulation, more targeting of transfers).

18 This combination can be considered to be in the tradition of Josef Steindl and Michal Kalecki. See J. Steindl, *Maturity and Stagnation in American Capitalism* (Oxford: Blackwell, 1952) and M. Kalecki, *Selected Essays in the Dynamics of the Capitalist Economies, 1937–1970* (Cambridge: Cambridge University Press, 1971).

19 G. Tichy, 'Die 'Neue Unsicherheit' als Ursache der europäischen Wachstumsschwäche', *Perspektiven der Wirtschaftspolitik*, 6, 3 (2005), pp. 385–407.

8

The European Social Model: Gender and Generational Equality

Jane Jenson

Contemporary economies depend upon high employment rates, and therefore upon women being in work. For the 30 years after 1945, when European countries designed their social models, policy communities assumed that 'full employment' meant employment of *only half* the population together with a labour market that provided wages sufficiently high to meet the needs of a family of two adults, several dependent children and perhaps an elderly relative or two. Policy design followed directly from these two assumptions, including ways of providing care for dependants at home and the norms for sharing family responsibilities among women and men as well as with the state.

When in the 1970s women began to make claims for greater autonomy as well as for access to income security for themselves, adaptations were made. Directives from the European Union promised protection against discrimination in the labour market, and many countries added proactive policies to counter stereotypes and encourage the full integration of women into employment and entrepreneurship as well as their full inclusion into public life. Services and other supports for reconciling work and family life were extended, including public support for childcare.

Important as these adjustments have been – and as generously as they have been advanced in several member states – this vision of 'equal opportunities' has only partially worked. Many women have achieved full integration into political life as well as labour market success, yet three-quarters of the working poor are women and many women have only low-paid and/or part-time work. Immigrant women, especially from the global South, are often concentrated at the bottom of the job ladder and among the low-income earners. Many families have access to childcare – some of it of very high quality – but the fertility rate is in steep decline. Many men share childcare and household tasks, but most caring tasks are still done by women. Levels of stress and concomitant health costs to individuals and medical systems are high, as people juggle heavy loads of work and care for family members in the ordinary course of life, whether in early childhood, turbulent adolescence or vulnerable old age. Others face even more serious time and income crunches when a family member lives with a significant disability.

The premise of this chapter is that there are fundamental choices to be made about directions for social models and in particular the ways in which they address inequalities of gender and across the lifecycle. The commitment to activation as the way to ensure a modernized social model has brought a redefinition of 'full employment' from its Keynesian meaning of the male half of the population to employment of virtually all adults, and renders inoperable long-standing assumptions about the best mix of public and private responsibility for care. Rising life expectancy rates and falling birth rates, as well as transformations in family forms, all raise new challenges about how to ensure intergenerational equity and also promote gender equality.

This chapter examines this situation, in two ways. The first half sets out a framework and principles for achieving gender and intergenerational equality. The second uses that framework to examine and make proposals in two areas constantly evoked in any discussion of European social models – demography and labour markets.

A framework for gender and generational equality

This analysis starts from the 'Lisbon position', that good economic outcomes depend on solid social policy arrangements. It also assumes that the 'European social model' is a mechanism for market-correction, in a situation in which most of individuals' and families' well-being will be provided by market activity and income earned by themselves or a family member. Third, most of the instruments for achieving gender and intergenerational equality remain within the competence of member states.[1] Fourth, three basic principles for gender equality provide a measuring rod of the extent to which this commitment is realized.

Social inclusion

Any social model that sets the boundaries of inclusion into the community and one founded on social justice will contain guarantees of social inclusion for women as well as men of all ages; these guarantees will go beyond the economic.

Social inclusion includes first and foremost the recognition of one's legitimate membership and belonging in society. It also includes the capacity to make claims and to participate in collective choices, which depends on much more than having a right, although that is clearly a minimum. Capacity includes having the means and the time to participate. The 'double day' of work and family life makes it difficult for many women and for men with young families to participate in community, workplace and political life. Linguistic and cultural barriers also sometimes block minorities, and often the women among them, from participating.

Security

Most social models place security at the top of the list of objectives. As often as not, we think of income security, and the idea that everyone needs to have sufficient material security to be included and function as a member of society. Other forms of security are also important, however, including that provided by good health, housing and sufficient food. In addition, access to safe communities, streets and play spaces is crucial to the well-being of women, their families and children.

Autonomy

Too often, autonomy is a taken-for-granted goal of social models, the assumption being that adequate income will provide autonomy via market choices. It is, however, important to keep this third principle front and centre, and this for three basic reasons. First, much analysis has pointed to the gender structures in employment that mean many women do not have access to sufficient employment. In an era of low-wage work and high rates of low income for lone-parent families, the issue of autonomy has not gone away. In addition, for young people thinking of starting their own families, their lack of capacity to maintain an autonomous household is a central concern.

Second, as social policy focuses more on 'poverty' and therefore on household income, there is a potential conflict with one of the major gains of gender equality initiatives of previous decades – that is, the individuation of benefits and the separate treatment of women's and men's income situations. Women advocated individuation precisely so as to achieve an autonomous status when it came to making claims for unemployment benefits, pension rights and so on.

Third, as the ageing of societies becomes an everyday reality, older adults make claims for the right to live autonomous lives as long as possible, often in their own homes and without falling into dependency on their children, the state or the community. In addition, those who have vulnerable family members – whether parents, children or other relatives – also claim the right to be able to choose whether to provide care themselves or to rely on others' caring work. In other words, some wish *to be able* to care, and to have the support of their community and the broader society when they make that choice. Others, however, claim support, in the form of public services such as home help, home care and other services so they will not be forced to choose between their own employment and ensuring the well-being of a relative.

Finding an equilibrium among principles

Ensuring equal levels of autonomy, security and social inclusion for women and men is an objective. The goal is to maximize each of them, while recognizing that certain contradictions or unintended consequences may exist. For example, providing too many incentives for families to choose parental childcare (the autonomy to choose to care) may have unintended consequences such as: (1) the developmentally important services of early childhood education are not provided or, if available, not used; (2) over the long term, women's income security may be threatened by their choice to remain out of the labour market in order to provide care; (3) social programmes that depend on contributions may be undermined by a dependency ratio that is out of balance.

For example, focusing attention on programmes that provide income security to women *because* they have children (such as those described as fighting 'child poverty') may have unintended consequences: (1) they may encourage early child-bearing as a mechanism to establish an autonomous household; (2) they may leave large numbers of adult women without security because they responsibly choose not to have a child when they are in a low-income position; or (3) the problem of women's economic insecurity may simply be postponed until the moment when they lose their income support because the youngest child reaches the age of 18.

A multitude of such examples exist and it is important, therefore, to minimize such unintended consequences. Because it is impossible, in the space provided, to address all possible challenges to doing so, I concentrate on two that are particularly relevant to current discussions of the ESM – demography and labour market activity. These provide the focus for the rest of this analysis.

Demography I: gender in the ageing society

When the European social models were first being designed, demographic patterns were quite different from what they are now. In 1950, only 8.9 per cent of the population of EU(25) was older than 65 and fully 25 per cent was younger than 14; two of every five were under 25. The average life expectancy of men was not much higher than the official retirement age. Between 1960 and 2002 the gap in life expectancy between men and women widened. Demographers project, however, that it will decrease significantly in the next decades.[2] Men as well as women are now living much longer, and their post-retirement lives are stretching. As everyone knows, such statistics mean that pension systems are under stress. Nonetheless there are issues of autonomy, security and social inclusion that go *beyond* the sustainability of pension regimes, and these merit attention.

Patterns of informal care

The amount of informal care work that is being done is significant. Eurobarometer data report close to 17 per cent of adults in the EU(15) caring for a frail elderly or disabled person not living with them and the same percentage caring for a person living with them.[3] In the past, the assumption was that care for elderly relatives was solidly located in the family, with wives, daughters and daughters-in-law having the bulk of the responsibility. Such assumptions are no longer valid, and this is for three reasons.

First, elderly people do not want to become dependent on their relatives and they aspire to high levels of social inclusion. We must, in other words, become accustomed to thinking about older women (and men) as being in need of equal access to social inclusion and autonomy as much as meriting security of all types, and not just income security via adequate retirement income (important as it is!).

Second, care for frail relatives is currently the responsibility of the family first, which may in turn rely on the market and some community supports. When care work in the ageing society is considered by member states as well as the EU, the tendency is still to call for supports for the family, with the implication being that younger people are providing the care. In many cases, however, older people (both men and women) and increasingly the very elderly (80+) are being asked in their retirement years to take up new types of work, for which they have no training. They are providing significant amounts of nursing care to frail relatives and are often responsible for overseeing complicated medication regimes.[4]

Finally, as activity rates increase, working-age women have employment responsibilities which do not leave them 'free' to care for frail relatives. In cases where they must do so, or when they autonomously choose to do so, there is a ticking bomb for the future, in the form of the threat to their own retirement incomes. While many countries now provide schemes for care allowances and paying for care that incorporates carers into the social security system, this inclusion is usually at the lowest level, and will therefore leave these carers with minimal security for their own old age.

Gender equality concerns raised by practices of informal care will need to be incorporated into any discussion of intergenerational solidarity. Only by doing so will social models avoid structuring a situation in which care and supports for the vulnerable elderly are provided, but in ways that reinforce structures of inequality among carers, including those who care for a living.

The market for household services and an ageing society

The expansion of a market for household services and therefore a labour market for providers tracks the other socioeconomic and demographic changes mentioned already, including rising rates of women's labour force participation and the ageing society. While household services are by no means limited to services for the elderly, persons older than 65 are more likely to be the consumers of four of the five standard types of service.[5]

In many European countries the market for household services is growing at the same time that the community sector – termed the self-help movement, the third sector, the social economy, non-profit organizations and so on – is called upon to play a larger role in providing both services and social inclusion.[6] The result is that household service provision is also frequently organized in partnership form, either between the state (providing some financing) and the private sector or between the state and the community sector, with the latter often mixing voluntary and paid work.[7]

This increase in the availability of services does contribute to elderly persons' security, autonomy and social inclusion. Household services, whether home care or help with domestic tasks, allow many people to remain in their community, stay active in that community and be secure in their homes even when they live alone. However, the labour market rarely provides quality employment to this overwhelmingly feminized workforce. Of those responsible for care for the elderly and domestic cleaning (as well as childcare) never fewer than 90 per cent are female in any country of the EU(15).[8] Working conditions are stressful even when contractual and other conditions meet standard norms. Pay rates are tremendously substandard.[9]

Therefore, if policy design in the ageing society is not to promote an increase in poor quality jobs for many women in order to provide security, autonomy and social inclusion for the elderly, then this labour market needs to be seriously analysed and opportunities identified for making it function more fairly.

Demography II: too few children

Falling birth rates are a worldwide phenomenon. In the EU (as in most other OECD countries) fertility rates have been below the replacement level of 2.1 for several decades. But it is only in the last decade that a major political concern has taken shape. Following our framework, we must ask whether women and men have the autonomy to choose the number of children they wish, the security to decide to give birth and raise a child, and the social supports to raise their children. This analysis will demonstrate (and many have done it before) that much in the way the market sector is performing is making it very difficult for young women and men to choose to found and raise a family with several children.

Fertility patterns have experienced dramatic change over the last four decades.[10] No matter their welfare regime, no matter the social model and no matter their female activity rates, the drop in fertility is across the board.[11] All member states of the EU(25) have a rate below 2.1 (that is the rate necessary to reproduce the population). Overall, this decline represents a huge reduction in what was once a major social risk – that of unwanted pregnancy and the inability to provide for all one's children. This capacity marks a huge improvement in women's lives and a significant increase in their capacity for autonomy. It enables parents to judge whether they have the means needed to bring a child into the world.

There is, however, a dilemma. Many worry that the European Union's future as an economic and political force in the world and its quality of life may be in danger. Falling or low fertility rates may cause economic growth to falter, government budgets may be stretched to pay for pensions and health services, and there may be too few adults of working age to provide care and support for older people. On the other hand, however, the right and ability of individual women and couples to control their fertility is not only widely supported but also viewed as a private matter in which governments have little right to intervene. It is also accepted as a prerequisite of women's emancipation, and as a basic feature of modern European civilization.

In order to move beyond the macro-micro dilemma, some policy experts have advanced the notion of the *fertility gap*. This involves lining up the results of surveys and fertility rates. When this is done – and despite the fact that women of prime child-bearing age hope to have fewer children than their older sisters and mothers[12] – there is a numerical *gap* between women's stated fertility aspirations (the ideal number of children reported in surveys) and the reality of slumping

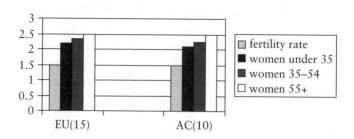

Figure 1
Fertility rates and ideal number of children, by age (2001)
Source: Fahey and Spéder, *Fertility and Family Issues in an Enlarged Europe*
(Dublin: European Foundation for the Improvement of Living and Working
Conditions, 2004), p. 27

fertility rates.[13] In addition, the gap seems to be widening. The numerical distance between young women's fertility aspirations and the number of children is growing.

Data such as these have been widely cited as evidence that women are having fewer children than they might if services were available for reconciling work and family. The policy objective is to close this widening gap.[14] The situation is not so simple, however. Demographers have examined this gap in detail and their data and conclusions point to the need to think more deeply about the reasons for any gap between aspirations and behaviour, as well as about its size.

A thorough study is available, one designed directly to assess the usual European hypotheses about how to confront the demographic challenges. The conclusions, based on 2001 data, are worth citing at length,[15] before moving to policy proposals (also see figure 1):

> Despite falling family size ideals, there is a gap between ideal and actual family size: people's ideals are generally higher than their attainment. Furthermore, evidence from the present data indicates that the gap between ideal and actuality has widened over recent decades, particularly in the EU(15) and to some degree also in the AC(10) [i.e. the 10 accession countries].
>
> From this, it might be tempting to conclude that the pressures which prevent women from realizing their fertility ideals are on the increase and, therefore, that falling fertility can at least partly be seen as an indication of narrowing options when it comes to family formation. However, a closer look at the data cautions against accepting this interpretation too readily. The widening gap between ideal and actual fertility turns out to be a consequence of a falling incidence of over-attainment of fertility rather than a rising incidence of under-attainment. It therefore reflects an increase in women's ability to avoid excess childbearing rather than a decrease in their ability to reach their ideal family sizes. . . .
>
> The gap between ideal and actual fertility is itself a complex thing, since it is an average arising out of an amalgam of quite different components. It is made up of a majority (something over half of those with completed fertility) who attain their ideal number of children, a minority (usually around one third) who fall short of that ideal, and a smaller minority (usually between 10 and 15 per cent) who over-attain their ideal: they have more children than they would want. This third group is important because it reminds us that the gap between ideal and actuality is not always on the deficit side but can arise also on the excess side. From a quality of life perspective, where the freedom to choose the style of life that best suits oneself is the central issue, the problem of attaining fertility ideals is two-fold rather than one-fold. It is a problem of too much *and* too little rather than just of too little.

What to do?

A first step: listen to Europeans

Europeans have views on the reasons the fertility gap exists, and they can tell us why there was a difference between their own behaviour and their own aspirations. They also have ideas about what to do. A first set of data comes from the Eurobarometer in 2001, unfortunately available only for the 13 countries that were candidates to join the Union at that time.[16]

It is worth noting that health (often no doubt related to either male or female infertility) is the major reported reason for any gap between aspirations and reality, and this for one in five respondents. After that, however, financial concerns top the list, either in general (18 per cent) or because children are costly (an additional 9 per cent). Finding adequate housing was mentioned almost twice as often (12 per cent), as was the category of reconciling work and family life, which included access to childcare (7 per cent).

When Europeans are asked to identify what should be governments' priorities in supporting families and family life, the 'fight against unemployment' tops the list.[17] In 6 of the EU(15) countries, it is first on the list, and for fully 12 of the 15 it is among the top three factors mentioned. Flexible working times and better childcare are linked, being at the top for three countries each.[18] In what are now the ten new member

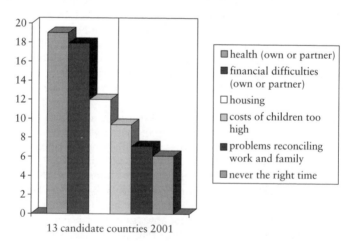

13 candidate countries 2001

Figure 2
Reasons for gap between number of children and fertility aspirations at 20
Source: Adapted from Fahey and Spéder, *Fertility and Family Issues in an Enlarged Europe* (Dublin: European Foundation for the Improvement of Living and Working Conditions, 2004), p. 40

states, in contrast, the fight against unemployment made the top of the list only in two of them, while four put child allowances highest – an item that topped the list nowhere in the EU(15). Child allowances are, of course, a policy instrument to increase income security.

Second step: recognize there is no silver bullet

What does all this mean? A first and key conclusion is that there is no one magic instrument to increase the birth rate.

The Barcelona targets for childcare spaces must be met, because childcare is good for children and it will help parents. It is a legitimate instrument for promoting women's equal inclusion in the labour force and helping to ensure greater security. There are strong labour market reasons as well as reasons of gender and intergenerational equality to promote good quality early childhood education and care. *Alone*, however, it is unlikely to prompt much change in fertility practices.

Increasing access to healthy and safe housing is a policy objective appropriately identified as a key factor for intergenerational fairness. It is also mentioned frequently by Europeans in public opinion surveys as one of the major factors influencing their fertility decisions (usually coming before work/family reconciliation matters). Therefore, ensuring access to good housing is needed as part of the policy mix.[19]

If, however, the main objective is to create a virtuous circle in which people will choose to have more children, then an even larger perspective is needed, one that addresses the underlying financial insecurity which many Europeans – and particularly women – face. They report, whenever they are asked, that they lack confidence in bringing children into a world in which their own economic prospects are uncertain.

Labour markets: how much income security, autonomy and social inclusion?

Rates of female labour market activity are climbing, while men's stagnate, indicating women's increased access to what has become the major institution for assuring not only income security but also social inclusion and autonomy. Yet, stubborn inequalities persist. On the demand side these are related to segregation of labour markets and systemic patterns of discrimination and on the supply side continuing lack of access to benefits and services for reconciling work and family in some places or the specifics of the design of these benefits and services.

Taking the supply side first, it is clear that good policy design fosters women's income security and autonomy; less attractive design can actually undermine both. First, access to affordable and high-quality services for early childhood education and care is a basic need. The OECD's work in the *Babies and Bosses* series continues to identify not only the gaps in availability of affordable places in many European countries, but also the importance of design. For example, Barcelona childcare targets are sometimes met by creating nursery school places. Being by definition only part time, they require parents to find a second form of childcare for the rest of the day (and/or the week) and to find means of transferring the child from one place to another. This policy design increases the difficulty faced by couples holding down two full-time jobs and lone parents holding one. Therefore, while perhaps enabling mothers to move from labour market inactivity to labour market activity, the latter is likely to be only for a few hours and therefore generating little income.

Second, parental leave is very important to the supply-side equation. Leave can be designed in ways that allow parents to take a short time off (up to 12 months) and then return to their employment without loss of skills and knowledge. Such arrangements encourage not only labour force participation but also enable women to take and maintain good jobs, because their absence from the workplace is limited. However, long parental leave (for three years, for example), that is sometimes offered so as to avoid the necessity of providing infant childcare, works against women's full inclusion in the labour force. Not only does this increase employers' reluctance to hire women, but also the women are likely to require retraining before they return to work.

On the demand side, on all measures of labour market success women still do less well than men. They are more likely to be unemployed both in the short and in the long term. They are also more likely to live in a jobless household, and are significantly more likely to be at risk of falling into poverty even after all social transfers have been made. These negative gender gaps exist *despite* the fact that women are less likely than men to halt their investment in their human capital and leave school early.[20]

After several decades of recognition by the EU and by many member states that labour market segregation and outright discrimination work against women's full integration into the labour force and against actions intended to overcome them, improvements are hard to identify.[21]

- The wage gap that has not narrowed in a decade. For EU(15), the average gap was 17 per cent between men and women's wages in 1995 and by 2003 the average had declined to . . . 16 per cent.
- Gender segregation in the labour market remains high.
- Low-wage work is overwhelming done by women. Whereas only two of every five (42 per cent) wage earners are female, fully three-quarters of low-wage earners are women. In several member states (Germany, the Netherlands, Austria and the United Kingdom), women's share is greater than four of every five low-paid workers.[22]

Such a difference in earnings can follow from several conditions: lower wages, shorter hours, or both. In their review of the literature on the working poor, Peña-Casas and Latta explode the myth that women work for fewer hours but for good wages.[23] Without being the only cause for women's low pay, the rise of part-time working cannot be ignored as a factor contributing to labour market results for women that lag behind men's. This increase in part-time work is attributable in large part to the expansion of the tertiary sector in which labour markets are increasingly non-standard with respect to hours.[24] Second, it has also been promoted in policy circles (since the 1970s in the Nordic countries) as a way to reconcile work and family life.

These two reasons together – secular expansion of a sector traditionally highly feminized and encouragement of part-time work for women with young children – have resulted in a form of work which is significantly gendered.

- The percentage of women working part time rose from 29 per cent in 1992 to 34 per cent in 2002.
- Men working part time are overwhelmingly young or over 65. The low overall rate of men's part-time work (6.6 per cent) is due to the behaviour of prime age workers: only 4 per cent of men aged 25–49 work part time and only 7 per cent of pre-retirement age male workers are employed part-time.
- Many women working part time are of prime working age. Among women aged 25–49, 32 per cent work part time; 37 per cent of women aged 49–64 are working part time.[25]
- Not only, therefore, is women's take-home pay lower than it would be if they were working full time, but so too are the benefits that they are accumulating – such as pension rights – if they are lucky enough to be working in a job or for sufficient hours that provide such benefits.[26]

Part-time work is also sensitive to policy choices. The Nordic countries first made innovations with part-time work, promoting it since the 1970s. Part-time work came with significant social protections and was also presented as an ideal solution for women with children. The result is that Nordic labour markets have long been among the most gender-segregated in the OECD. It is now necessary to make efforts to lower these rates of segregation.

The Netherlands, which focused on increasing the employment rate, has become the champion of part-time work for women. Fully 73 per cent of Dutch women active in the labour force work part time. This figure is far ahead of the other member states, with higher than average part-time employment for women: Germany at 40 per cent and the UK at 44 per cent.

Policies that emphasize job-sharing and more equitable gender relations can have an effect. The Netherlands also has a much higher than average rate of male part-time work (23 per cent) than the European average of 7 per cent. Nonetheless, despite all the efforts of the state sector to alter the labour market and family practices, systemic inequalities are stubborn. Despite efforts for decades to encourage men to share family responsibilities more equally, Denmark's percentage of men working part-time (11 per cent) is only a third the female rate (31 per cent) and the same is true for Sweden (11 per cent and 33 per cent). Few men take advantage of parental leave and the other possibilities available to them.

Therefore, if part-time work is to be promoted as a response to both employers' preferences and families' needs, it is important that protections long available to full-time workers are fully available to part-timers and that there are innovative responses to meet the particular needs the needs of these workers.

Household composition and the working poor

The working poor population is on the rise in the EU and, as we have seen, women make up more than three-quarters of it. Several factors already mentioned contribute to their low earnings: discriminatory practices, low pay in heavily feminized sectors and fewer hours of work. An additional major factor that contributes to their being poor is the number of adults available for employment in any household.[27]

Households with only one earner have a much higher rate of poverty than do those with two (or more) employed adults; one in every five such households is classified among the working poor. Of lone-parent households, 22 per cent are classified as working poor; of households with more than one adult and one or more children, 20 per cent are among the working poor. On average, it is only families with two earners that are protected from poverty. Nonetheless, the effect can be attenuated in countries with generous supports for families (such as family allowances and housing allowances).[28]

Much discussion about modernizing social models focuses on the situation of lone-parent families, over 90 per cent of which are headed by women. This is obviously the case in the United States, where 'welfare mothers' have been the target of reformers, and in Canada, where lone-parent families are identified as one of the groups 'at risk of poverty'. It is an error to focus too much on family type, however. UNICEF, for example, has concluded that 'the overall effect of lone parenthood on child poverty rates is small'.[29] The international organization arrived at this conclusion after a thought-experiment. It calculated that child poverty rates and the ranking of countries – its 'league tables' – would hardly change if each country had one in ten families headed by a single parent.

The problem is, then, that it is not the *type of family* but the *type of household*. Households with only one earner are at significantly greater risk of being among the working poor. Secondly, the problem is not the *type of family* but the *type of worker*. Women are significantly more likely than men to be among the working poor, even when they work full time.

Confronted with findings such as these, governments have begun to design new social policy instruments. These have taken the form of either making it less expensive for employers to hire low-wage workers or supplying income supplements, many of which are linked to labour force participation and/or are 'child-tested.'[30] Supplements are often justified as support for families with children, and as such they seem to have somewhat improved levels of child poverty.[31]

These findings lead to the conclusion that such instruments may be effective for addressing child poverty, and therefore responding to the social policy imperatives expressed in terms of 'social investment'. As such, they are important indeed, because, as is well known, a childhood spent in poverty is more likely to lead to an adolescence characterized by problems in school and perhaps with the police, and an adulthood of lower earnings.[32] In and of themselves, however, they do little to address the issues of gender equality or a social model guaranteeing autonomy, security and inclusion to women as well as men. Why not?

- When states take over some responsibility for the income package, by supplementing low-wage earnings, they do nothing *to shape* the labour market. Income supplements cannot improve working conditions, and especially pay rates, that leave many working women in poverty.

- Supplements do not address the fundamental problem of access to *sufficient* hours of work, which is the problem faced by many women.

Concluding remarks

The European Union and most of its member states have had a long-standing commitment to fostering gender equality, and more recently eyes have also turned to intergenerational solidarity. Many steps have been taken towards promoting equality between women and men on the dimensions of security, autonomy and social inclusion. Nonetheless, there is still much to be done, and this for several reasons.

First, while there is widespread and cross-European recognition of the importance of childcare and parental leave in any policy mix, which will enable women's equal labour force participation, this recognition often remains at a high level of abstraction. For example, the Barcelona targets for childcare are a benchmark of the number of children having a childcare place, but set no quality standard. Policy design counts immensely in these matters. All childcare spaces are not equal; they do not all provide the same level of early childhood education and care for children and of support for parents' labour force participation. Parental leave (even if paid) does not provide the same level of support to parental labour market activity and access to quality jobs. There is a need for much more attention to design and its consequences, in bench-marking processes at both member state and European level.

Second, actions to ensure income security must confront a rapidly changing labour market. Part-time work constitutes both an opportunity and a threat to women's security. It is an opportunity when it allows flexibility for balancing work and family responsibilities at the times when the latter are most demanding. It is, however, menacing to women's current – and future – well-being when it becomes a feminized ghetto, with low wages, without opportunities for career advancement, and with no chance of moving to a full-time job. Therefore, it is important to avoid the too easy invocation of 'flexible working times' as a mechanism for fostering gender equality.

Nor is part-time work the only reason for the wage gap between men and women. Segregated occupational patterns and discriminatory behaviour still exist, despite being targeted by Directives of the Commission since the 1970s and in much national legislation. Therefore, lawmakers cannot retire from their efforts to shape labour markets and to make them more responsible for delivering equitable gender outcomes.

Policy initiatives in the past have often been creative and solid. Unfortunately, there is sometimes a tendency to 'forget' them as other issues rise to the fore. Therefore a key recommendation is to 'stay the course'.

Recommendations

- *that the issue of design of both childcare services and parental leave be placed front and centre in discussing and benchmarking for services for reconciling work and family.*
- *that the EU and member states remain firmly committed and actively engaged with long-standing goals of fighting discrimination and labour force segregation in all labour markets.*
- *that, in particular, attention go to the labour market for household services. Wage rates are a particular problem in this labour market. More research is needed about its functioning and best practices. It should be seen as a labour market like any other, and therefore providing the same levels of protection and quality of work.*
- *that part-time working conditions and quality of work receive continuing surveillance so that they are not an additional structured form of employment hindering access of women to full equality.*
- *that attention go the limits of income supplements for promoting gender equality and more attention to the need for labour markets to produce quality jobs.*

Balancing governments' hopes of a higher birth rate with women and men's achievement of autonomy in reproductive decisions constitutes a significant challenge. In the recognition that raising children for a twenty-first-century future both takes longer and is more costly than in the past, families have significantly altered their aspirations and behaviour about fertility. For much of the European population, it now takes two incomes to remain above the poverty line, and even a short break for child-raising has to be carefully considered.

There is clearly space for the state to share responsibility with families, via the provision of high-quality early childhood education and care and well-designed parental leave, as well as housing. However, parents also recognize that responsibility for children stretches well into the future, with implications for income security often stretching over 20 years. These issues have yet to be fully addressed in most discussions about the 'fertility agenda.'

Recommendations

- *that discussions of fertility are solidly anchored in a wider consideration of equality and intergenerational solidarity, which includes attention to parents' concerns about economic security for several decades. Adequate earnings are as important as services such as childcare or as housing.*
- *that parental concerns about access to sufficient of hours of work and to adequate wages be incorporated into the policy discourse. In this way potential and current parents will recognize their own way of framing a fertility decision.*

The ageing society has placed a set of equality issues on the table, ones that have been much less systematically discussed than those concerning income or reconciling work and family, either by governments or by civil society and academics. Providing equal opportunities to the elderly is an area that merits a great deal of attention as we move into 'a Europe for all ages'.

Recommendations

- *that European governments recognize that concerns about security, autonomy and social inclusion reach well past retirement age, and that policy choices are therefore assessed in accordance with these goals which have long been applied to decisions about the young and working-age Europeans.*
- *that European governments recognize that 'families' providing care are very often elderly partners caring for each other. They need services in the area of housing, home help, home care and so on, if this caring is not to become an overwhelming burden and threat to their own well-being.*
- *that policy choices and design are made in full recognition that there may be tensions between the interests of working-age women and the elderly, and that the needs of both merit consideration. A decision to care, made by working-age relatives, cannot be permitted to mortgage their future well-being. A job in household services should be a quality job.*

- *that policies designed to provide services to the elderly so as to ensure their security, autonomy and social inclusion recognize the rights of care workers to quality work and reasonable wages.*

Notes

1 European Commission, *Report from the Commission to the Council, the European Parliament, the European Economic and Social Committee and the Committee of the Regions on Equality Between Women and Men* (COM, 2005) 44 final, pp. 6ff.

2 European Commission, *Confronting Demographic Change: A New Solidarity Between the Generations*, Green Paper (COM, 2005) 94 final, pp. 19, 25–6.

3 J. Alber et al., *Quality of Life in Europe* (Dublin: European Foundation for the Improvement of Living and Working Conditions, 2004), p. 37.

4 The Quality of Life survey found only a very slight difference between the rate of daily care work done by those over 65 (6 per cent of respondents) and that of the so-called and much discussed 'sandwich generation' of 35–64-year-olds (7 per cent). Alber et al., *Quality of Life in Europe*, p. 37.

5 'Household services are defined as all those services provided by public or private organisations, or by the third sector, which substitute paid work (in the form of a job or self-employment) for work which was formerly performed unwaged within the household. Therefore, all services provided inside and outside the home of the user are included, as long as they maintain and support members of a private household', A. Cancedda, *Employment in Household Services* (Dublin: European Foundation for the Improvement of Living and Working Conditions, 2001), p. 8. The major types of services are: childcare, care of the elderly, domestic cleaning (of the house, linen, clothes, etc.), catering, domestic maintenance and gardening.

6 See ibid., 'Introduction', for an overview of EU initiatives fostering this reliance on the community sector.

7 Ibid., ch. 1 and p. 44.

8 Ibid., p. 46.

9 In the mid-1990s in France only 7 per cent of employees in household services earned the minimum wage. Over half of household employees declared a monthly income of FRF2,500, at a time when the SMIC (*Salaire minimum interprofessionnel de croissance* – minimum wage) was at FRF7,000. A child minder in Portugal earned between PTE20,000 and 30,000, when, on average, workers in 'personal and protective services' earned PTE102,400 and the average wage was PTE132,800. R. Peña-Casas and M. Latta, *Working Poor in the European Union* (Dublin: European Foundation for the Improvement of Living and Working Conditions, 2004), p. 34.

10 All the data in this section, unless otherwise indicated, are from T. Fahey and Z. Spéder, *Fertility and Family Issues in an Enlarged Europe* (Dublin:

European Foundation for the Improvement of Living and Working Conditions, 2004).

11 The drop in fertility rates is a very widespread phenomenon. Demographers debate the reason, but most point to large-scale secular trends such as falling infant mortality rates, rising levels of women's education, and knowledge about as well as access to reliable contraceptive methods.

12 No matter the level of public services available, or their access to the labour market, in 24 countries the women now of prime child-bearing age aspire to fewer children than their older sisters and mothers hoped for. Only young French women hope to have more children than what women over 55 identify as the ideal number. Fahey and Spéder, *Fertility and Family Issues*, p. 27.

13 Women and men agree almost completely on these matters. 'Among men . . . the decline in fertility ideals is found in all countries. Generally speaking, patterns of decline differ little by gender. Men have slightly lower ideal family sizes than women, but the difference is slight' (ibid., p. 26).

14 See, for example, High Level Group, *Report of the High Level Group on the Future of Social Policy in an Enlarged European Union* (Brussels: European Commission, DG Employment and Social Affairs, 2004), p. 65.

15 Fahey and Spéder, *Fertility and Family Issues*, pp. 56–7.

16 Ibid., p. 40.

17 Ibid., pp. 73ff.

18 The countries putting childcare as the highest priority are two with good services (Sweden and Finland) and one with improving services (the UK). In contrast, respondents in the countries with the lowest fertility rates among the EU(15) (Spain, Italy and Greece) did not put services as one of their top three priorities, and for the other two countries located below the mean of the fertility rate (Austria and Germany) childcare services arrived in third place among the top three government priorities.

19 For example, the High Level Group on the Future of Social Policy (2004, p. 66) did just that, listing housing as one of three public policies needed.

20 *Joint Report on Social Protection and Social Inclusion* (Brussels: European Commission, DG Employment and Social Affairs, 2005).

21 European Commission, Report from the Commission, pp. 1–5.

22 Peña-Casas and Latta, *Working Poor*, pp. 34–5.

23 Ibid., p. 35.

24 Part-time work is concentrated in the same sectors as low-paid work. Unless otherwise noted, the data on part-time work are from European Foundation (2005).

25 Even among the youngest workers, where part-time work is sometimes considered 'normal', women aged 15–24 have a rate of part-time work almost double that of men.

26 While in 1997 the social partners at the EU level set out a *European Framework on Part-time Work* that sought to eliminate discrimination

against part-time workers and so on, matters concerning statutory social
security were also recognized as falling to the competence of member
states, with consequences for levels of variation.
27 Peña-Casas and Latta, *Working Poor*, pp. 40–1.
28 UNICEF, *A League Table of Child Poverty in Rich Nations*, Innocenti
Report Card #1 (Florence, Italy: UNICEF Innocenti Research Centre,
2000), p. 15 and passim.
29 Ibid., p. 11.
30 These are benefits that are accessed by adults responsible for a dependent
child, usually under the age of 18 or still in school. They are sometimes
called 'child contingent' benefits.
31 UNICEF, *Child Poverty in Rich Countries 2005*, Innocenti Report Card
#6 (Florence, Italy: UNICEF Innocenti Research Centre, 2005).
32 J. Jenson, *Canada's New Social Risks: Directions for a New Social
Architecture*, Report F|43 (Ottawa: CPRN, Inc, 2004), at <www.cprn.org>.

9

Social Justice Reinterpreted: New Frontiers for the European Welfare State

Patrick Diamond

Introduction: social justice in a changing world

The renewal of social democracy and the revitalization of welfare states in Europe are great challenges for the new century. The chapter argues that for these objectives to be satisfied, social democrats need to reinterpret the values of justice and equality, while inventing new policy instruments to pursue them: traditional *ends* as well as means are inadequate.

European social democrats should adopt a strategy of egalitarian modernization. This implies, in essence, a dual conceptual shift. The basic ideals of egalitarian social democracy must be reinterpreted. A rationale for the welfare state in Europe with new frontiers then needs to be defined: existing institutions and policies have to be examined, carefully considered, and revised. In the discussion that follows, the focus is on the relationship between the welfare state and economic equality, especially equality of income and wealth.

The European social model as I will define it should no longer be concerned merely with tackling poverty, inequality or insurance against predictable risks – the traditional objectives of the welfare state, it argues – but with strengthening aspiration: ensuring every individual has the opportunity to fulfil their potential. Indeed, the expression 'welfare state' itself, though best known in its English form, comes from the German original – *Wohlfahrtsstaat* – which refers to 'prosperity' rather than welfare.[1]

The active welfare state must be a trampoline for success,[2] not a safety net that cushions people from failure for the rest of their lives, extending personal freedom to all, not only those with wealth and power: the historic mission of European social democracy since the mid-nineteenth century.

The task of renewal must be undertaken at a time when the conviction that the welfare state is in crisis has established itself as the new orthodoxy with astonishing rapidity in the advanced capitalist countries.[3] Since the early 1990s, leading member states in the EU have begun to recast their welfare systems – but while several reformist steps have been take, more remains to be done. Meanwhile, a reformed welfare state must tackle new inequalities in an age of individualization, globalization and accelerating demographic change.

The European cross-class consensus in favour of shielding citizens from the misfortunes inflicted by the market remains intact.[4] The German poet Hölderlin has written: 'Where there is danger, possibility grows as well.' But if the welfare states of Europe are to be revitalized, a fundamental revision of traditional social democratic doctrine is required. The need for a restatement of doctrine is hardly surprising since each is the product of a particular kind of society. As society changes, so again a restatement of doctrine is called for.

Committed revisionists seek always to make their values relevant to modern circumstances in the light of changes in politics and the economy. In a democratic polity, egalitarian social democrats must pursue a variety of strategies, varying the emphasis between each of them according to contingent circumstances.[5] This chapter argues the case for exactly that approach. It insists that the European centre-left must launch a further wave of programmatic renewal.

Social democratic parties in the midst of profound intellectual upheaval need to assert their core values – while also revising their application. Social democracy does not describe a particular definition of society that may be empirically observed, or policies that create such a society – but consists of emotional and ethical aspirations. The maxim is clear: means and image will change, yet basic value commitments must also be revisited.

The history of the welfare state in Europe

Welfare states embody the inspirational ideals of solidarity and justice, but over time the exact meaning of those values has been lost. In twentieth-century Western Europe, welfare systems restrained rising market-generated inequalities while protecting the vulnerable from the oppressions inflicted by industrial capitalism. The welfare state was principally concerned with security rather than social justice, nonetheless.

The history of European welfare states helps to illuminate the roots of the present crisis: why social justice must be revised, and a new rationale for the social model developed. During the twentieth century, interest group pressure led to an explosion of rights-based claims in the welfare system. It is too easily forgotten, as the political theorist Daniel Wincott reminds us, that socialists saw the welfare state not as the means of tackling inequality, but, 'to facilitate solidarity among workers by partly insulating them from the whip of the market'.[6] The needs of the vulnerable were increasingly marginalized.[7]

Meanwhile, the normative philosophy of social justice that underpins the welfare state was under sustained attack by the 1970s. Neoliberalism produced an intellectually potent rhetoric of reaction against the social democratic state from which it has barely recovered in Britain and the Anglo-Saxon world, though its influence on the European continent was less marked.[8]

It is worth reflecting on the nature of this neoliberal critique of social democracy and its commitment to social justice and greater economic equality, as it helped to provoke precisely the confusion over means and ends that is witnessed today.

Neoliberalism and the social democratic state

The philosopher Raymond Plant argues that it was 'a rhetoric of reaction with a vengeance, because against the background of a rather timid moral case for social democracy, the neoliberal critique has developed a great deal of moral force and political acumen'.[9] The neoliberal position most strikingly articulated in the writings of the German theorist Friedrich Von Hayek is that social justice must be treated as a moral and political illusion, for reasons brilliantly articulated elsewhere.[10]

The right drew the conclusion that the welfare state as broadly conceived should not be the instrument of greater equality, but reduced to a safety net for those who could not provide for themselves. This is not merely the result of empirical weaknesses in the welfare state, but the consequence of fragile moral and philosophical justifications.

Social democrats have been rather too complacent about the fundamental durability of the post-war collectivist state. Liberal theorists of European industrial society were often inclined to treat the welfare state as a 'completed' phenomenon, undergirding the stable liberal democratic order of late twentieth-century capitalism. It was seen as the completion of a centuries-long movement towards full and equal citizenship.[11] The welfare state dissolved class conflict in any sense close to that analysed by Marx.

It is more prescient to insist, however, that welfare states are chronically enmeshed in class conflict, rather than replacing it altogether.[12] The welfare state is thus a relatively fragile institution, highly sensitive to ideological shifts and the changing balance of power within the state. It became increasingly vulnerable as the argument with neoliberalism was gradually lost in the 1980s and early 1990s. So if a reformed welfare state is to tackle new inequalities, social democracy as a moral and political project needs to be reinstated; its core values must therefore be reinterpreted.

What is social justice?

Revising social justice necessarily requires a counter-critique of the neoliberal position. Von Hayek was incorrect to assert, for example, that social justice has little salience because the outcomes of the marketplace are unintended, and therefore cannot be considered *unjust*. Social injustice arises whether or not the actions that led to the result were foreseen or intentional.

Neither is the assertion that liberty requires the negation of social justice really morally convincing. For the political right, it is the freedom to lead a life shaped by one's own purposes and interests, not those of others. But if freedom is merely freedom from coercion and restraint, in what sense is it really valuable to us? It is possible to recognize immediately that freedom and 'ability' are linked.[13] The ability to do and to be is precisely what makes freedom precious.

It is in the context of this neoliberal critique that social democrats must also reinterpret and analyse afresh their value commitments and egalitarian philosophy.

A viable governing project is not sustainable if redistribution and the welfare state are secured only on pragmatic grounds. An explicit ideological rationale is necessary for the dual conceptual shift in the welfare state advocated here to occur. In his seminal work *Liberals and social democrats*, the historian Peter Clarke reminds us of the distinction between moral and mechanical reformers in politics.[14]

Moral reformers are essentially bottom-up reformers who believe that values are only effective in politics if widely shared. They seek to transform the values by which people live in a direction compatible with the broader ethical commitments of their moral philosophy. The mechanical reformer, in contrast, believes that political, social and economic strategies exist that will lead to the desired outcome irrespective of the underlying moral culture of citizens.

The costs of mechanical reform have been very high indeed for social democracy since 1945. If one attempts to pursue a political strategy that does not draw deeply on the values held by the population at large, it will collapse quickly when challenged by a more salient and self-confident belief system. Revitalizing the welfare state requires a strategy conceived as moral, not mechanical, reform.

But the philosophical case itself also needs to be greatly refined. It is necessary explicitly to frame political arguments that fit with wider public understandings of fairness and desert.[15] We should be suspicious of large general ideas that on closer examination turn out to have no precise content. Highly generalized concepts of justice and equality are less useful as the analysis of poverty and social exclusion has become more fine-grained since the 1990s.

Traditional deductive notions of social justice that attempt to pin down a single view inevitably unravel. The political theorist Geoff Mulgan draws on the philosopher Jon Elster's writings, emphasizing that essentially moral conceptions such as social justice are highly context specific.[16] If many highly differentiated factors are woven together in a single aggregation, important insights are lost and complex moral dimensions soon reappear. Social justice becomes harder to sustain in the real world of political argument.

Revisionist social democracy: reinterpreting justice and equality

In this context, precisely how should justice and equality be refashioned? Traditionally, European welfare states saw egalitarian social justice as demanding the equitable distribution of commodities and services – regardless of the effective functioning that this achieved for the individuals concerned. This is palpably insufficient and reflects the inadequacy of social democratic interpretations of concepts of justice. Efforts to equalize economic outcomes do not necessarily strengthen the individual's life-chances, since human needs are highly diverse.

As the development economist Amartya Sen reiterates, individuals are unequal in their capabilities given the same level of monetary resources.[17] A conception of the universal welfare state as the guardian of equality disguises the need to treat individuals not as the same, but to reflect their complex capabilities. The British sociologist R. H. Tawney emphasized this brilliantly in the 1930s:

> Equality of provision is not identity of provision. It is to be achieved not by treating different needs in the same way, but by devoting equal care to ensuring that they are met in the different ways most appropriate to them. . . . The more anxiously, indeed, a society endeavours to secure equality of consideration for all its members, the greater will be the differentiation of treatment which, once their common needs have been met, accords to the special needs of different groups and individuals among them.[18]

The precondition of a revised conception of social justice is an emphasis on diversity of treatment according to need – not uniformity as the guarantor of equality in name only. Individuals rather than the state are agents of their own interests. Public policy must strengthen autonomy, self-esteem, integration into society and adaptation to ever-changing economic challenges.[19] The welfare state, as this chapter argues, requires customized, individually tailored measures precisely and efficiently targeting the most vulnerable. Active welfare should replace the unitary post-1945 interventionist state.

There are several advantages to this new conception derived from Amartya Sen and the American philosopher John Rawls.[20] It uses the concept of the individual as the point of departure, taking into account the individualization of values and lifestyles in the post-industrial societies of the twenty-first century. Rawls suggested that his egalitarian principles were best realized through some form of 'property-owning democracy' or liberal socialism, rather than a capitalist welfare state.[21] *Ex post* income redistribution would leave untouched large inequalities in property and human capital, thereby perpetuating economic inequality, as the economist James Meade also emphasized.

Rawls' and Sen's notions of justice emphasize individual freedom, protecting people against authoritarian or paternalistic impositions by the state or society. Yet Rawls' second principle, enunciated in *A Theory of Justice*, requires considerable redistribution, as long as it promotes equal and fair life-chances for the least privileged.

How should social justice therefore be defined? The German political scientist Wolfgang Merkel has listed five priorities of social justice in a post-industrial society:[22]

1 The fight against poverty – not just because of economic inequality itself, but on the grounds that poverty (above all enduring poverty) limits the individual's capacity for autonomy and self-esteem.

2 Creating the highest possible standards of education and training, rooted in equal and fair access for all.
3 Ensuring employment for all those willing and able.
4 A welfare state that provides protection and dignity.
5 Limiting inequalities of income and wealth if they hinder the realization of the first four goals or endanger the cohesion of society.

The formula provides a sound ideological basis for the egalitarian modernization strategy developed in this chapter. It acknowledges the reality of a highly differentiated society and economic imperatives. It also makes clear that tackling child poverty remains absolutely critical.

There are, of course, still passionate philosophical disagreements on the left about the nature of equality.[23] The traditional account of equality of opportunity in contrast to equality of outcome is a weakly conceived proposition, as both Rawls and the leading British political theorist and politician C. A. R. Crosland argued. Opportunity-based egalitarianism pays too little attention to starting-points and unequal endowments such as family background and genetic legacy. As welfare policy expert Julian Le Grand concludes, differences in people's incomes arise in large part because of factors beyond their control; hence such differences are rarely fair.[24] Inevitably, opportunities and outcomes are inextricably intertwined.

The income and wealth gap between rich and poor still matters since it gravely hinders mobility chances. As numerous empirical studies have highlighted, social mobility is closely linked to the prevailing conditions within families. A fairer society will not be constructed from the bottom-up alone: a concerted strategy to prevent social exclusion among the rich is essential.

Perversely, some continental welfare states have maintained entitlements that encourage an insidious conception of negative freedom: remaining outside work in the most agreeable income conditions possible. This undermines active participation – the precondition for dignity and self-fulfilment – and the effective freedom to act and to choose. The opportunity to participate actively in society should be the right of everyone. The social bases of self-respect, as Rawls puts it, must be distributed equally.

This reinterpretation inspires an ideal of social justice focused on freedom – nurturing personal capabilities, while neutralizing the disadvantages of being born into a disadvantaged class position. It is less concerned with where the individual is located at any given temporal point in the income distribution, more with self-development and the avoidance of poverty. No one should lead a life trapped in cumulative disadvantage, locked into precarious and insecure labour. A specific theory of distributive justice is required, sustaining the individual throughout life while concentrating its efforts to remove specific clusters of disadvantage.

If egalitarian principles are radically revised, the twenty-first-century welfare state will serve as a more effective instrument, combating the social inheritance[25] of under-privilege while extending opportunity and justice to all.

The economic and social challenge for the welfare state

In the meantime, revisionist social democracy requires a rigorous assessment of social and economic change. In reinterpreting social justice, the centre-left needs carefully to assess the broader drivers reshaping welfare policy in modern Europe and, in particular, continuing high levels of income inequality.

The real issue is not whether we have a welfare state, but what sort of welfare regime it will be in the future.[26] Other changes over the coming decades mean that the state must play an increasingly influential role in addressing poverty and inequality, while strengthening individual capabilities.

The first set of trends concerns demographic change within countries: Western industrialized societies are composed of increasingly aged populations. The ratio of active to inactive adults is falling in many EU member states. In much of Europe, extensive protection is now provided against the risks of old age, but there is too little protection from new social risks in the earlier stages of life, such as casual employment, family breakdown, mental illness and inadequate skills.[27] There is a compelling need to rewrite the generational social contract. The sustainability of the twenty-first-century welfare state depends in particular on reconciling higher female labour market participation with women's increasing willingness to have children.

These trends reflect the growing disconnection between work, welfare and family. This has depressed fertility rates and worsened child poverty in many EU member states. The overall income distribution of a country is strongly affected by its household composition: the number of household members who are economically active or inactive.

A recent study of income distribution in Finland found household composition – one or two income earners, number of dependants – more important than class in determining disposable income.[28] Class determined no more than 15 per cent of the variation in individual

income after tax and transfers, but household composition determined more than 25 per cent. Empirical studies by the Institute for
Public Policy Research show that a substantial proportion of the rise
in inequality in Britain between 1979 and 2003–4 occurred because
of demographic factors – changes in household composition, fertility
patterns and population ageing.[29]

Other recent evidence also indicates that high birth rates and
women's involvement in the labour market can coexist if social policy
is appropriately integrated. According to ECHP (European
Community Household Panel) data, there are no differences in the
rate of labour market participation between women with children and
those without children in the Nordic countries, which is presently
higher than 75 per cent.[30]

The rise of child poverty with many long-lasting effects is another
damaging trend. Infancy is a formative environment that plays a critical role in the development of individual human capital. There is a
mounting weight of evidence on the effects of early years' experiences – from diet and parenting to cognitive development in schools –
on subsequent achievements. In countries such as Germany, Spain,
Italy and the Netherlands, the rate of child poverty now exceeds
poverty among the elderly.[31]

We come, second, to the impact of globalization upon the boundaries of the nation-state: the erosion of economic sovereignty has
rendered unworkable traditional demand-management approaches,
and weakened counter-cyclical policies. The declining performance of
the continental economies and their failure to tackle rising unemployment since the early 1990s has further highlighted these weaknesses.

Raising the rate of growth and employment within the European
economy requires more than modest adjustments to the Stability and
Growth Pact. Fundamental reforms of regulatory structures and corporatist institutions are needed, especially in labour markets. The
benign assumptions of the post-war welfare state appear increasingly
tenuous. Attempts to pursue social democratic policies in a single
nation-state have proved untenable.

Hirst and Thompson argue that the 'radical expansionary and
redistributive strategies of national economic management are no
longer possible in the face of a variety of national and international
constraints'.[32] Yet internal exogenous or socio-demographic factors
are far more decisive in urging a transformation of welfare arrangements than economic forces attributed to globalization.

A third set of variables concern immiseration and the related shift
in the demand for skilled labour: the basic threshold required to
participate in the knowledge economy is rising. The accepted level of

cognitive skills such as basic literacy and numeracy has increased since the late 1970s. The new economy is raising the threshold of skills and competencies required to attain secure, well-paid employment. The low skilled are no longer able to access stable jobs, as was the norm in the post-war industrial economy, while the risk of permanent entrapment in poverty grows steadily worse.

Until the early 1990s, it was widely believed, as Esping-Andersen argues, that rising income inequality was wholly confined to the UK, the United States, New Zealand and Australia – apparently consistent with the institutional characteristics that distinguish these economies from continental Europe.[33] The deregulated Anglo-Saxon model allows wages to be set by the market – generating jobs, but not equity. In the rest of the EU, larger welfare entitlements and labour market regulations constrain rising inequalities.

However, the latest data suggest that the Anglo-Saxon economies are hardly the exception at all: the new inequality is a structural feature of almost all advanced capitalist societies.[34] Most experienced a long phase of income equalization between 1945 and 1973, as a result of the increasing returns to labour of unskilled and semi-skilled workers, and the impact of redistributive social policies. But research indicates that most countries have experienced a remarkable rise in inequalities since the early 1990s – with a sharp divergence in wages at the top and bottom of the distribution.[35]

The trends have been most dramatic in Germany, France, the Netherlands, Denmark and Norway. In France, for example, the ratio at which wages at the top outpace the bottom of the distribution has risen from 1:8 to 1:16 since 1991. Moreover, the UK – contrary to the view that it has comparatively large earnings gaps – displays average figures, and in fact sits below France.[36] Wage differentials have increased exponentially as lower returns at the bottom interact with weakening employment protection in the form of the minimum wage, unionization, incomes policies and national wage-bargaining. This produces powerful social dualisms: today, even the French speak of the *societé de deux vitesses*, and the Germans of the *Zweidrittelgesellschaft*.

Finally, there is also Europeanization. This is the contested political space defined as Europe, in which governments are able to steer national economies and welfare systems to achieve greater economic, social and institutional coordination. The development of the EU, however, remains dominated by negative integration arguments such as the neoliberal belief in a larger internal market and free trade – rather than positive integration such as strengthening the social dimension. These debates are likely to persist long into the future.

How are governments responding: an audit of social justice in Europe?

It is also necessary to consider how effectively welfare states have responded to the present challenges. The socio-demographic transition and the transformations in economic life open up the scenario of greater well-being, wider opportunities and new freedoms in Europe.[37] But new social risks are also emerging associated with the incompatibility of work and care, lack of access to knowledge, the obsolescence of professional skills and the risk of marginalization and actual exclusion from the very fabric of society.[38]

The common reflex in more traditional welfare states involves, as Ferrera notes, 'resorting to compensatory measures aimed at rectifying damage to individuals or groups that occurs after the event'.[39] Only when an undesirable outcome has occurred is the social safety net activated.[40] These measures include transfer payments, professional re-training, subsidies for the most disadvantaged workers and measures to combat exclusion. Such policies, however, merely cushion the blow of poverty and unemployment rather than anticipating the risks that generate it.

More proactive and preventative strategies are required that focus on the most vulnerable groups such as women, younger families and children. Such systems have to escape from the reliance on precautionary aftercare. The social democratic welfare state should concentrate on promoting opportunities – rather than providing compensation after the event for individual crises that have already occurred. This requires a shift from old to new social risks, and a more equitable distribution of safeguards and social protection than European welfare states have hitherto allowed. The new welfare state must reconcile the demands of efficiency and economic modernization with distributive justice and equal opportunity for all.

How are welfare states in Europe performing? Wolfgang Merkel has ranked a selection of OECD countries' level of social justice on five key indicators in order of significance: poverty, education, employment, welfare state, and income distribution (see table 1).[41] Poverty has the highest weighting in determining the level of social justice, and income distribution the least: higher numbers indicate a greater level of social justice. The final column of Z-scores reflect a country's overall performance.

As Merkel concludes, it is not surprising that the four Scandinavian welfare states lead on rankings of social justice. The continental European countries tend to be located in the middle of the

Table 1   Comparative welfare state performance

	Poverty (5)	Education (4)	Employment (3)	Welfare State (2)	Income Distribution (1)	Z-scores (weighted)
Denmark	8.51	6.99	3.08	1.13	1.80	4.30
Norway	5.22	7.68	4.48	−0.06	0.80	3.62
Sweden	3.18	4.58	2.54	2.55	1.47	2.86
Finland	7.57	1.58	0.65	1.51	1.52	2.56
Austria	4.90	3.21	1.13	1.57	1.26	2.41
France	3.65	1.99	−1.92	2.09	0.24	1.21
Switzerland	−0.12	2.11	3.76	−1.22	0.47	1.00
Netherlands	3.49	−2.28	0.64	0.70	0.83	0.68
Belgium	4.12	−1.48	−2.92	0.42	0.39	0.10
Canada	−3.41	1.79	1.94	−2.38	0.06	−0.40
Germany	−0.27	−3.12	−0.88	1.62	0.13	−0.50
Australia	1.14	−3.02	0.72	−2.84	−0.46	−0.86
UK	−2.78	−2.42	1.56	−0.70	−0.64	−1.00
USA	−11.41	1.46	3.56	−2.36	−1.46	−2.04
Spain	−1.37	−4.42	−5.98	−0.15	−0.97	−2.58
Ireland	−2.94	−3.22	−3.27	−2.59	−0.94	−2.59
Italy	−7.64	−1.79	−5.26	2.63	−1.48	−2.71
Portugal	−9.53	−1.21	−0.04	−2.23	−1.76	−2.96
Greece	−2.31	−8.42	−3.77	0.33	−1.25	−3.09

Source: Merkel, 'A reformed welfare state will tackle new inequalities', in M. Browne and P. Diamond, eds., *Rethinking Social Democracy* (London: Polity Network, 2003)

distribution: Germany, for example, ranks poorly on levels of social investment critical for individual life-opportunities. This harms both equality between the generations, and impairs its long-term economic prospects. The specific structure of the German welfare state also massively hinders advances in gender equality. What Merkel terms the conservative orientation of Bismarck's social insurance state is scarcely beneficial in securing justice and opening up the possibilities for social mobility, especially for women, the young and the unemployed.

More specifically, the British 'Anglo-social' model is frequently overlooked, but it has notable strengths.[42] Various labour market measures have been introduced since 1997, raising the UK employment rate to 78 per cent – compared to 70.3 per cent across the EU. More than two million more people are in work and unemployment is at its lowest for 30 years. Policies to promote employment include benefit conditionality and targeting, additional childcare places, and measures to provide more flexibility and part-time work, significantly increasing rates of female labour market participation.

Progress in tackling more generic poverty in Britain has also been strong. The numbers who have trouble heating their homes has halved. Infant mortality is at a record low. Britain has also moved away from the American model in some important ways, since its welfare state mixes economic dynamism and high employment with public services funded through general taxation, and an active social policy. Labour's welfare to work approach, for example, has been influenced by Scandinavia rather than the US. Through competent economic management, it is laying the foundations of a markedly fairer society. Some fundamental problems persist, however. The stock of economically inactive individuals in Britain remains high. Indeed, more than seven million people are not participating in the labour market. In 1997, one in five households (20.1 per cent) had no one in work. By 2003, this figure had fallen only very modestly to 17 per cent.

Child poverty remains deeply ingrained in British society. There are still large numbers of the working poor who depend on tax credits to provide a living income. The UK has, to some extent, sacrificed equity for growth since 1997. On spatial measures of poverty, the gap between the poorest neighbourhoods and the rest has also widened.

Meanwhile, there are still powerful dualisms that exclude sections of the middle class from public services such as health and education. More than half a million children, for example, are educated in private sector independent schools outside the state system each year; in London more than one-fifth of pupils are educated in private schools. This has a deleterious impact on social cohesion. As the philosopher Michael Sandel has written: 'The new inequality does not simply prevent the poor from sharing in the fruits of consumption and choosing their ends for themselves; it also leads rich and poor to live increasingly separate ways of life corrupting the idea of citizenship.'[43]

The challenges facing continental welfare states are very different. Their vulnerability lies not in widespread poverty and problems of skill-formation, but in the chronic inability to stimulate employment growth. The main policy response has been to induce labour force exit leading to less favourable population dependency ratios.

First, the continental welfare states are bedevilled by unsustainable models of financing with a rise in budgetary strains and higher unemployment. Second, there are seemingly intractable insider-outsider cleavages. As Ferrera argues, these systems, 'are to a large extent characterised by a labour market segmentation syndrome . . . there is evidence of excessive insurance benefits for "guaranteed" workers, who almost own their job, as against the lack of adequate protection for those employed in the weaker and more peripheral sectors'.[44]

High fixed employment levels also inhibit job-creation. The

main obstacle to private jobs growth lies in high wage floors created by larger labour costs. At the same time, public employment is constrained by the fiscal burden of supporting a very large inactive population. As Esping-Andersen concludes, 'the continental Western European welfare states are coming into conflict with the emerging needs of a post-industrial economy'.[45]

Finally, we turn to the Scandinavian social democratic model. These states appear to have achieved, 'the elusive combination of social equality and economic efficiency'.[46] They are small, open economies that are highly dependent on competitive exports. Sweden in particular is frequently cited as the paradigmatic example of social democracy. Here, the high proportion of dual-earner households keeps child poverty low. Its employment activation policies have also been successful – combined with a high rate of social expenditure. The Scandinavian social democratic parties have also adapted their programmes since the early 1990s, described as the 'three tiers strategy'.[47]

The Nordic countries have contained private and public costs to restore profitability and fiscal prudence. They have improved incentives by fine-tuning their welfare systems and liberalizing part-time work as well as product markets. These economies have also significantly increased investment in future growth, surpassing the larger West European countries on R&D, educational expenditure and ICT innovation.

But in the early 1990s, fears of a crisis in Scandinavian welfare state social democracy arose. Some analysts argued that the Scandinavian growth and employment model was far less effective.[48] This, in turn, made welfare state entitlements unaffordable. Fortunately, this was too negative a picture – but major concerns remain. As John Stephens suggests, '[j]ob growth in Scandinavia has been almost entirely a product of the expansion of public services in the past two decades and it is widely agreed that this pattern cannot continue'.[49]

New frontiers for Europe's welfare states

The European welfare state needs to be recast, with a revised conception of equality and justice at its heart. If social democracy is to recover itself intellectually and politically in Europe, both the fundamental doctrine and the policy instruments through which it is pursued need to be re-examined.

The welfare state requires institutional frontiers that strengthen social protection in a world of rapid change and uncertainty. This involves a broader effort than merely providing more institutions of life-long learning. Labour market flexibility and a more proactive training system do not constitute adequate social protection in a globally competitive economy. In many countries and sectors, new secure jobs requiring advanced skills are not expanding quickly enough to absorb those liberated from low-skilled agricultural, industrial and menial work.[50]

While the long-term goal of a high-skill economy may be greatly desirable – resolving many of the conflicts and problems that have bedevilled the welfare state since the late 1970s – it is an end-state that is tricky to reach. Only a minority of the population is involved in producing internationally traded goods and services. Also, competitive niches require higher labour market productivity – reducing the total number of workers required for a given level of output. Skill-creation strategies do not necessarily create more jobs.[51]

The EU requires more, not less, welfare – with an intelligent, proactive welfare state resting on a refashioned social contract. The strategy of egalitarian modernization would reflect five core premises that draw on Richard Freeman's synthesis in *The New Inequality*:[52]

- shifting redistributive strategies away from income transfers, towards the distribution of productive assets that strengthen individual capability;
- moving redistribution forward in the life-course, targeting interventions on the young;
- raising the social wage but taxing it progressively;
- encouraging the growth of citizens' organizations such as trade unions that protect the terms and conditions of the most vulnerable employees; and
- targeting urban areas for regeneration as the building-blocks of a more egalitarian economy.

The welfare state must also remain broadly universal sustaining popular support for these arrangements. In this context, it requires certain conditions. First, a family contract maximizing the proportion of dual-earner households through the equitable distribution of income and services. This acknowledges the limits of human capital strategies and invests in families through egalitarian social institutions. It requires, for example, a new European childcare guarantee. This would set minimum childcare standards covering all member states as a powerful symbol of Europe's commitment to social values.[53]

Second, a gender contract moving beyond more maternity and paternity leave entitlements and workforce flexibility. The old gender mainstreaming policies will not work any longer. Western capitalism needs to better reconcile work and care through deeper cultural change.

Third, an employment contract preventing individuals from being trapped in disadvantage throughout their lives. It requires more public service jobs for the lowest skilled as a route into the paid labour market. It also offers ladders for the working poor – careers, not just jobs.

Finally, it requires a behaviour contract, since responsible personal behaviour has to be encouraged and irresponsibility sanctioned – such as estranged fathers who fail to provide maternity payments. It is impossible to tackle new social risks such as single parenthood and a lack of marketable skills unless the link with personal behaviour is clearly acknowledged.

The next stage of welfare reform is in turn likely to involve a shift away from the contributory principle and a work-focused model to one that acknowledges a wider range of activities that society believes to be valuable, including caring for dependants, education and training, and voluntary work, as well as paid employment. The policy analyst Lisa Harker envisages a reinvigorated social insurance system, with entitlement based on participation rather than contributions.[54]

This strongly conforms to Amartya Sen's emphasis on capability and active participation. It is likely to reignite interest in the concept of a participation income: a universal flat-rate payment in recognition of desirable activities, reducing the need for means-testing and enabling men and women to make independent choices at work. However, there are major political and administrative obstacles to such a scheme, while it would increase replacement ratios and diminish incentives to take up paid work.

There are also, of course, big divergences between European countries in their welfare systems. The European social model is not a unitary concept, but a set of values and aspirations that vary greatly between member states.[55] What is sketched below is a series of proposals that might be adopted in varying ways by specific reforming countries. The key to developing a new social democratic contract for the welfare state in Europe – reapplying the basic ethical commitments of social democracy in novel ways – is deeper public policy innovation:

- services for babies and the elderly to lighten the burden of unpaid care chiefly shouldered by women, including an EU childcare guarantee;
- transitional employment insurance through the new EU globalization fund so that those who lose their jobs re-enter the labour market quickly;

- an 'individual learning account' for every adult of working age to purchase education and training of their choosing, subsidized by the EU;
- effective preventative screening and interventions such as basic literacy and numeracy classes for those in the labour market at risk of unemployment;
- advancement agencies for the unemployed and low skilled to get seamless advice about retraining and educational opportunities;
- public service employment schemes creating intermediate labour markets for the low skilled;
- incentives that reassign caring duties from mothers to fathers breaking with an entrenched culture;
- forms of financial assistance that encourage women quickly back into the labour market following maternity;
- substantial tax deductions that lighten the load of raising a family;
- benefit sanctions where individuals fail to take up opportunity-enhancing social goods such as early years' provision, training or parenting classes.

Conclusion: a twenty-first-century welfare state

The reform of the European welfare state is deeply contentious, creating new divisions and fault lines within centre-left parties. But internal conflict must not deter social democrats from ideological and policy renewal.

The tensions involved in reconceiving welfare policy are very real. The rate of economic growth in Europe may not be sufficient to fund the active welfare state: activation policy, often targeting the hardest to reach, is notoriously expensive. The electoral coalition that sustains the universal welfare state is also fragile. Certain policy instruments may be less salient than in the 1960s and 1970s – but traditional social democratic values need to be reinterpreted, not abandoned altogether. Equally, the social democratic welfare state is a cherished ideal on the left, yet it cannot be regarded as untouchable. What Anthony Crosland terms the psychological barriers to revisionism must be overcome.[56]

The pace of change in Europe also means that attention will inevitably shift rapidly to new problems in the next 15 years, and social democrats have only just begun to anticipate them. The immobility of individuals in low-paid and low-skilled service jobs is set to worsen. The proportion of households with no one in work is growing in the EU. Meanwhile, the contribution of poor public health to social exclusion is becoming clearer. The multiple disadvantages suffered by ethnic minority groups in Europe are also coming into focus, raising controversial issues of family structure and culture.[57]

There are indeed also pressures, as Christopher Pierson notes, for welfare to bypass the state altogether, returning to more localized, non-hierarchical and non-bureaucratized forms of self-administration.[58] Securing responsive services through the mass institutions of the twentieth-century legal-administrative state has proved testing, and social democrats need to heed the warnings of bureaucratic stagnation and over-centralization.

The problems faced by policy-makers are changing rapidly, revealing a more complex picture than even a decade ago, tied up with behaviour and culture, as well as economics. In response to a revised conception of justice and equality, the European welfare state must advance new frontiers: the dual conceptual shift outlined in this chapter.

Social democrats in late nineteenth-century Europe were bravely radical in redefining traditional values of community, equity, solidarity and security in response to industrialization and urbanization. Their willingness to be innovative and bold helped to create the twentieth-century welfare state. The task in the twenty-first century is to be similarly ambitious in responding to the twin challenges of globalization and the post-industrial economy. This chapter sets out the case for a new revisionism – a refashioned conception of social democracy and the welfare state rooted in moral values and aspirations.

Much scope for optimism remains: as the American sociologist Lane Kenworthy notes, '[e]galitarian shifts are possible even in circumstances in which institutional forces are relatively inhospitable'.[59] Political reform, as well as moral vision, economic ideas and social policy – the essence of revisionism – will need to be skilfully weaved together if social democracy and the welfare state are to be revived together. But as Donald Sassoon concludes: 'Moving forward is no guarantee of success. Standing still offers the certainty of defeat.'[60]

Notes

I would like to acknowledge the assistance and advice of Professor Anthony Giddens, Professor Julian Le Grand, Professor David Held and Professor Mary Kaldor in producing this essay. I am extremely grateful to the Centre for the Study of Global Governance at the LSE and the German Marshall Fund in Brussels for providing such stimulating research environments and facilities. Roger Liddle, Juergen Kronig, Matthew Browne and François Lafond provided invaluable comments on successive drafts. I am also deeply indebted to Professor Maurizio Ferrera of the University of Milan, whose ideas have made a lasting impression on my interpretations of the European welfare state.

1 As quoted by Professor Norman Stone in his *Europe Transformed: 1878–1919* (London: Fontana Press, 1991).

2 This term was initially employed in the first *Social Justice Commission Report* (London: IPPR, 1995).

3 See C. Pierson, *Beyond the Welfare State* (Cambridge: Polity, 1996).

4 See T. Judt, *Post-War: A History of Europe Since 1945* (London: Heinemann, 2005).

5 See B. Jackson, 'Revisionism Reconsidered: Property-Owning Democracy and Egalitarian Strategy in Post-War Britain', *Twentieth-Century British History*, 16, 4 (2005), pp. 416–40.

6 D. Wincott, 'European social democracy and New Labour', in D. Leonard, ed., *Crosland and New Labour* (London: Macmillan, 1997), p. 112.

7 As is made clear in M. Ferrera, 'The caring dimension of Europe', *Progressive Politics*, 3 (London: Policy Network, 2004).

8 As is noted in G. Esping-Andersen, 'Welfare states without work: the impasse of labour shedding and familialism in continental European social policy', in G. Esping-Andersen, ed., *Welfare States in Transition* (London: Sage, 1996).

9 R. Plant, 'Social democracy', in D. Marquand and A. Seldon, eds., *Ideas that Shaped Post-War Britain* (London: Fontana, 1996), pp. 76–87.

10 Each of these arguments has been expounded at length in Plant, 'Social democracy'.

11 See Pierson, *Beyond the Welfare State*.

12 See A. Giddens, *Sociology: A Brief but Critical Introduction* (London: Macmillan, 1982).

13 As reiterated by Plant in 'Social democracy'.

14 P. Clarke, *Liberals and Social Democrats* (Cambridge: Cambridge University Press, 1982).

15 See G. Mulgan, 'Going with and against the grain: social policy since 1997', in N. Pearce and W. Paxton, eds., *Social Justice: Building a Fairer Britain* (London: IPPR, 2005).

16 Ibid.

17 See A. Sen, *Inequality Re-examined* (New York: Russell Sage Foundation, 1997).

18 R. H. Tawney, *Equality* (London: Allen & Unwin, 1931), p. 35.

19 See W. Merkel, 'A reformed welfare state will tackle new inequalities', in M. Browne and P. Diamond, eds., *Rethinking Social Democracy* (London: Polity Network, 2003).

20 These arguments are more fully explained in Merkel 'A reformed welfare state'.

21 See Jackson, 'Revisionism reconsidered'.

22 See Merkel, 'A reformed welfare state', pp. 204–5.

23 A. Giddens and P. Diamond, 'The new egalitarianism: economic equality in the UK', in Giddens and Diamond, eds., *The New Egalitarianism* (Cambridge: Polity Press, 2005).

24 See J. Le Grand, *The Strategy of Equality* (London: Allen & Unwin, 1982).

25 The concept of social inheritance was invented by Esping-Anderson, 'Welfare states without work'.

26 I am grateful for discussions with Professor Wolfgang Merkel in developing this section of the argument.

27 See Ferrera, 'The caring dimension of Europe'.

28 As cited in G. Therborn, *Between Sex and Power: Family in the World 1900–2000* (London: Routledge, 2003).

29 See M. Dixon, *Population Politics* (London: IPPR, 2006).

30 See Esping-Anderson, 'Welfare states in transition'.

31 See G. Esping-Andersen, 'Inequality of incomes and opportunities', in A. Giddens and P. Diamond, *The New Egalitarianism* (London: Polity, 2005).

32 See P. Hirst and G. Thompson, *Globalization in Question* (Cambridge: Polity Press, 1996).

33 See Esping-Andersen, 'Inequality of incomes'.

34 Ibid.

35 Ibid.

36 See European Commission, 'Employment in Europe 2005: recent trends and prospects', in *Employment and Social Affairs*, European Commission Directorate-General for Employment, Social Affairs, and Equal Opportunities (Brusssels, 2005).

37 See Ferrera, 'The caring dimension'.

38 These points are developed extensively in ibid.

39 Ibid.

40 See F. Vandenbroucke, *Globalisation, Inequality and Social Democracy* (London: IPPR, 1998).

41 See Merkel, 'A reformed welfare state,' pp. 204–5.

42 The case for the 'Anglo-social' model is well made by M. Dixon and H. Reed, *An Anglo-European Social Model* (London: Open Democracy, 2005), available at <www.opendemocracy.net>.

43 M . Sandel, *Liberalism and the Limits of Justice* (Cambridge: Cambridge University Press, 1996), pp. 154–5.

44 Ferrera, 'The caring dimension', p. 36.

45 Esping-Andersen, 'Inequality of income', p. 11.

46 J. D. Stephens, 'The Scandinavian welfare states: achievements, crisis, and prospects', in E. Esping-Andersen, ed., *Welfare States in Transition*, pp. 85–9.

47 See K. Aiginger and A. Guger, 'The ESM: from obstruction to advantage', *Progressive Politics*, 4, 3 (London: Policy Network, 2005), p. 64.

48 See Stephens, 'The Scandinavian welfare state'.

49 Ibid.

50 See C. Crouch, *Industrial Relations and European State Traditions* (Oxford: Clarendon Press, 1992).

51 These arguments are set out at length in ibid.

52 These points are adapted from an essay by the US economist Richard Freeman in *The Boston Review*. See R. Freeman, *The New Inequality* (New York: American Prospect, 2001).

53 For an excellent summary of this idea, see D. Clark, 'Why we need a social Europe', *Renewal*, 13, 4 (2005). A European childcare guarantee would set minimum standards covering all member states. Countries already meeting those standards could receive a rebate on their budgetary contributions. For the rest, the EU could provide funding directly to local providers.

54 L. Harker, 'A twenty-first century welfare state', in N. Pearce and W. Paxton, eds., *Social Justice: Building a Fairer Britain* (London: IPPR, 2005).

55 See A. Giddens, 'The world does not owe us a living!', *Progressive Politics*, 1, 3, (London: Policy Network, 2005).

56 C. A. R. Crosland, *The Future of Socialism* (London: Allen & Unwin, 1956).

57 See G. Mulgan, 'Rethinking Social Justice,' in N. Pearce and M. Dixon, eds., *Social Justice: Building a Fairer Britain* (London: IPPR/Politicos, 2005).

58 Pierson, *Beyond the Welfare State.*

59 See L. Kenworthy, *Egalitarian Capitalism: Jobs, Incomes and Growth in Affluent Countries* (US: Russell Sage Foundation, 2004).

60 Donald Sassoon, *One Hundred Years of Socialism: The West European Left in the Twentieth Century* (London: Fontana, 1997).

10

A Knowledge Economy Paradigm and its Consequences

Luc Soete

Introduction

From a traditional economic perspective, the easiest way for policy-makers to increase a country's welfare is to increase the supply of its input factors. The input factor which offers most scope for easy and at first sight straightforward expansion is, of course, labour. To judge from the experience in Scandinavian countries, the UK and the Netherlands, it appears that an active labour market policy aimed at raising the employment activity level can indeed result in an immediate improvement in output growth performance. Given the gap between the activity level targets set in Lisbon and current employment levels in many EU countries, there are still more opportunities for job-intensive growth in EU countries based on the further expansion of employment to underrepresented groups in the labour force: women, immigrants, 55+ citizens, students combining study with part-time jobs, etc. Relatively high Dutch economic growth performance in the 1990s, for example, was clearly associated with job-intensive growth.

However, at some stage, such expansion in the labour market in a high-income setting will result in decreasing returns: a decline in the willingness of those who are 'voluntarily non-active' in the labour force[1] to seek formal paid employment. Exchanging for paid work the various activities they are involved in outside the formal wage income sphere – not just leisure or time spent on hobbies, but also social and voluntary work, care, household and community activities – will barely be influenced by specific incentive schemes and the active labour market policy tools put in place. Following Becker, it can be argued that with the average rise in hourly levels of pay, the welfare value of leisure and voluntary 'non-work' activities has also risen. In short, there are limits to raising activity levels as sustainable engines for growth in high-income societies. By which I am not implying that these levels are currently being reached in EU countries,[2] but rather that sustainable growth opportunities of such labour-intensive growth are intrinsically limited, and particularly when the rapidly ageing structure of Europe's population is taken into consideration.

An even more straightforward economic argument holds with respect to the decreasing returns accompanying the accumulation of capital, the other traditional production input factor. For high-income countries, the only input factor which promises long-term sustainable output growth is, ultimately, knowledge accumulation in its various forms: embodied in more efficient capital goods, in human capital, in organizational methods, in new production techniques or products.

There is thus nothing peculiar about the priority given to and emphasis put on knowledge and innovation as engines for sustainable growth, both in the original and recently revised official Lisbon Strategy declarations.[3] In this chapter, I draw attention to a number of particular features of knowledge accumulation and innovation that seem to have been insufficiently addressed in the practical (past and present) implementation plans of the Lisbon Strategy.

First, there is the quite fundamental way in which knowledge accumulation and innovation have changed over the last century and is different today from what it was 20–40 years ago. As a result, realizing the welfare and efficiency gains that result from knowledge accumulation and innovation is today more closely and intractably linked to the dynamism and windows of opportunity offered by individual countries' social models. The European social model (ESM), as represented by its German continental version,[4] was first and foremost an industrial society model: a model very much in line with a process of technological accumulation characterized by incremental innovations.

As I will argue, proposals for reform of the ESM, however defined, will need to take into account the changing nature of technological change. Ideally, this might well involve recognizing more explicitly the emerging dual nature of the labour market. It is the 'knowledge workers' segment of that labour market which seems today to lack dynamism in Europe and which appears to undermine the financial sustainability of the ESM. Reform policies should focus on that particular segment of the labour force.

My third point addresses more directly the policies designed to increase knowledge investments in Europe as formalized in the so-called Barcelona R&D targets. As I argue, such R&D investment cost targets are somewhat odd. It would be better to focus more specifically on the underlying 1 per cent government expenditure target and what could be called the 'Lisbonization' of member countries' fiscal policies: the relative amount of public investment in knowledge and innovation in the broadest sense, i.e. including, for example, education. It is necessary here to recognize that apart from purely quantitative targets with respect to fiscal deficits aimed at economic stability, there is also a 'quality' side to member states' budgets. But the national focus on the need for investment in knowledge accumulation will also need to recognize the underlying shifts in the nature of technological accumulation and innovation which I highlight first. The one I wish to pinpoint at the end of this chapter is the international dimension. Achieving technological international competitiveness might well, to paraphrase Paul Krugman, have become a dangerous European obsession, certainly when viewed against the global challenges and threats to national welfare.[5] The balance of sectors and areas where technological competitiveness is essential for maintaining European welfare (aerospace, information societies technologies, advance manufacturing, etc.) as opposed to sectors where global diffusion and access to knowledge is becoming much more crucial to Europe's long-term welfare (energy saving, sustainable development and climate change, health and diseases, security) is shifting rapidly. Is it not time for a shift in the importance given by European policy-makers to the strengthening of international intellectual property in favour of access to knowledge?

In short, the shift in the knowledge economy paradigm agenda has implications that go way beyond the traditional research and innovation policy agenda discussed by European member countries' respective ministers and administrations on research and innovation. A truly integrated Lisbon Strategy will have to take these implications more fully into account, as highlighted in my conclusion.

On the changing nature of technological accumulation and innovation

From S&T to industrial R&D

Science and technology has been the subject of public interest and support for centuries. The acceptance of a utilitarian argument for the public support of basic scientific research predates the Industrial

Revolution itself.[6] Although government and university laboratories had existed earlier, it was only in the 1870s that the first specialized R&D laboratories were established in industry.[7] What became most distinctive about this form of industrial R&D was its scale, its scientific content and the extent of its professional specialization. A much greater part of technological progress now became attributable to R&D work performed in specialized laboratories or pilot plants by full-time qualified staff. It is this sort of professional work that is today recorded in official, internationally harmonized R&D statistics. Already in the early days of defining what was to become the OECD Frascati Manual definition of 'R&D', it was obvious that it would not be possible to measure the part-time and amateur inventive work of typical nineteenth-century research. The present industrial R&D statistics are therefore a reflection, and also a measure, of the professionalization of R&D activities. And while the extent of specialization should not be exaggerated – even today in many manufacturing firms, the 'technical' or 'engineering' departments, or 'OR' sections, contribute far more to the technical improvement of an existing process than the formal R&D department, more narrowly defined – the balance significantly changed over the course of the twentieth century, with a gradual further specialization of the R&D function. It is the emergence of this particular function which can be most closely identified with the emergence and growth of the industrial society.

This industrial research 'revolution' was, however, not just a question of a change in scale. It also involved a fundamental change in the relationship between society, on the one hand, and technology and science, on the other. The expression 'technology', with its connotation of a more formal and systematic body of learning, only came into general use when the techniques of production reached a stage of complexity where traditional methods no longer sufficed. The older, more primitive arts and crafts technologies continued to exist side by side with the new 'technology'. But the way in which more scientific techniques would be used in producing, distributing and transporting goods led to a shift in the ordering of industries alongside their 'technology' intensity. Thus, typically, in most Western industrial societies of the twentieth century there were now high-technology-intensive industries, having as a major characteristic high sector internal R&D investment, and low-technology craft-based industries, with very little R&D. And while in many policy debates, industrial dynamism became somewhat naively associated with the dominance in a country's industrial structure of the presence of high-technology-intensive sectors, so the more sophisticated studies on the particular features of intersectoral technology flows, from Pavitt to Malerba, brought back to the forefront many of the unmeasured, indirect sources of technical progress in the analysis.[8]

At the same time, the 'science' and 'technology' parts of research developed with an increasing degree of independence from each other, certainly when compared to the early phases of the Industrial Revolution. The latter have been described by Mokyr as a period of 'industrial enlightenment': a period of close and fruitful interactions between industrialists searching for a better scientific understanding of their technological inventions, and scientists keen on understanding the underlying scientific principles of those new industrial technologies.[9] Thus the development of the steam engine influenced thermodynamics, whilst scientific knowledge of electricity and magnetism became the basis for the electrical engineering industry. The two bodies of knowledge were nevertheless generated by distinct professions in quite different ways and with largely independent traditions. The scientific community was concerned with discovery and with the publication of new knowledge in a form which would meet the professional criteria of their fellow scientists. Application was ultimately of secondary importance or not even considered. For the engineer or technologist, on the other hand, publication was of secondary or negligible importance. The first concern was with the practical application and the professional recognition which came from the demonstration of a working device or design.

Elsewhere, I have described the growing dichotomy between science and technology in recent decades as a 'Dutch knowledge disease' phenomenon – a process which was set in motion in the 1970–80s and consisted of a dual 'crowding out':[10] a 'crowding out' of fundamental, basic research from private firms' R&D activities on the one hand, and a process of 'crowding out' of applied research from public, primarily academic university research, on the other. The first process found its most explicit expression in the reorganization of R&D activities, from often autonomous laboratories directly under the responsibility of the Board of Directors in the 1960s to more decentralized R&D activities that were integrated and fully part of separate business units. Today, only firms in the pharmaceutical sector and a couple of large firms outside this sector are still involved in the funding and carrying out of fundamental research (as reflected, for example, in the number of scientific publications coming out of private firms). For most firms, the increased complexity of science and technology has meant a greater focus on applied and development research and a more explicit reliance on external, university or other, often public, knowledge centres for more fundamental research input. Firms now 'shop' on the world market for access to basic and fundamental research and choose the best locations to locate their R&D laboratories. In doing so, they will not only hope to make their own, in-house R&D more efficient, but also look to the efficiency, quality and dynamics of the external universities and public R&D institutions.

At the other end of the spectrum, public research investments in universities and other public research institutes became, in most advanced countries, increasingly subject to national public scrutiny during the 1980s and '90s through systematic performance assessment and academic peer review. As a result, academic performance became even more explicitly the dominant incentive in public research institutes, while applied, or more immediately relevant, research was second rated. As a result, in many countries, particularly in Europe, applied research became 'crowded out' of the university environment.

These opposing trends in the nature of private and public research have to some extent accompanied the gradual shift in the economy from an industrial society to a more service-based, immaterial economy, in which industrial production is no longer the prime recipient and carrier of technological improvement.

The emerging knowledge economy paradigm

In the last couple of decades or so, there has been a major shift in the understanding of the relationships between research, innovation and socioeconomic development. First, economists have come to accept that knowledge accumulation can easily be analysed, like the accumulation of any other capital good. In short, that economic principles can be applied to the production and exchange of knowledge; and that knowledge is intrinsically endogenous to the economic and the social system, not an external, 'black box factor, only to be opened by scientists and engineers', in Christopher Freeman's celebrated words.[11] Hence, while knowledge has some specific features of its own, it can be produced and used in the production of other goods, even in the production of itself, like any other capital good that is used as an input in the production process. It can also be stored and will be subject to depreciation, when skills deteriorate or when people no longer use particular knowledge and, in the extreme case, forget about it. It might even become obsolete, when new knowledge supersedes and renders it worthless – as in the case with leading-edge technologies.

However, there are some fundamental differences with traditional industrial capital goods. The production of knowledge will not take the form of a physical piece of equipment, but will be embedded in some specific blueprint form (a patent, an artefact, a design, a software program, a manuscript, a composition), in human beings or even in organizations. In each of these cases there will be so-called positive externalities: the knowledge embodied in such blueprints, people or organizations cannot be fully appropriated; at little cost to the knowledge creator, it will flow away to other firms or to the public knowledge stock. Knowledge is from this perspective a non-rival good. Many people can share it without diminishing in any way the amount available to any one of them.

Second, the emergence of the cluster of new information and communication technologies (ICTs) has also had a direct impact on research, international knowledge access and innovation. ICTs are, in the real sense of the words, an information technology, the essence of which consists of the increased memorization and storage, speed, manipulation and interpretation of data and information. In short, it is what has been characterized as the codification of knowledge. As a consequence, information technology makes codified knowledge, data and information much more accessible than before to all sectors and agents in the economy linked to information networks or with the knowledge of how to access such networks. But ICTs have also had a direct impact on the R&D process itself. Research laboratories are today equipped with sophisticated ICT equipment allowing more precision, reliability and expanding dramatically the scope for research in many different scientific fields. The intensive use of sophisticated ICT instruments in the process of R&D is one of the major factors contributing to the increase in the efficiency in research over recent decades.

At the same time, the increased potential for international codification and transferability of knowledge linked to the use of ICTs implies that knowledge, including economic knowledge, becomes to some extent globally available. While local capacities to use or have the competence to access such knowledge will vary widely, the access potential is there. ICT, in other words, brings to the forefront the enormous potential for catching-up, based upon cost advantages and economic transparency of (dis-)advantages, while at the same time stressing the crucial tacit and other competence elements in the capacity to access international codified knowledge. For technologically leading countries or firms, this implies increasing erosion of monopoly rents associated with innovation and shortening of product life-cycles. Research efforts may no longer be profitable in this setting, from the perspective of a single firm. The ability of each economic actor to innovate single-handedly in such a global setting is becoming more risky, and stresses the role of strong technology clusters and government investment in knowledge.

Third, the perception of the nature of innovation processes has changed significantly since the 1990s. In Paul David and Dominique Foray's beautifully narrated historical analogy, innovation capability is today seen less in terms of the ability to discover new technological principles than in terms of the ability to exploit systematically the effects produced by new combinations and use of pieces in the existing stock of knowledge.[12] This new model, closely associated with the emergence of numerous knowledge 'service' activities, implies to some extent more routine use of a technological base allowing for innovation without the need for leaps in technology, a process which has sometimes been referred to as 'innovation without research'. It requires systematic access to state-of-the-art technologies; each industry must introduce procedures for the dissemination of information regarding the stock of technologies available, so that individual innovators can draw upon the work of other innovators. As David and Foray highlight, this mode of knowledge-generation – based on the recombination and re-use of known practices – raises also much more information search problems and must confront the problems of the impediments to accessing the existing stock of information that are created by intellectual property right laws.

The new concept of a 'science, technology and innovation system' is, in other words, shifting towards a more complex, socially distributed structure of knowledge-production activities, involving a much greater diversity of organizations. The old system reviewed above was, by contrast, based on a simple dichotomy between knowledge-generation (R&D laboratories and universities) and production and consumption activities, where the motivation for acting was not to acquire new knowledge but, rather, to produce or use effective outputs. The collapse (or partial collapse) of this dichotomy leads to a proliferation of new places having the explicit goal of producing knowledge and undertaking deliberate research activities, which may not be readily observable but which are nevertheless essential to sustain innovative activities in a global environment.

To summarize, traditional R&D-based technological progress, which is still very much dominant in many industrial sectors ranging from the chemical and pharmaceutical industries to motor vehicles, semiconductors and electronic consumer goods, has been characterized by the ability to organize technological improvements along clearly agreed-upon criteria and a continuous ability to evaluate progress. At the same time, a crucial part of engineering research consisted, as Richard Nelson put it, 'of the ability to hold in place': to replicate at a larger industrial scale and to imitate experiments carried out in the research laboratory environment. As a result, it involved first and foremost a cumulative process of technological progress: a continuous learning from natural and deliberate experiments.

The more recent mode of technological progress described above, which is associated more with the knowledge paradigm and the service economy (with, in its extreme form, the attempts at ICT-based efficiency improvements in, for example, the financial and insurance sectors, the wholesale and retail sectors, health, education, government services, business management and administration), is based much more on flexibility and confronted with intrinsic difficulties in replication. Learning from previous experiences or from other sectors is difficult and sometimes even misleading. Evaluation is difficult because of changing external environments: over time, among sectors and across locations. It will often be impossible to separate out specific context variables from real causes and effects. Technological progress will, in other words, be based much more on trial and error, but without – as in the life sciences – providing 'hard' data, which can be scientifically analysed and interpreted. The result is that technological progress will be less predictable, more uncertain and ultimately more closely associated with entrepreneurial risk-taking. Attempts at reducing such risks might involve, as Von Hippel has argued, a much greater importance given to users who are already in the research process itself.[13]

This shift, as I argue in the next section, has major implications for the functioning of the ESM as typified in the German version of that model. The German social model was to some extent the 'ideal' type of social industrial model (with Japan), with strong incentives for firms to invest in the internal learning and upgrading of their workforce, a close and privileged interaction between firms and higher education establishments (dual learning systems) and specialized industrial R&D and engineering departments, guaranteeing a continuous improvement in production and organizational efficiency. It resulted in continuous improvements in the international competitiveness (unit labour costs) of German production, as reflected in German trade surpluses – still the case today. It also explains the high expectations of economists in the 1980s of the German (and Japanese) *Standort* likely to take over US industrial technology dominance.

However, compared to the new mode of technological progress, the previous advantages of this social model are now quickly turning into disadvantages primarily associated with major emerging inflexibilities, which are to some extent at loggerheads with the flexibility that is now required in the new knowledge paradigm.

The knowledge paradigm and the European social model

The organizational and social challenges associated with the emerging knowledge paradigm described above, and also closely associated with the service economy and the 'e-conomy', were, and maybe somewhat paradoxically given the original emphasis on e-Europe in Lisbon, not really addressed in the discussions leading up to the Lisbon summit. Most of the discussions focused on the technological aspects of knowledge-creation and development, the lagging position of the EU vis-à-vis the US, the need for a European research area and better coordination of member states research policies, the shortages of scientists and engineers, etc. The challenges of the emerging knowledge paradigm for the social models in European members states were barely addressed.

Yet it is clear that in a knowledge-driven society as described above there are likely to be many institutional, social and cultural bottlenecks to entrepreneurial risk-taking, trial and error innovation and the ensuing creative destruction, which touch directly on the functioning of the ESM. To some extent, the Lisbon declaration was not only an expression of a political desire to strive for a Europe belonging to the world's most knowledge-intensive regions in ten years, but also that this was to happen within the context of a strengthened, 'activated' social Europe that would have an eye for past social achievements. The question that was *not* addressed was how activating labour markets would enhance the shift towards the new knowledge paradigm.

Economists such as Giles Saint-Paul have analysed the relationship between labour market institutions, and in particular the costs of hiring and dismissing employees, and the development of innovations from a purely theoretical perspective.[14] Hiring and firing costs are in many ways the most explicit manifestation of the industrial employment 'security' that is embedded in European continental social welfare states – the Bismarck model. They have led to stability in labour relations and have represented a useful incentive for employers and employees alike to invest in human capital. However, in terms of the new knowledge paradigm, and in particular the accompanying process of 'creative destruction' which might accompany the development of new activities – whether concerned with new product, process or organizational innovations – this model will dramatically raise the costs with which 'destruction' can be realized. Thus, as shown in Saint-Paul's model, the US, with lower firing costs, will eventually gain a competitive advantage in the introduction of new, innovative products and process developments onto the market, while continental Europe will become specialized in technology-following activities, based on secondary, less radical improvement innovations.

In other words, the dynamics of innovation, of entrepreneurship, and of creative destruction thrive better in an environment that provides higher rewards for creativity and curiosity than in one that puts a higher premium on the security of employment, internal learning and efficiency improvements in the production of existing products. Viewed from this perspective, the gap between Europe – and in particular continental Europe – and the United States in terms of innovative capacity, efficiency and wealth-creation may look like the price Europe has had to pay for not wanting to give up the social securities and achievements associated with its social model. Many of the proposals on 'activating the labour market' with by now popular concepts like 'empowerment' and 'employability' appear to go hand in hand with innovation and growth dynamics; others, though, do not. Some European countries, such as the UK and Denmark, appear to have been more successful in reducing dismissing costs than others, and appear to have benefited much more from the knowledge paradigm in terms of growth dynamics.

The central question, which must be raised within this context, is whether the social security model developed at the time of the industrial society is not increasingly inappropriate for the large majority of what could be described as 'knowledge workers': workers who are likely to be less physically (but by contrast possibly more mentally) worn out by work than the old type of blue-collar, industrial workers. The short working hours, the early retirement schemes and the longer holidays might well appear to knowledge workers less as a social achievement – work not really representing a 'disutility' – than as an essential motivating activity, providing even a meaning to life.

There is, in other words, I would argue, a need for a fundamental rethinking of the universality of European social security systems. That rethinking should explicitly recognize the emerging duality in the labour force between work involving *labour*, i.e. an exhausting physical or mental activity, and work involving *pleasure*, i.e. activities primarily providing self-satisfaction in terms of recognition, realization and creativity. Workers involved in the first sort of activity will consider the social achievements, including employment security, a relatively short working life and short weekly working hours, as important social achievements and intrinsically associated with their quality of life, which they will not be prepared to give up. Workers involved in the second sort of activity have been given similar social rights by extension, because of the universality principles of labour law. At the same time, such an automatic extension of social rights appears by and large to be inappropriate and could be considered to be behind the lack of dynamism of knowledge workers in Europe. Furthermore, the full application of the social model to the growing proportion of knowledge workers undermines the sustainability of the social model itself. In short, when work involves significant positive externalities as in the case of knowledge work, it appears particularly inappropriate to apply social 'security' guarantees to employment aimed first and foremost at reducing the negative externalities of physical work.

Increasing knowledge investments in Europe

Whereas the 2005 spring summit of EU heads of state and government made the Lisbon goal a longer-term and less formal objective, the knowledge investment targets set at the Barcelona European Council meeting in 2002 remain a major policy priority for EU member states. As agreed in Barcelona, research, development and innovation investments in the EU will have to be increased to 3 per cent of GDP by 2010, up from the 1.9 per cent of GDP in 2000. The innovation part of those expenditures is difficult to measure, so most countries have focused on the R&D expenditures part. An increase in the level of business R&D funding has been called upon rising from its current level of 56 per cent to two-thirds of total R&D investment, a proportion currently achieved in the US and in some European countries. Public investment in R&D and innovation should amount by 2010 to 1 per cent of GDP.

The Barcelona R&D and innovation investment objectives arose from the recognition that strengthening Europe's private R&D and innovation systems appeared essential in realizing the Lisbon strategic goal. The assumption behind this was that domestic private R&D would be a crucial driving force for a competitive and dynamic knowledge-based economy. The impression of a clear Lisbon failure is also closely associated with the failure to improve in any sense over the last five years the private R&D intensity in most member countries.[15] Notwithstanding the political importance of setting such a long-term knowledge investment target, in terms of economic policy the 3 per cent objective is somewhat odd.

First and foremost, it is an investment cost target. Equally important, if not more so, is the question of what the results – in terms of efficiency and effectiveness – of such investments will be. Firms are not interested in increasing R&D expenditures just for the sake of it but because they expect that the new or improved production processes, technology concepts or new products responding to market needs emerging from these activities will improve their efficiency and hence their long-term competitiveness. Furthermore, these same basic economic rules apply of course also to the increasingly costly R&D process itself: if at all possible, firms will try to license such technologies, or alternatively outsource at least part of the most expensive or risky knowledge investments. In the current international environment, firms are constantly being pressed to increase the efficiency of their internal R&D by rationalizing, reducing the risks by outsourcing R&D to separate small high-tech companies which operate at arm's length but which, once successful, can be taken over. None of these features, characteristic of the new knowledge paradigm and which from an economic growth and competitiveness perspective appear essential, is captured in a 3 per cent R&D objective.[16]

Second, as a policy target spread between a dominant private industry target (2 per cent) and a relatively weak public sector target (1 per cent), the 3 per cent objective does not appear to be very credible: the main investment efforts needed to achieve it are with the private sector, something most governments have at best some indirect influence over, whereas the weaker public sector target is itself subject to the fiscal policy constraints (the other 3 per cent target) under the Stability and Growth Pact (SGP).

Conceptually, the weakening of the 3 per cent Barcelona objective in a double R&D effort of the private sector for every single public R&D effort again appears odd and not based on a careful reflection of the different roles of each of those sectors in knowledge investments in different member states. It appears to be based on the current US private versus public decomposition of R&D expenditures, thus ignoring the quite fundamental differences between the US and European countries' business profits and income tax regimes and the implications thereof for private and public parties in the funding of research and development (and higher education and training). It also ignores the dominance of publicly funded military research carried out in private firms in the US, and the much more diversified picture in Europe (significant in the UK, France and Sweden, of low importance in Germany and Italy).

In particular, the differences in income taxation regimes appear at first sight to be important: in countries with progressive tax regimes, such as the Scandinavian countries, The Netherlands or Belgium, there is a natural expectation amongst private investors (businesses and individuals) to assume that governments will take on a stronger role with respect to investment in public research infrastructures and, in particular, higher education.[17]

Third, and from the small, open economy perspective characteristic of many European member states (19 out of 25), but also the case for the larger ones, the question must be raised whether any national domestic knowledge investment target has any real economic significance. With increased globalization, the relevant R&D which will act as a driving force in any European country[18] is much more likely to come from abroad; at the same time, domestic R&D activities might have little impact on the domestic economy in which such R&D activities happen to be located.[19] Although many enterprises recognize the increased importance of investing in R&D, they do so only to the extent that they can exploit results effectively within their (often international) organizational borders, and expect sufficient returns to balance the risks inherent in such investment. Here too, the same argument holds: firms will do so no longer from a domestic but only from a global perspective.

In short, the 3 per cent knowledge investment target seems odd not only from an analytical economic perspective, it makes also little sense within a global knowledge world in which private R&D has become by and large a mobile production factor, with firms locating such activities where the local conditions appear optimal. Among the most important factors in this regard is a sufficient supply of highly qualified human resources, in particular in science and engineering, the availability of a strong public research base that is flexible and open to interactions with the private sector and a local environment characterized by a dynamic entrepreneurship culture, particularly with respect to potential suppliers and users. These appear to some extent the crucial 'attractor' factors which domestic policy-makers should address.

As I will argue in the next section, national policy goals will often be misleading in this area. Whereas innovation and technological developments, even in the new knowledge paradigm, might need a strong R&D production system (both public and private) and sophisticated human skills, they ultimately depend on the national or local ability to utilize new knowledge produced elsewhere and to combine it with the available domestic stock of knowledge. Most European countries are not just dependent on foreign R&D activities; they are also unlikely to be able to capture all the benefits of their R&D investments domestically. The absorptive capacity of domestic actors with regard to new knowledge, produced in the country or elsewhere, their capacity to create linkages with foreign R&D actors, should be equally key elements of attention in addition to the 3 per cent target as an expense target.

A possibly more interesting knowledge and innovation investment target might well consist of a combination of R&D and innovation expenditures with education expenditures, both public and private.[20] Combining the 3 per cent Barcelona R&D and innovation/GDP target with the OECD's 6 per cent education/GDP target would probably give much more leeway to individual member countries to adjust the knowledge investment targets to their own situation, taking more fully into consideration the size of the country, its industrial structure and its attractiveness to foreign investment. At the same time, the amalgamation of both public and private funding would offer member countries the freedom to design their own knowledge investment boosting policies: through public funds or through the design of appropriate incentive schemes to raise more private funds. Finally, broadening the knowledge and innovation concept to include education more systematically would also enable member countries to address particular weaknesses of their education systems as an integral part of their investment target.

Strengthening Europe's technological competitiveness: a dangerous obsession?

The national and European focus on the need for investment in knowledge accumulation within its own EU borders, as exemplified by the targets described above, is not just at odds with the global decision-making about knowledge investments of multinational firms; it appears also to ignore the increasingly global nature of long-term sustainable problems likely to affect directly the future welfare of the EU and its member states.

The programmes were designed at a time when strengthening the international competitiveness of particular high-tech firms and sectors was considered essential for Europe's long-term welfare. It led to the strengthening of a number of industrial firms/sectors, some of which became successful at the world level, others of which failed dramatically. Today, most EU research programmes benefit European and foreign firms equally, as long as they are located in Europe. The same holds for universities and other public research institutes. Elsewhere, I have pointed to the inherent knowledge 'diversion' and European 'cocooning' implications of such a European research networking strategy.[21]

At the same time, the broadening of research priorities to include both local as well as global long-term issues increasingly raises questions about the European territorial nature of the research being carried out and funded through such programmes. In many research areas, European welfare will in the long term be directly influenced not by the development of local knowledge through the programmes, its international commercial exploitation and intellectual appropriation, but by global access to such knowledge, the development of joint global standards and the rapid worldwide diffusion of such new technologies to other, non-EU countries. One may think of energy-saving technologies, research on sustainable development and climate change, health and the spreading of diseases, food safety, security, social sciences and humanities, etc. In all these areas, the limitation of the funding of research to academic, public and private research institutes located in Europe appears contrary to the need for global solutions to safeguard European welfare in the long term.

Somewhat at the opposite end of the spectrum of such trends, the global multinational enterprises have been successful in pressurizing both the EU and the US to strengthen worldwide the intellectual property regime, within which knowledge can now effectively be traded globally – such as the TRIPS agreement under the WTO and the various so-called TRIPS+ bilateral trade agreements enforced by the US. This more or less universal imposition by the EU and the US of the new international intellectual property regime raises many questions about global welfare and access to knowledge, particularly for emerging and developing countries. The current intellectual property regime has actually become greatly skewed in favour of protecting private knowledge goods, without taking into account the social costs incurred. As Richard Nelson put it: 'While patents are the primary incentive for profit-motivated invention in some key technologies, they are actually causing harm in other areas, including some "high-tech" industries involved primarily in R&D.'[22] In areas such as drugs, bio-prospecting and software, questions can be raised as to whether alternative research funding systems that provide less negative externalities for consumers worldwide, and in particular in developing countries, than the current patent system might not be more appropriate.[23]

In short, is it not time for a completely different approach in the EU to knowledge appropriation that recognizes much more the global nature of knowledge accumulation and the importance of access to knowledge for most emerging and developing economies? From the perspective of what Europe could contribute to worldwide welfare, it might, I would submit, contain a vision with much more political appeal to European citizens than the somewhat Eurocentric perspective of Lisbon.

Conclusions

The new Lisbon Strategy, 'Integrated guidelines for growth and jobs', following the mid-term review (July 2005), consists of a long list of guidelines brought together under four broad headlines: 'Macroeconomic policies for growth and jobs'; 'Knowledge and innovation – engines of sustainable growth'; 'Making Europe a more attractive place to invest and to work'; and 'More and better jobs'. In this discussion, the focus has been on the second of these political priorities: knowledge and innovation. Europe's failure to achieve significant progress under this heading since the end of the last century has as much to do with the interaction between knowledge and innovation as with the guidelines under the three other headlines. The knowledge society which has emerged in Europe is, as has been argued here, indeed not an exogenous one, external to Europe's macroeconomic policy, competition policy or social model, but fully endogenous to those other areas of economic policy.

In this sense, the various areas discussed in this chapter highlight different aspects of the lack of integration of the knowledge and innovation Lisbon priority within the other areas of the Lisbon Strategy. They suggest a number of straightforward recommendations.

First, the Lisbon Strategy interpretation of 'knowledge and innovation as engines of sustainable growth' represents still, I would argue, and despite brave attempts of the Commission to prove the contrary,[24] a very segmented policy approach, addressing first and foremost the traditional R&D and innovation member countries and EC policy constituencies.[25] The proposed guidelines and the further detailed proposals from the Commission are, from this perspective, more reminiscent of the old industrial R&D model than of the emerging knowledge economy paradigm model described earlier on in this chapter.[26] The only shift in attention is with respect to potential regulatory barriers to research and innovation, reflecting the broadening of vision no longer to limit support policies to just R&D, but also to include more systematic innovation, raising new competition policy issues. However, no attention is paid to interactions with Europe's social model, or to education policy. The result of this relatively narrow focus is that the proposed integrated guidelines are anything but integrated and convey an impression of 'over-structure', with target-setting on a multitude of particular aspects of knowledge and innovation which are by and large outside the control of policy-makers.

Second, given the increasingly global nature of the social, economic, environmental and demographic problems that Europe is currently and in the future likely to be confronted with, a unilateral focus on the strengthening of knowledge and innovation activities, with the aim of improving European competitiveness, reflects increasingly, I would argue, a rather outdated 'Eurocentric' approach. It certainly does not do justice to the much broader societal and global impact that knowledge accumulation is having on European citizens' welfare. In a growing number of research fields, European welfare will in the long term be directly influenced not so much by the development of local knowledge, its international commercial exploitation and intellectual appropriation, as by global access to such knowledge, the development of joint global standards and the rapid worldwide diffusion of such new technologies to other, non-EU countries. While the shift from the old to the new Lisbon Strategy sounds at least less 'Eurocentric', the question remains whether it is not time for a different approach in the EU to knowledge appropriation, one that recognizes more explicitly the global nature of knowledge accumulation.

Third, there is a need for a fundamental rethinking of the universality principles of social security systems as they were developed in Europe in the twentieth century, in a variety of ways, in broad synergy with the emerging industrial society. Such a rethinking should recognize the duality in the labour force between work involving '*labour*', i.e. a physical or mental wearing out activity, and work involving '*pleasure*', i.e. activities providing primarily self-satisfaction in terms of recognition, realization and creativity. As I argued above, workers involved in the first sort of activity are likely to consider the past social achievements of the European social model as important achievements intrinsically associated with their quality of life. They will consider any change of those conditions as a clear deterioration in their quality of life and reject it. Workers, involved in the second sort of activity, call them knowledge workers, are not so much in need of social measures aimed at reducing negative externalities of physical work. Their work involves primarily positive externalities. Obviously they also will appreciate social 'security' guarantees to their employment, but these will rather be used as substitute rather than as complement for own life-long learning efforts and investments. Effectively, knowledge workers are 'free riding' on social 'security' guarantees designed in another industrial age and aimed at a different category of workers.

The Lisbon initiative was a unique attempt to deal with what could be considered an institutional failure in the formation of the EU.

Until then, there were really only two areas where, in institutional terms, European power was clearly dominant over individual member countries' power: competition policy and monetary policy in the case of the Eurozone countries. Competition policy has, one could argue, an internal dynamics leading to a continuous broadening of its influence: an enlargement of the sphere of the working of market forces, a further harmonization of rules such as the Services Directive or the European patent proposals. While this is likely to bring about a general efficiency-enhancing effect across the EU, it has not contributed in any direct sense to knowledge accumulation or innovation improvement. On the contrary, in areas of research and innovation, competition policy has created growing legal uncertainty in member countries with respect to their own R&D and innovation support policies, which explains the efforts by the Commission in developing a new State Aid Action Plan. Monetary policy, on the other hand, as implemented by the European Central Bank, has put a priority on addressing the regional diversity in the union in growth and inflation pressures. Here too there is a sheer natural broadening of the influence of monetary policy over domestic member countries' fiscal policies. In principle, the Stability and Growth Pact provides Europe with an instrument with which it can determine in purely quantitative terms member countries' fiscal policies. But here too, there is no inherent incentive to promote knowledge and innovation as engines of sustainable growth.

Not surprisingly, the emphasis put by the Lisbon Strategy on knowledge and innovation capacity building in Europe was by and large dependent on member countries' efforts and willingness to give domestic priority to knowledge accumulation in all its facets, including innovation and knowledge diffusion, education and training. This is an area where, contrary to the two areas described above, there is no European power over and above member countries. Furthermore, the relevant policy areas involve a wide spectrum of fields ranging from research to education policy, with sometimes little, sometimes growing European involvement (as in the case of the proposed European Research Council). From this perspective it is actually not surprising that little progress has been achieved in bringing forward the Lisbon Strategy.

The revised Lisbon Strategy following the mid-term review undoubtedly offers new opportunities to revitalize knowledge and innovation capacity-building in Europe. As it stands, though, and as I have argued here, there are a number of structural weaknesses which will have to be urgently addressed if Lisbon is to live up to its promises.

Notes

1 I am hence not referring to the unemployed.
2 As Aiginger and Guger stress, the average employment ratio of the continental European countries Germany, France, Belgium and Italy is well below that of the group of active labour market policy countries. See Karl Aiginger and Alois Guger, *The European Social Model. Difference to the USA and Changes Over Time* (Vienna: WIFO, September 2005).
3 European Commission, *Implementing the Community Lisbon Programme: Communication from the Commission to the Council, the European Parliament, the European Economic and Social Committee and the Committee of the Regions: More Research and Innovation – Investing for Growth and Employment: A Common Approach* (Brussels: SEC, 2005).
4 Europe's social model cannot be described in precise terms. It consists of rather different diversified models across Europe. Broadly speaking, though, one might consider two main models: one financed through general taxation (the 'Beveridge system') and the other based on social security contributions (the 'Bismarck system'). Denmark, Greece, Spain, Ireland, Iceland, Italy, Norway, Portugal, Finland, Sweden and the UK all belong more or less to the first system. The 'Bismarck model' can be found in Belgium, Germany, France, Liechtenstein, Luxembourg, the Netherlands, Austria and Switzerland.
5 Paul Krugman, 'Competitiveness: a dangerous obsession', *Foreign Affairs*, 73, 2 (1994).
6 The first clear and forceful advocacy of a national S&T policy based on public support for research was attributed by Freeman to Francis Bacon (1627). In *The New Atlantis*, he advocated the establishment of a major research institute ('Salomon's House') which would use the results of scientific expeditions and explorations all over the world to establish the 'knowledge of causes, and secret motions of things'. See C. Freeman, *The Economics of Industrial Innovation* (London: Penguin, 1974). See also, for more detail, C. Freeman and L. Soete, *The Economics of Industrial Innovation*, 3rd edn (Cambridge MA: MIT Press, 1997), part IV of which gives a detailed overview of the historical development of public support for science, technology and innovation.
7 See D. Mowery, 'Industrial research and firm size, survival and growth in American manufacturing, 1921–46: an assessment', *Journal of Economic History*, 25, 5 (1983).
8 K. Pavitt, 'Patterns of technical change: towards a taxonomy and a theory', *Research Policy*, 13, 6 (1984), pp. 343–73; F. Malerba, ed., *Sectoral Systems of Innovation* (Cambridge: Cambridge University Press, 2004).
9 J. Mokyr, *The Enlightened Economy: An Economic History of Britain 1700–1850* (Penguin New Economic History of Britain, forthcoming 2006).

10 L. Soete, 'The Lisbon challenge: designing policies that activate', in R. Liddle and M. Rodrigues, eds., *Economic Reform in Europe: Priorities for the Next Five Years* (London: Policy Network, 2004).

11 Christopher Freeman and L. Soete, eds., *The Economics of Industrial Innovation*, 3rd edn (London: Pinter, 1997).

12 P. David and D. Foray, 'An introduction to economy of the knowledge society', *International Social Science Journal*, 54, 171 (2002), pp. 9–23.

13 E. Von Hippel, *Democratizing Innovation* (Cambridge MA; MIT Press, 2004).

14 G. Saint-Paul, 'Employment protection, international specialization and innovation', *European Economic Review*, 46 (2002), pp. 375–95.

15 As the recent Commission report notices somewhat schizophrenically: 'The 3% objective and the follow-up Action Plan for more investment in research have had a mobilising effect on member states. Nearly all have set targets, which – if met – would bring research investment in the EU to 2.6% of GDP by 2010. However, instead of rising, EU research intensity is more or less stagnant. In most member states, increases in public and private research investment and the range and ambition of policy initiatives fall far short of what their national targets, let alone the EU target, would require. Private investment is particularly low. At the same time, European innovation performance has not increased enough.' (European Commission, Implementing the Community Lisbon Programme: *More Research and Innovation – Investing for Growth and Employment: A Common Approach*, SEC, 2005).

16 One may also notice, e.g., that corporate funding in the US dropped by nearly $8 billion in 2002, or 3.9 per cent, the largest single year decline since the 1950s.

17 This explains amongst others why the 'tuition debate' is strongly resisted by the population at large in most continental European countries with progressive income tax regimes, even if it is widely accepted that most of the current systems of free or cheap higher education are effectively resulting in subsidies from the poor to the rich.

18 See e.g. the results obtained by Griffith et al. on the importance of US R&D for British firms' research: R. Griffith, R. Harrison and John Van Reenen, *How Special is the Special Relationship? Using the Impact of US R&D Spillovers on UK Firms as a Test of Technology Sourcing*, Discussion Papers dp0659 (London: Centre for Economic Performance, LSE, 2004).

19 To highlight that such argument isn't purely theoretical, an example: Flanders with IMEC has a top research facility in semiconductors, including clean room facilities. However, it has no national production anymore. Flemish policy-makers are of course requesting from private partners with IMEC proof of national/regional spill-over effects when applying for public R&D support. Yet, for most of the private partners of IMEC the spill-overs (at least in terms of blue-collar labour) are likely to accrue elsewhere in the world, where they have their production facilities.

20 The Dutch Innovation Platform, chaired by the Dutch prime minister, proposed such a new investment target, called KIQ: the knowledge investment quote.

21 L. Soete, 'Technology policy and the international trading system: where do we stand?', in H. Siebert, ed., *Towards a New Global Framework for High Technology Competition* (Tübingen: J. C. B. Mohr, 1997).

22 See UNU-INTECH, 'Experts urge reform of international patent system', at eve of WIPO Assembly, 26 September 2005.

23 See e.g. the proposal for a Medical Innovation Prize Fund in the US (HR417), whereby patents would be kept in place until registration of the new drug, but then freely copied by generic competitors. As a result, the developer of the drug would not control the market, but there would be competitive valuation of the medicine whereby each new drug would compete with other new drugs for prize money. The most important changes in the IP paradigm are: the budget for innovation is fixed, the incremental cost to innovators of using the new innovation is zero, and there are no economic incentives to restrict access to the newest technologies.

24 As in the case of the recent Communication from the Commission to the Council, the European Parliament, the European Economic and Social Committee and the Committee of the Regions: *More Research and Innovation – Investing for Growth and Employment: A Common Approach* (EC, 2005).

25 These range from the science, technology or research ministries and the various advisory committees to the trade and industry, economic affairs or innovation ministries and their various advisory committees. Within the EC these comprise primarily the DG Research and DG Enterprise constituencies.

26 See European Commission, *Implementing the Community Lisbon Programme.*

11

The Environment in the European Social Model

Måns Lönnroth

Understanding tomorrows

The present political discussion in Europe about social policy and environment protection is a rather defensive one, based as it is on the worry about competitiveness. The Cardiff summit in 1998 repeated the need for integration of environmental protection into Community policies, as stated in the Amsterdam Treaty. The principle that major policy proposals by the Commission should be evaluated also in terms of their environmental impact was reindorsed. The Lisbon summit set new goals for economic reform and social cohesion and the Gothenburg summit added the environmental dimension to these goals. But the Cardiff-Lisbon-Gothenburg agendas of policy integration do not correspond to an integrated academic agenda. Policy areas have their own academic traditions, concepts, models and languages and are by and large mutually incomprehensible.

The social models of the EU(15) represent the culminations of the European nation-states and were well established long before the internal market of the European Community. Neither social security nor labour market policies have ever belonged to the core competences of the EU. There is a distinct European social model when seen from the US and Japan, and there are at least four different models when seen from within.

European environment policies have followed a different course. While they originated as nation-state policies, they were deeply integrated into Community policy as a consequence of the Single

European Act. Two arguments were important: first, 'a race to the bottom' of environmental standards should be avoided; and, second, a single environment policy would strengthen the political legitimacy of the EU.

However, very little has been written about the environmental policies of different countries and their broader impact on social or economic issues; there is no Gøsta Esping-Andersen, André Sapir, Fritz Scharpf or even Anthony Giddens in that field. There is a huge need for a better understanding of how different environment models interact with competitiveness and with social policy. This chapter seeks to shed light on the nature of this interaction.

Is there a distinct European environment model?

The emergence of environment policy is best described as a history of waves of policy innovation. Three peak waves and three troughs with respect to policy breakthroughs can be identified.

The first peak wave occurred between the late 1960s and the early 1970s and was the founding period of institutions for national policies. National legislation and environment protection agencies were established with the aim of reducing air and water pollution from industrial plants. The improvements in air and water quality that we now see in cities, rivers and lakes in developed nations are due to this work of the institutions of the first peak wave.

There then followed a trough of almost 15 years as the environment slipped down the political agenda. The second peak wave was the period of internationalization and lasted from between the second half of the 1980s until the Rio summit in 1992. Europe led the way, since national environment policies in Europe are highly dependent on transboundary agreements. Improvements were noted on acid rain, and in the river Rhine, the North and the Baltic seas. Also, the three global conventions for the protection of the ozone layer, the climate and biodiversity were agreed upon. Only the first has so far been an unqualified success.

The second peak wave was followed by a second trough, as US and European economies slumped in the early 1990s. The international institutions of the second peak wave were superimposed on the national institutions of the first wave, and progress continued to be made. Air quality improved markedly in many cities in Central and Eastern Europe as they applied the experiences of the West European countries.

The third peak arrived in the second half of the 1990s with two distinct additions: first, internationalization turned into globalization; and, second, the need for policy integration in Europe (Cardiff/Lisbon/Gothenburg). Product chain management was a key issue, with obvious WTO implications.

This last peak was a short-lived one. The movement went sharply downhill well before the Johannesburg summit in 2002 (the best summary was a newspaper headline stating: 'Disaster averted, opportunities lost'). The EU saved the Kyoto protocol from being dismantled during the spring of 2001.

As I write, we are stuck in a new and very deep trough and waiting for a possible fourth wave. It is time to take stock.

If European progress is a glass, it is, at most, half full. Many environmental problems caused by industry and with straightforward technological solutions are on their way. Others, such as chemicals and climate, are not. The same goes for transport, erosion of critical ecosystems, and depletion of biological resources such as marine fish and fresh water. Globally, the glass is not even half full.

Let us look at differences between regions and countries, notably the EU, the US and Japan. As a start, three cases will be looked into: air pollution from transport, air pollution from large-scale industrial plants and, less extensively, producer responsibility. The first two are success stories of the twentieth century. The third opens up to the twenty-first century and to the debate about globalization. Then I will look at chemicals and climate change, two twenty-first-century cases that illustrate the complexities of policy-making within a much wider field of risk and uncertainty.

Air pollution from transport

There is now only one global model (even if Europe lagged behind the US and Japan until the late 1980s). This convergence has three reasons. First, the car industry – and the truck industry – is nowadays a global industry. Second, the standards for cars are essentially set within one market. Car manufacturers that want to be present in the Californian market have to participate in the technological race. Third, all car manufacturers have accepted that standards are becoming progressively stricter. Differences between European, Japanese and US standards are now reduced to timing.[1]

This is a classic example of a global innovation system. Issues are well defined and technological solutions are there to be developed. Risk levels are comparatively low and the future predictable. The major uncertainty now is the role of climate change in the future of regulation.

Air pollution from large-scale industrial plants

There is a European/Japanese model for air pollution from large-scale industrial and power plants. The US lags behind. These pollutants have effects on health and the environment that are similar to those of air pollution from transport, but the regulatory experiences are rather different.

Japan leads the field and had already started in the late 1960s. In 1983, Japan had more than 1,400 plants equipped with flue gas desulphurization compared to 10 in Germany. The Federal Republic had a change of heart in the early 1980s. The single European Act then made it possible for Germany to convince the other members of the EC to enact the Directive on existing large-scale combustion plants.

Today, the differences in both city air quality and overall emissions between Japan, the US and the EU are rather dramatic. In the mid 1990s the US had more than twice the level of emissions per unit of GDP compared to the EU, which in turn had more than twice the level compared to Japan (which, per unit of GDP, had one-sixth of the US level). In terms of city air quality, the differences are not as large, but the US still has by far the highest level (roughly four times that of Sweden, twice that of Germany and some 25 per cent higher than Japan).[2]

The main reasons for these differences lie in political priorities. Japan has been concerned with public health. The EU has, in addition, been concerned with eco-system damage. US policy has been mainly health-driven and only later became driven by concerns for eco-systems (under pressure from Canada).

Europe and Japan have followed roughly the same path, with Japan leading and Europe catching up. The European policy has its own diversity between member states (city air quality in Spain and Italy are roughly on the US level) and has also been very effective in reducing acid rain. Emissions have been brought down and the pressure for technological change has now diminished.

The difference between industrial plants and car emissions is explained by the fact that the electricity generation industry is at most a regional industry. The impact on the competitiveness of other industries is not strong enough to enforce the type of global harmonization of standards that the car industry has experienced. Climate change policies might well make a difference, however.

Producer responsibility

There is a distinct European model in producer responsibility, with Japan as a follower and the US as a laggard. Land scarcity has driven waste policy in Europe and Japan. For that reason, both the EU and Japan are shifting the responsibility for waste from the consumers (and by implication local authorities) onto the producers. Thus producers and importers of goods such as cars, electronics etc. will have to organize the scrapping and recycling of their waste. The US has not been so concerned with this issue. Products regulated under producer responsibility legislation will thus affect trade, as components produced in one country are assembled in another and shipped to a third one.

Producer responsibility also lends itself to a new type of activism down the supply chain. The Forest Stewardship Council is a cooperation between different NGOs aimed at creating standards for sustainable forestry that are agreed upon by environmental NGOs, forestry, wood-using industries such as furniture, paper and pulp industries, and the like. As a model, it illustrates a new form of environment action for the twenty-first century. Other areas of concern for producer responsibility include marine fishing (the Marine Stewardship Council), child labour, anti-union activities, corruption and so on and so forth. It remains to be seen whether this type of activism will be translated into government policy.

Chemical policy

A distinctly European model is now emerging in this area. Chemicals policy represents a technological and regulatory frontier which generates a diversity of possible futures. It is also about risks that cannot be experienced by the senses (in contrast to the three examples above), about globalization of markets and about a global flow of effects.

Chemicals policy is, when compared to other cases of environment policy, much more complex. There are at least three reasons for this:

1 The complexity of scale. Air quality concerns a handful of substances; chemicals policy several thousands.
2 The complexity of impact. Chemicals can have vastly varying impacts on vastly varying geographic scales and on vastly varying organisms. Some chemicals accumulate in food chains and can be found far away from point of release. The scientific uncertainty remains significant in many cases.

3 The complexity of use. A given chemical can be used in a large number of different applications, each with its own pattern of release.

Present regulations concerning chemicals within the EU and the US have two basic elements: first, the legislation makes a distinction between existing and new chemicals. Second, the burden of proof for allowing access to the market lies with industry for new chemicals and with the authorities for existing chemicals. Thus chemicals that were already on the market when the existing legislation was enacted are allowed to be marketed unless or until the authorities can demonstrate that the costs to human health or eco-systems outweigh the benefits to industry and the consumers. For new chemicals, the reverse applies: the manufacturer in question has to demonstrate that benefits outweigh costs. Overall, the system probably tends to favour existing chemicals over new ones. If so, it is innovation-inhibitive. The area is a virtual quagmire of contention. The most important issue is how to manage risk when scientific uncertainty still exists in large measure.

The EU has by and large been more stringent in regulating chemicals than the US. The main reason appears to be that the legal systems work differently. The US Environmental Protection Agency's proposed regulations are almost invariably challenged in courts, which then rely heavily on economic models of cost-benefit analysis that in turn tend to err on the conservative side. The European system relies more heavily on administrative decisions which on the whole have not been challenged in the European Court of Justice.

The REACH proposal (at the time of writing in conciliation between council, the Commission and the European Parliament) within the EU will reinforce these differences with the US.[3] The linchpin of REACH is to do away with the distinction between existing and new chemicals. In early versions of the proposal, the right of industry to market existing chemicals without adequate data would disappear, and the burden of supplying data for risk assessment and risk management would shift from the authorities to industry. REACH would thus strengthen the position of the chemicals-using industry vis-à-vis the chemicals-producing industry.

If, as seems likely, the REACH proposal is implemented in some modified form or another, the differences with, primarily, the US could become critical. The political battle is about different pictures of the future. From one perspective, the present situation is a runaway experiment with market liberalization, even though science frequently cannot provide conclusive answers. From another perspective, the present situation is not qualitatively new. It is just a continuation of what has worked well in the past. Nothing has changed and nothing needs to be changed.

So, is there a separate European environment model? I would argue yes, for the following reasons. First, the EU environment policy is by and large a product of the internal market legislation. It is designed to create a level playing field within the Union as a condition for access to markets. Environment legislation adds legitimacy to the internal market. Second, EU legislation is to a large degree based on the concept of 'best available technology'. When new plants are built or existing plants retrofitted, the legal requirement is to use the best available technology ('*Stand der Technik*' in German parlance). This ensures rapid reduction of emissions in the plant in question. Third, EU environmental policy relies somewhat less on cost-benefit analysis compared to the US (although this may change). US legislation is mostly decided in the courts. Economists thus have a larger role than they so far have in the European system. The net effect is probably to slow down change.

Thus, as we are looking for a fourth wave of environment policy innovation, the US has lost the leadership. The EU is increasingly leading in terms of policy development and Japan keeps its technological advantage. With the dominant political currents in the US having turned increasingly anti-government, the US is likely to continue on its '*Sonderweg*'.

Relations between environment policy and competitiveness

Not much needs to be said about the relations between environment, energy and economic growth. The energy link is a natural one, since the use of fossil fuels is a major source of pollution and also of climate change. In an article by Jorgenson and Wilcoxen, it is argued that the US GDP trajectory would have been somewhat higher had it not been for the environmental policies of the 1970s and 1980s.[4] The conclusion (presented with three decimal places) is of course heavily dependent on the structure of the economic model, but does make some intuitive sense. The OECD estimates that the member states allocate some 2 per cent of GDP to pollution control, so the theoretical thought experiment of no environmental policies at all could well imply a somewhat higher GDP.[5]

A more important issue concerns the relations between environmental policies and trade. The conventional argument is that environmental policies that are too stringent will lead to reallocation of pollution-heavy industries to countries with more lax policies. Here again, much academic work has been done, essentially based on economic general equilibrium growth models. Jaffe et al. reviewed some 100 articles in 1995 and concluded:

> [O]verall, there is relatively little evidence to support the hypothesis that environmental regulations have had a large adverse impact on competitiveness, however that elusive term is defined . . . [and] studies attempting to measure the effect of environmental regulation on net exports, overall trade flows, and plant location decisions have produced estimates that are either small, statistically insignificant or not robust to test of model specifications.[6]

Copeland and Taylor conclude: 'Most available studies suggest that the effect (of free trade on the environment) is small.'[7] More detailed studies relate Foreign Direct Investments (FDIs) to the difference in environment standards in different countries. One study in particular (completed by Javorcik and Wei, two economists at the World Bank and the IMF) looks at whether investment flows into the countries of Central and Eastern Europe and the former Soviet Union have been influenced by differences in environment standards. Their conclusion is that there is no such influence, partly, perhaps, since so many other factors intervene (such as corruption and weak governance). In fact, they find that cleaner industries are more likely to migrate to these countries.[8] An overview article from 2004 concludes that most, if not all, studies disregard the interrelation between trade, environment and technology and states that 'the relationship . . . is not well understood but potentially very important'.[9]

The reason why the academic literature does not provide a clear answer is probably that there is no clear answer. It is perhaps impossible to analyse different environment policy options and their impact on trade within the existing set of economic models. These models come with a price: the more sophisticated the economics modelling, the cruder the modelling of the environment policy – and vice versa.

There are other attempts. The revisionist argument is that well-designed environment policy can stimulate innovation and thus competitiveness, and goes under the name of the 'Porter hypothesis', after Michael Porter and Claas van der Linde's article in the *Harvard Business Review*.[10] The revisionist argument exists in two versions:

- The weak version: 'Top environmental performers do not appear to have suffered in terms of economic growth.'

- The strong version: 'Countries with forward-leaning environmental policies and programs will enhance their competitiveness.'

Esty and Porter have made a statistical analysis of environmental performance and regulation and the relationship to competitiveness and GDP/capita. Competitiveness here is defined by the World Economic Forum questionnaire and not within general equilibrium models. Their conclusion is that the weak version is consistent with data and that existing data does not disprove the strong version. Indeed, looking at the OECD countries only, it is obvious that the high performance of environmental quality, GDP per capita and competitiveness as defined by the WEF go hand in hand. Esty and Porter state that 'the countries that have seen the most aggressive environmental policies also seem to be the most competitive and economically successful'.[11] The smaller countries around the Baltic and the North Sea (Sweden, Denmark, Finland, Norway, the Netherlands) tend also to come up at the top in the rankings on social justice.

Needless to say, economists who start from general equilibrium models do not agree with Esty and Porter's hypothesis. In a general equilibrium model there is no such thing as a free lunch and Jaffe et al. conclude: 'Just as we have found little consistent empirical evidence for the conventional hypothesis regarding environmental regulation and competitiveness there is also little or no evidence supporting the revisionist hypothesis that environmental regulation stimulates innovation and improved international competitiveness.'[12]

Fast forward to climate change

The environmental policy of the EU has up to now largely developed without any explicit reference to social policy. The future may well be different, however.

A potential fourth peak wave of environment policy innovation will stand and fall with climate change. A failure to move ahead on climate change would demobilize opinion on many other issues.

Climate change is by far the most complex of the environmental issues that the EU or the world has faced so far (leaving even chemicals policy far behind). There are several reasons for this:

- complexity of the climate system with interlocking positive and negative feedback mechanisms and thus large remaining uncertainties in modelling;

- complexity of mitigation of greenhouse gas emissions and their links to the use of fossil fuels;
- complexity of the impact of climate change and the need for adaptation;
- complexity of time perspective, which lies outside the normal thinking of industry, politics, finance and economics.

Climate change policy is an enormous challenge to existing institutions. It is an indeterminate series of issues linked to a partial understanding of globalization. Scientific uncertainty is only one element; equally important are technological uncertainties as well as uncertainties about the impact on economic and political institutions. Nevertheless, a consensus is emerging that climate change has to be addressed. An increasing number of multinational corporations are accepting that climate change is for real. So is China.

Global climate change policy stands and falls with the EU. The EU policy will have to strike a balance between competitiveness and innovation, between today and tomorrow. The total EU policy, of which emissions trading is only one component, will have to demonstrate that climate change may be different, but it is not that different – economic growth and emissions can be decoupled. If this works, the global political log-jam might well break.

Emissions trading is the keystone of the EU policy and so far covers some 40 per cent of EU emissions of greenhouse gases. The allowed quotas have been rather generous, so the effect during the coming three to five years will be more psychological than real. Companies will get used to the concept that greenhouse gas emissions come at a price. The crunch will come within a few years.

This is an area where the European environment model and the European social model will have to merge. Any successful attack on the European greenhouse gas emissions is bound to have structural effects also on European industry and everyday life. Thus there is a need for a coordinated technology policy as well as a strong social policy.

Can the European social model cope with climate change?

This chapter started with the statement that there is no academic agenda under which economic, social and environmental policy interactions can be analysed. So far, this has not been a major problem. Most environment problems that emanate from industrial causes and that have clear-cut technological solutions have not led to the type of major economic or social dislocations that would need a well thought through policy integration. This statement can also be turned on its head: environment issues that require major policy integration have been put on the back burner. Examples include transportation, agriculture, fishing, biodiversity and so on. This is the lesson of the twentieth century and of the first three waves.

The twenty-first century will be different. Issues will be global rather than national or regional. Producer responsibility and product chain management comprise one illustration, chemicals another and climate change a third. Managing these issues requires a capacity to manage a multitude of organizations, layers of legal systems and different value systems. There will not be one harmonized outlook; rather, a disjointed system of cross-cutting perspectives – Picasso rather than Vermeer.

I would argue that we do not even have a language for understanding what is ahead and much less any analytical framework. Some elements would include the following:

- Global environment issues will add to already existing pressures for industrial restructuring from new EU members (not to speak of China and India).
- These pressures will have to be met by forward-looking social and labour market policies that welcome structural change. Technology policy will be as important as education and active labour market policies.
- Supply chain management by private–public partnerships will have to be developed. Corporations, NGOs and governments will be increasingly involved. Trade disputes will have to be kept within bounds (or the dispute settlement mechanism would be completely overburdened).
- New actors will be involved, ranging from new forms of NGO to the financial industry. The former may have to develop new carbon-offsetting mechanisms. The latter will have to adapt its time perspective.

The financial sectors are particularly important. They have to create new trading mechanisms for various climate-related activities. They also have to factor in climate change-related issues in their understanding of uncertainty. In fact, the financial sectors will have to revisit their own rather insular perception of risk. Today, the financial sectors tend to relate risk and opportunities mainly in the shorter term.

Pension funds and other institutional investors should develop investment strategies that are based on streams of income that in turn are based on explicitly positive visions of globalization and the world that generates this stream of incomes. They need to think through their perception of risk and uncertainty and integrate climate change into their investment strategies.

As for the European social models, taken together they are, in my view, the potential Achilles heel of a progressive European climate change policy. The European social models have to balance protection and risk, looking back and looking forward.

There is an essentially backward-looking European social model which puts a high premium on job security together with unemployment benefits and a corresponding low premium on labour market policies that stimulate individuals to take the risk of moving from a low-productivity job to a high-productivity job. There is also the potential of a forward-looking European social model which puts less emphasis on job security and a corresponding higher emphasis on labour market policies that stimulate individuals to move from lower- to higher-productivity jobs.

The forward-looking European social model would facilitate structural change and may even add impetus to it. Strong supply-side pressures such as technology policies (like the technology platforms now under discussion within the EU) would add further impetus for innovation. The bottom line of the forward-looking social model is that it depends on a high general level of employment. High levels of unemployment would increase the pressures on the systems of social protection and thus increase the risk of low labour mobility.

So far, the Scandinavian social model appears to be the closest to a forward leaning social model, a model that actively promotes structural change.

Finding a common academic language – the risk society needs a new Keynes

The time has come for universities to create a science of sustainable development. Economics is where society and the biosphere meet. We need a science that integrates economics with the biosphere sciences and the social sciences. My inspiration here is John Maynard Keynes.

His main achievement, possibly, was to redefine the role of government vis-à-vis the economy of nation-states and thereby, it should be added, the role of economists in the administration of the state. In 1919 he left the Versailles negotiations in disgust, when the governments of the day persevered in enforcing indemnities on a defeated Germany – a move that Keynes thought utterly counterproductive. He called for an integration of foreign and economic policy that would help stabilize social conditions. He reinterpreted the role of governments in the depression of the 1930s much as Franklin D. Roosevelt (who was not overly impressed with the economists of the day when it came to their understanding of the social effects of their recommendations). Keynes failed after the First World War but persevered during and after the Second World War in the negotiations leading up to the Bretton Woods institutions.

I would like to believe that had he lived today Keynes would have strived for yet another redefinition of the place of economics in public affairs. He would have been sufficiently iconoclastic to take on the whole of the economics profession and the peculiar kind of rationalism, expressed in mathematics and so-called rational choice, which for the time being has taken hold of the subject. He was, as I have understood it, scathing about the preponderance of using statistical models to predict the future. Having started in philosophy and written his thesis in probability theory he had a much more sophisticated view of how uncertainty and risk guide action than what could be captured by mathematical models then, now or in the future.

Economics as if the long term mattered: surely this means the integration of economics with the sciences of the biosphere and the sciences of social justice. So, will the Keynes of the twenty-first century please step forward. You are sorely needed!

Notes

1 OECD, *Sustainable Development in OECD Countries. Getting the Policies Right* (Paris: OECD, 2004).

2 OECD, *Economic Aspects of Extended Producer Responsibility* (Paris: OECD, 2004).

3 On REACH, there is a great deal of literature both from the EU and from REACH. See, e.g., the European Parliament, the European Commission or Chemsec (<www.chemsec.org>).

4 D. W. Jorgenson and P. J. Wilcoxen, 'Energy, the environment and economic growth', in Allen V. Kneese and James L. Sweeney, eds., *Handbook on Natural Resource and Energy Economics*, vol. 3 (Amsterdam: North Holland, 1993).

5 OECD, *Economic aspects*.

6 Adam B. Jaffe, Steven R. Peterson and Paul R. Portney, 'Environmental regulation and the competitiveness of US manufacturing: what does the evidence tell us?', *Journal of Economic Literature*, 33 (March 1995), pp. 132–63.

7 Brian R. Copeland and M. Scott Taylor, 'Trade, growth and the environment', *Journal of Economic Literature*, 42 (March 2004), pp. 7–71.

8 B. S. Javorcik and S. J. Wei, 'Pollution havens and Foreign Direct Investment: dirty secret or popular myth?', *Advances in Economic Analysis & Policy*, 4, 2 (2004), Article 4.

9 Scott M. Taylor, 'Unbundling the pollution haven hypothesis', *Advances in Economic Analysis & Policy*, 4, 2 (2004).

10 Michael Porter and Claas van der Linde, 'Green and competitive: ending the stalemate', *Harvard Business Review* (September–October 1995).

11 D.C. Esty and Michael E. Porter, 'Ranking national environmental regulation and performance: a leading indicator of future competitiveness?', in *The Global Competitiveness Report 2001–2002* (New York: Oxford University Press, 2001), pp. 78–100.

12 Jaffe et al., 'Environmental regulation'.

12

Immigration: A Flexible Framework for a Plural Europe

Patrick Weil

The Amsterdam Treaty, which came into effect in 1999, committed the EU to developing a common immigration and asylum policy. Since then, European Immigration Policy has made some progress and achieved some of the goals defined without completing all the objectives set in the Amsterdam Treaty. In reality, the European immigration framework is founded on common principles, instruments and goals, but is sufficiently flexible to allow at the same time the development of policies adapted to the particularities of member states.

Until 1940, every nation-state had the freedom to determine who could cross into its territory and who could acquire its nationality. After the Second World War, in reaction to Nazism and later to Communism, the liberal democracies submitted themselves progressively and voluntarily to some legal norms independent of changes in political or economic circumstances: they renounced all selection of immigrants based on ethnic or national quotas, which implied a hierarchy between 'desirable' and 'undesirable' nationalities.[1] They ratified the Geneva Convention of 1951, to which was added the New York protocol of 1967 on the status of refugees, and thus guaranteed the most protected status to political refugees admitted to their territory. They recognized the right of foreign residents to a normal family life, and thereby allowed a permanent influx of the families of citizens as foreign residents. They also had to accept that an unwritten rule would enter into statute: foreigners would acquire, by the successive renewal of their residence permit, the right of abode in a democratic state; they could not be repatriated against their will if, for example, the economic climate changed, since they had acquired the right to integrate. Finally, the liberal democracies recognized some rights for illegal immigrants (care, schooling of their children, recourse against certain legal or administrative decisions), which are also in the interest of the host society.[2]

These rules, which form the policies of states, are of different orders: they are inscribed in international conventions or in constitutions, but they can also result from practices progressively validated by jurisprudence. They constitute a common framework, notably for the policies of the Old Europe of 15 countries, which today have all become countries of immigration (the most recent of these are Italy, Spain, Greece, Portugal and Ireland). However, these principles have not formed a common policy. National policies remain different and the flow of immigration varies from state to state, not at all proportionate to the demographic weight of each state.

These divergences can be explained by the permanence of numerous differential factors. The geographical situation is the first of these: it is more difficult to land on an island than to cross a terrestrial frontier. Frontiers are thus crossed more easily through Germany, Italy or even Spain, than through the United Kingdom or Ireland.

The respective demographic situations of each of the countries of the Union are also very different. A report published in 2000 by the Population Division of the United Nations clearly demonstrated that immigration can be a realistic solution to combat the decrease of the total population of the European Union. But the report also shows that Italy or Germany need a level of immigration far more numerous than in the past; whereas France or the United Kingdom need less. It is to maintain – for the stability of their retirement systems – an active population at the same level that all EU countries would need to increase their net immigration flow. But here again, the situations are very different: between 2000 and 2050, the net immigration needed to maintain the active population at its current level would be 5.459 million (110,000 people per annum) for France, 25.2 million for Germany (500,000 per annum) and 19.6 million for Italy (fewer than 400,000 per annum).[3]

Each European state is in a different situation with regard to the migratory cycle. If all the 15 'old' members of the Union are now countries of immigration, the majority of the flows of the oldest ones (Germany, France, the UK, Belgium and the Netherlands) are composed of families with indirect access to the labour market.[4] In the more recent countries of immigration (Spain, Italy, Portugal or Greece), immigration is still principally labour migration.

Political traditions can also influence the management of immigration: in continental Europe, the possession and inspection of identity documentation appears 'normal'; this is still not the case in the UK or Ireland, neither of which has yet ratified the Schengen Agreement, which has presaged since 1985 the abolition of static controls on the internal frontiers of signatory countries, and its replacement with internal controls on the territories of member states.

The techniques and regulations linked to the management of immigration can equally vary. The asylum procedure can have effects on the configuration of the migratory phenomenon in each country; irregular immigrants remain hidden in Italy where the procedure for asylum is less protective, but they will be counted as asylum applicants in the Netherlands where the procedure lasts three years and allows the applicant to benefit in the meantime from housing and employment rights. We also find significant procedural differences in family reunification (length of stay before the procedure may be opened, age of children/minors, conditions for access to resources and housing) and in admission to the labour market (systems of quotas or individual criteria).

These national particularities explain why European harmonization has only been partial. By 2005, harmonization was complete for visa policy between the countries of the Schengen zone. It had achieved a great deal for all the member states of the EU in the domain of asylum, where a common rule already existed – the Geneva Convention that remains the foundation stone of the asylum system in Europe.

On the other hand, harmonization is minimal in the field of family reunion, where each national system has been preserved. It has still not been achieved in the domain of labour migration, where states retain a considerable margin of manoeuvre to adopt their policies to diverging necessities.[5]

In each state, immigration policy is defined at a crossroads of common principles and common European regulations on the one hand, and geographical, demographic, institutional and political contexts on the other. The examples of Germany, the UK, Italy, France and Spain demonstrate this.

Germany

By the end of the 1950s, Germany had set a programme for the introduction of 'guest workers': foreigners were permitted to come and work temporarily and without their family, returning when their contract expired. Work and residence permits were renewed when a business requested it. Their number passed a record level of 2.6 million (12 per cent of the labour force)[6] at the point where Germany called a halt to the entry of further guest workers in November 1973. Five years later, in September 1978, the Constitutional Court annulled a Bavarian state decision to refuse to renew the residence permit of an Indian immigrant, who had been in Germany since 1961: this right of renewal, which was thus guaranteed after a certain period of time on German soil, transformed Germany into a de facto country of immigration.[7] In 1983, the relative failure of an aided voluntary repatriation scheme entrenched this situation.

In the mid-1980s, Germany faced a strong growth in asylum applications from 103,000 in 1988 to 438,000 in 1992, since article 16 of the Basic Law of 1949, together with the Geneva Convention, guaranteed asylum to anyone persecuted for political reasons. The Europeanization of asylum policy within the Schengen Agreement allowed the government of Helmut Kohl to adopt a constitutional amendment aligning German law with the laws and practices of other European countries. Since then, the number of asylum applications has fallen progressively to 50,563 in 2003, the lowest figure since 1984.

Since the beginning of the 1990s, Germany has set bilateral accords concerning the entry of seasonal workers, cross-border workers and apprentices. The number of seasonal workers has risen from 137,819 in 1994 to 318,000 in 2003. Although Germany won a seven-year delay on the opening of its borders to permanent migration from the new member states from its European partners, more than 80 per cent of seasonal workers in 2003 were Poles (271,907).

In 1999, Chancellor Gerhard Schröder announced the creation of a quota of 20,000 visas for foreign IT workers. The result did not meet the government's expectations: the Indian IT workers being sought by Germany preferred to go to the UK or the US where they spoke the language and were offered a better status. Four years after the announcement of the quota, which was intended as an annual figure, it still had not been completely fulfilled: since 2000, 15,658 visas have been issued, of which 2,285 were in 2003.

In 2004, a new law, adopted as a compromise between the opposition and the majority, ratified the status of Germany as a country of immigration (in fact, the most important in Europe: in 2004 the foreign population was around 7.335 million or 8.9 per cent of the total population). In order to facilitate integration, the law put in place compulsory training in German for new arrivals. The right to a family life is still recognized, even if the immigration of a child older than

12 can be refused on the grounds that its foreign education could impair its integration into Germany.

Finally, the system of quotas was abandoned. The current law organizes German immigration policy with the aim of facilitating recruitment of qualified immigrants by businesses in a pragmatic way:

- a student who, after the completion of his or her studies in Germany, finds a job can remain as a permanent resident in Germany; he or she may also remain in Germany for one year after studying to look for work;
- senior managers and scientists immediately receive the right of permanent abode;
- finally, provision is made for those who invest more than one million Euros or who create at least ten jobs, which allows them to obtain a three-year right of residence before obtaining the permanent right of abode.[8]

The United Kingdom

Soon after the Second World War, the UK became a country of high immigration, principally from the countries of the Commonwealth. By 1962, more than 500,000 Indians, Pakistanis and West Indians had installed themselves and were soon joined by their families.[9] From 1962 onwards, this wave of immigration was progressively halted and British governments put in place the most restrictive and efficient policy of immigration in Europe. Forced into having to choose to integrate these immigrants – they became British citizens from the point of their arrival – successive governments benefited from their insular situation, and also from the still relatively open character of other European policies, to make their policy of strict control a success.[10] They also implemented a regulation concerning family reunion which gave an implacable power of discretion to British consular officials. All of this allowed the UK to get close to the objective of zero immigration,[11] so that, at the beginning of the 1990s, the flow of legal immigrants was reduced to a level of 50,000 per annum.

Since then, the UK has had to face a heavy increase in asylum applications. This flow was attracted by Europe's most flourishing economy, which offered many precarious jobs; legal restrictions that prevented identity controls on British territory after crossing the border; and finally by the hardening of immigration controls in the rest of Europe. In reaction to this, asylum procedures were restricted, cooperation with the rest of Europe reinforced and for several years asylum applications have been falling. Even if it is not yet fully part of the Schengen Agreement, the UK participates actively in all the other European policies.[12]

In contrast to this, a clear change came about in autumn 2000, in response to the need for more qualified immigrants. The objective of the British government was no longer merely to control immigration (the 'control' remains, however, in place for asylum applicants) but also to 'manage' it in response to the need for economic growth: the UK competes with other European states – and indeed with all industrialized countries – to attract elite workers.

In May 2001, the Home Secretary concentrated in his own hands the power to give work permits, which until then was held by the Minister of Employment. These were valid for five years with immediate effect. More measures were put in place to allow innovators, businessmen and investors, as well as new graduates undergoing training, to come and work in the UK, passing through accelerated procedures. The Highly Skilled Migrants Programme, launched on 28 January 2002, allowed highly qualified immigrants move to the UK without already holding a job, on condition that they were able to provide for their own needs. Finally, since May 2004, citizens of the ten new member states of the EU have been authorized to work in the UK.[13]

The statistics demonstrate the effectiveness of that policy: of 139,000 permits issued in 2003 (a 20 per cent growth on 2002), 29,600 were given to qualified workers (a 50 per cent increase), 65,800 were given to facilitate family reunion (a 20 per cent increase), whilst the number of asylum applications fell by 30 per cent.

Italy

Since the beginning of the 1970s, Italy has become a country of immigration. But it was not until 1986 that a first immigration law was voted in on the regularization of illegal immigrants.[14] In 1989, through a decree that became law in 1990, the then deputy Prime Minister Claudio Martelli put in place what became the framework for Italian immigration legislation: respect for family life, taking into account the needs of the Italian economy and the putting into place of instruments of control as well as the fight against illegal immigration. The 1990 law enlarged the protection of the Geneva Convention to those persecuted in regions of the world beyond Europe. But above all, the total number of immigrant admissions became subject to a national quota fixed after consultation with professional organizations of employers and trade unions.

In the context of the weakening of the labour market, the first quotas were restricted to the entry of families, asylum applications and foreign workers coming in under the old system.[15] It was not until 1995 that the quotas took into account the introduction of new immigrant workers. After the Turko-Napolitano law of 1998, the Prime Minister's office fixed the quotas directly each year. Finally, in exchange for more efficient cooperation in the readmission of their illegal immigrants, Mediterranean countries (Albania, Morocco and Tunisia) received privileged quotas for several thousand entry permits each year, guaranteed for a limited period of time.[16]

What were the results of this policy? Between 1995 and 2004, the quota passed from 25,000 to 79,500 after achieving a record in 2001 of 89,400. At the same time, five *sanatorie* – regularizations (of illegal immigrants) – were put into effect from the mid-1980s: in 1986 (120,000), in 1990 (220,000), in 1996 (246,000), in 1999–2000 (250,000) and finally in 2003–4 (750,000).

One could say that Italy has accumulated a strong demand on its labour market as a result of its ageing population, the increase in life expectancy and its weak birth rate (since 1990, the number of children per woman has hovered between 1.2 and 1.3); it finds also itself in the first stage of the migratory process, thus the needs of its labour force have not until the present been fulfilled by family immigration flows (however, the regularization of immigration in 2003–4 will bring a strong growth in familial immigration which passed from 2,000 in 1990 to 64,000 in 2001, since, after one year's stay in Italy, the families of immigrants may enter outside of the quota).[17]

Finally, the Italian example shows that quota plays an important role in encouraging illegal immigration, as a result of its announcements: if the government posts in advance a quota of 80,000, many more potential immigrants will hope to benefit from it than there are places available. But if one compares the regularization of 2003–4 and that of 1999–2000, one can see a net change in the composition of illegal immigration: today, it comes more from Central and Eastern Europe (Romania and Ukraine) than in 1999–2000, which was more from the Mediterranean (Albania and Morocco). Immigrants from Eastern and Central Europe have benefited from a relative freedom of movement, whilst controls on those arriving from the Mediterranean have been reinforced; this has had a marked impact. Clearly, in both legal and illegal immigration, Italy favours Eastern and Central Europe over Mediterranean and African countries.[18]

Spain

In 1985, as it approached accession to the EU, Spain adopted its first legislation on immigration, highly restrictive and focused on the control of frontiers and illegal immigration.[19] Following it closely, the Spanish government proceeded with a first, small regularization of illegal immigrants (23,000 permits were issued for 44,000 applicants).[20] The government proceeded in a similar vein in 1991, when the imposition of a visa requirement for citizens of South American and North African countries to enter the Schengen area was accompanied by a second regularization which concerned 116,000 foreigners for 133,000 applicants. It was at this point that immigration became a political and social phenomenon. In trying to regulate this flow of illegal immigrants and to respond to the needs of the labour force, quotas were instituted at the level of 20,000 to 30,000 per annum from 1993, divided almost equally between seasonal and permanent workers.[21] This system allowed thousands of hidden workers to legalize their situation each year. It failed, however, to regulate immigration. Spain signed agreements with several South American countries (Ecuador, Colombia, the Dominican Republic), and with Morocco and Romania: in exchange for greater cooperation on the control of their frontiers and the readmission of illegal immigrations, these countries were given priority in the allocation of visas.

But after the vote of the law of April 2000, which developed a policy of integration, a new regularization brought in 164,000 foreigners out of 250,000 applicants, and again after the August 2002 law when there were 184,000 regularizations for 350,000 applicants.

A new country of immigration, endowed with a narrow maritime border and also a terrestrial frontier with Africa (Ceuta and Melilla), Spain is also one of the countries of Europe with a weak birth rate (1.2 children per woman). The need of an unskilled workforce offers an opportunity to immigrants from Morocco, but also from Latin America and Eastern Europe. Just as in Italy, the system of quotas has the effect of an appeal for immigrants. It is bureaucratic: determined by the Director-General of Migration in the Ministry of Labour and Social Security, since 2002, after consultation with trade unions and employers in each province, it is now divided between 12 economic sectors and 52 geographical areas (which gives, for example, 5,300 seasonal workers for Huelva in the south of Spain, but also one services worker for Soria).[22] The demand is obviously greater than the fixed quota (for example, 97,000 applications were made in 1999 for

30,000 available places), and often serves to regularize immigrants already present for a long time on Spanish territory.

At the end of August 2004, the government of José Luis Zapatero announced, in response to the presence of several hundred thousand illegal foreign workers, the legalization of all foreigners working illegally, provided they had a contract of at least six months. It is estimated that this legislation concerns between 500,000 and 1,000,000 illegal immigrants.

France in a comparative perspective

An old country of immigration, the legal system in France, as in the UK and Germany, mostly supports familial immigration. The number of refugees – in the sense of the Geneva Convention – is small, and labour migration is even smaller.[23] In total, in 2002, 124,000 non-EU foreign citizens obtained permanent residency.[24] The impact of the 1998 law voted in by the left has been important: 51,333 permanent residence permits were issued in 1997. If one adds the 30,000 residence permits given to EU citizens, one is not far off from the net figure of 110,000 migrants that the United Nations suggested for France (the country with the strongest birth rate in Europe: 1.9 children per woman) in order to maintain its present level of active population 50 years hence.[25]

On temporary migrations, the impact of the 1998 law was also important, even if not always forecast by the government. The number of foreign students admitted into French universities grew by 60 per cent between 1997 and 1998 and 2003 and 2004. But the number of asylum applications has also grown: from 21,146 in 1997 to 51,090 in 2002, whilst those asking for territorial asylum grew from 1,414 in 1998 to 28,372 in 2002. This increase is the result of a poor administrative choice. In order to manage asylum applications, a swift procedure, managed by independent, professional judges, has only desirable effects. It allows for the speedy award of legal status to those who need protection and at the same time dissuades the greater part of those whose claims are unfounded. Forgetful of these realities, the left-wing government concentrated applications for the new status of 'complementary' asylum in the hands of the Ministry of the Interior, rather than with the French Office for the Protection of Refugees and Stateless Persons, a specialized organ that manages applications for asylum made under the Geneva Convention, as a result of their fear of its 'liberalism'. The result of this was that an asylum application could be made twice: once before OFPRA for the Geneva Convention; the second time before the Minister of the Interior for territorial asylum, doubling the length of time it took to process applications. It would give legal residence to applicants for three years, even if their application was rejected.

The statistic of 124,000 residence permits also includes the effects of a mechanism of continued and individual legalization (as opposed to 'exceptional' and 'collective'), rather like the mechanism of 'prescription' or the statute of limitation that exists for the violation of many laws. Let us take the example of fiscal legislation, or the highway code. If sanctions for breaking the rules are not enforced, no one will respect the law. But if no prescription is set even after years have passed since the violation of the law, citizens will have the impression of being under the permanent threat of state control and investigation of a quasi-totalitarian nature. In the field of immigration, it means that in the years following their arrival illegal immigrants should be removed back to their country of origin. But with the passing of the years, and as immigrants become integrated into society, it is a better policy to allow them to adjust their status if strong and durable links with the society of their residence can be proven.[26] Without this individual and selective process, the French experience (1981, 1991 and 1997) and the more recent Italian and Spanish experiences show that the number of illegal immigrants grows cumulatively; a massive and exceptional regularization becomes inevitable, with all its perverse effects: administrative disorder, an incoming flow of candidates for regularization coming from neighbouring countries and, in the end, even more illegal immigrants. In 2002, the new Minister of the Interior, Nicolas Sarkozy, used this instrument of individual regularization to respond to the mobilization of illegal migrants, thus avoiding massive regularization. He thus kept this instrument as a part of French legislation that was modified by parliament on his initiative in November 2003.

His impulse toughened immigration legislation – more resources required from tourists, fewer facilities for family unification, more numerous conditions and longer delays before obtaining a residency permit or French nationality by marriage or adoption. The law accords special new powers to mayors: to issue or refuse to issue a certificate of residence, to meet a future spouse before the celebration of a marriage to check their consent, and to be consulted before the issuing of a residence permit. Another law merged the procedures for asylum under the Geneva Convention and those of subsidiary asylum,[27] while opening this protection to individuals persecuted by non-state agents; this aimed to reduce the time spent in processing applications and allowed for the drawing up of a list of 'secured' countries or countries of internal asylum.

Since 1974, as a result of the unemployment situation, the French authorities have closed their doors not only to unskilled workers, but also to the skilled ones.[28] In contrast to the UK, Germany or the Netherlands, it continues to close its door to qualified workers from OECD countries, just as it does for the countries of the South. Yet, graduates and skilled workers of all nationalities operate more and more in a globalized competitive marketplace.

France, just as in the UK, has been able to open immigration to the qualified, without any fuss and with a high degree of efficiency. On 16 July 1998, the Minister of Labour allowed French businesses to recruit foreign IT workers to help combat the millennium bug.[29] By the beginning of 2004, when the instruction on foreign IT workers was repealed,[30] 6,374 systems engineers had acquired a permanent residence permit. In the meantime, a circular of 15 January 2002 opened the labour market to students with the condition for students from the South that the vacancy should be in the nature of a co-development project. The main problem is mobilizing the relevant agencies and getting rid of ineffective procedures. Indeed, the number of work permits has actually fallen: from 8,811 in 2001, to 7,462 in 2002, 6,500 in 2003 and 6740 in 2004.

Finally, in contrast to the UK or Italy, France has made no gesture with regard to the employment of citizens – even the graduate ones – from the new member states of the EU.

Sedentary immigration and circulatory migration

In some member states, strong reservations with regard to skilled migration exist. It sometimes has racist or corporatist roots: the wish to reserve the most valuable professional positions in society for the natives. It can be based on 'third-worldism': in the name of development or co-development, they encourage foreign graduates to return to their country of origin.

This is both incoherent and absurd. African, Asian, South American or other non-EU citizens should, from the moment they receive a degree from a European university, enter the world market of graduates. If they do not want to return home, they will not do so. And if Europe refuses them residency, they will receive a job offer from the United States, Japan, Canada or Australia and will be 'lost' both for their country of origin and for the country where they received their training.

Europe should therefore have its own third way policy on qualified foreign workers: neither closing the door to the potential they offer nor falling into the North American trap – the brain drain, (i.e. attracting skilled immigrants who never return home). Rather, Europe should favour brain and labour circulation. Often, foreign graduates seek employment on the European labour market because they wish to gain the resources or the professional experience necessary to launch themselves into a career in their home country. They should not be prevented from choosing this path – on the contrary. If they later balk at the idea of going home, it is often because they fear losing the cultural, scientific or entrepreneurial environment necessary to maintain or enhance their skills base. It is essential, therefore, to accompany the liberalization of the recruitment of the most highly qualified with a better 'offer' that is both closer to the wishes of these high-skilled workers and more respectful – case permitting – of their home countries' interests. It is necessary to facilitate voluntary 'recirculation' between their country of origin and their country of training. Thus through the development of intellectual exchanges and a flow of business, they will become the private agents of co-development.

Conclusion

The European Immigration Policy is at a crossroad. Obviously, in the domains related to migration control and asylum, where common rules pre-existed the Amsterdam Treaty (with the Schengen Agreement and the Geneva Convention), convergence is reinforcing itself, directive after directive. This is not the case in the domain related to the admission of legal immigrants, where directives have either accepted the formalization of the gap between national policies (such as family reunification) or have been postponed (in the case of the admission of non-EU nationals working in the EU). In the case of labour migration, European states find themselves either in competition with one another (to attract the highest skilled) or in the position of producing potential undesirable side effects (for example, in the case of the legalization of all illegal immigrants, or, on the contrary, in the case of refusal to bring in any legalization at all).

The challenge here is to coordinate the action between nation-states whose need for legal migration will remain divergent for a long period of time. In the future, how can Italy, Germany and Spain attract three or four times more immigrants than France or the UK without undesirable side effects potentially coming from all sides? The solution has not been found yet because the outcomes of all the different national policies have not been put frankly on the table. The absence of a common and efficient statistical framework prevents any comparison based on credible data, and therefore its adoption should be a priority.

For the nation-state, immigration is one of the challenges of the future and not a problem of the past. We do not believe in either the maintenance of the state as it stands, or in its diminution, but rather in its reconfiguration. The state is retreating and will retreat from certain areas, but it is conquering new ones. Immigration is one of these areas of future conquest. And immigration policy, as complex as it is diverse, requires the investment that was not made in the past, in order to coordinate better the multiplicity of relevant administrations, to take on board better the wishes of migrant populations and to learn not only how to control the flow of migration, but also to manage their 'recirculation' over a longer period.

Seasonal workers could get the benefit of multi-annual permits: they would get the guarantee of a permit over the following five or ten years, if at the end of their season, each year, they return to their country of origin. Foreign graduate students from European universities could receive the benefit of a permanent visa.[31] It would permit them to return and recirculate from their country of origin without fear that any exit would be final. When an EU university or hospital recruits foreign professors or doctors, they should be offered the possibility of a joint recruitment. They would alternate work between an EU institution and an African or Asian one, keeping their salary and their European job. Their salary in the sending country could be funded by the EU as a concrete and pragmatic action in favour of development.

The facilitation of 'recirculation', according to a regime adapted to suit each category of migrants – for highly skilled workers, but also for seasonal workers – will be one of the new tasks for immigration policy in the twenty-first century. This will demand the most radical innovations in the immigration administration. The inert state of the nineteenth century liked stable populations and quotas. The twenty-first-century state must learn how to regulate immigration and not seek to 'control' it with rigid and unadaptable instruments. It must become more and more accustomed to managing the rights and the status of its nationals abroad, and of foreigners within its own territory, in short – as against sedentary immigration – of migrants in movement.

Notes

1 P. Weil, 'Races at the Gate: A Century of Racial Distinctions in American Immigration Policy (1865–1965)', *Georgetown Immigration Law Journal*, 15, 4 (Summer 2001), pp. 625–48.

2 If an illegal immigrant contracts a contagious disease and cannot treat himself, he puts the host society in danger. It is also in the interest of the society where the child of an illegal immigrant is attending school.

3 United Nations, Population Division, *Replacement Migration: Is It a Solution to Declining and Ageing Populations?*, ESA/P/WP.160 (New York: United Nations, 2000).

4 On the distinction between direct and indirect entries onto the labour market, see J.-F. Léger, 'Les Entrées d'étrangers sur le marché de l'emploi de 1990 à 2001', *Révue européenne des migrations internationales*, 20, 1, (2004), pp. 7–20.

5 See European Commission, Green Paper on *A Community Approach to the Management of Economic Migration* (Brussels: COM, 2004) 811 Final, 11 January 2005.

6 Philip Martin, 'Germany: managing migration in the twenty-first century', in Wayne A. Cornelius, Takeyuki Tsuda, Philip L. Martin and James F. Hollifield, *Controlling Migration, a Global Perspective*, 2nd edn. (Stanford: Stanford University Press, 2004), pp. 221–51.

7 Daniel Kanstroom, 'Wer sind wir wieder? Laws of asylum, immigration, and citizenship in the struggle for the soul of the new Germany', *Yale Journal of International Law*, 18, 1 (1991), p. 194.

8 Rainer Münz, 'New German law skirts comprehensive immigration reform', Migration Information Source, 1 August 2004.

9 See Randall Hansen, *Citizenship and Immigration in Post-War Britain* (Oxford: Oxford University Press, 2000), Introduction.

10 R. Hansen, 'Commentary', in Wayne A. Cornelius et al., *Controlling Migration*, pp. 338–42.

11 See Christian Joppke, *Immigration and the Nation-State, the United States, Germany, and Great Britain* (Oxford: Oxford University Press, 1999), pp. 100–37.

12 Hansen, *Citizenship and Immigration*, p. 256.

13 The UK, Ireland and Sweden are the only 'old' member states that have opened their labour markets to the new citizens of Europe. The 12 other member states have applied 'transitional arrangements' with regard to the free movement of workers across the Union. The restrictions that apply to eight of the ten new member states (Cyprus and Malta are exempted) last from two years (deadline May 2006) to seven years (deadline May 2011).

14 Salvatore Palidda and Alessandro Dal Lago, 'L'Immigration et la politique d'immigration en Italie', in Bribosia Emmanuelle and Rea Andrea, *Les Nouvelles Migrations, un enjeu européen* (Brussels: Editions Complexe, 2002), pp. 183–206.

15 Luca Einaudi, 'Programmation de quotas, regularisations et travail au noir: les politiques de l'immigration en Italie et en Espagne (1973–2003)', in Marie-Claude Blanc Chaléard, Stéphane Dufoix and Patrick Weil, eds., *Immigration, intégration, nationalité* (Paris: Éditions manuscript.com, 2005).

16 See Ferrucio Pastore, 'Quote et Gestione degli ingressi per motivi economici. Primi elementi per una valutazione dell'esperienza italiana (1998–2003)', in *Consiglio Nazionale dell'Economia e del Lavoro (CNEL), Regolazione dei flussi migratory tra programmazione e precarieta' degli interventi* (December 2003), pp. 45–57.

17 Einaudi, 'Programmation'.

18 For 2004, the quota reserved for the new member states was 36,000 for a total quota of 115,000 (excluding family reunion, asylum applications and the EU(15)). For 2005, it passed to 79,500 out of a total of 159,000.

19 The information that follows is taken from Francisco Javier Moreno Fuentes, *The Evolution of Migration Policies in Spain. Between External Constraints and Domestic Demand for Unskilled Labour*, CEACS Working Paper no. 211 (Madrid: Instituto Juan March, 2004), p. 37.

20 Only 13,000 permits were renewed after a stay of one year.

21 Except in 1996, 2000 and 2001; 20,600 in 1993 and 1994; 25,000 in 1995; zero in 1996; 24,690 in 1997; 28,000 in 1998; 30,000 in 1999; zero in 2000 and 2001; 32,079 in 2002 and 2004; 337 in 2003. Source: Einaudi, 'Programmation'.

22 L. Einaudi shows that 82 per cent of the seasonal workers affected are in agriculture, whilst 60 per cent of permanent workers are in services (hospitality, transport, domestic service). See his 'Programmation', pp. 42–3.

23 In 2003, 50,200 partners of French citizens, 26,700 family reunions, 11,500 refugees or families of refugees and 6,500 salaried workers.

24 Statistical report for the High Council for Integration (Paris, 2002).

25 United Nations, Population Division (2000), *Replacement Migration*.

26 In 2002, for those with more than ten years of residence, 2,155 permanent residence permits were issued; for those foreigners who arrived before the age of 10, there were 1,770 issued; for the parents of French children, 7,087; under the title of private and family life in France (Article 8 of the European Convention on Human Rights), 7,123; for sick foreigners, 3,370.

27 Substitute for territorial asylum.

28 As an exception, businesses have, however, the right to recruit foreign employees provided that their salary has attained a particularly high level (remuneration should be 1,300 times the minimum guaranteed hourly rate or €3,978 monthly before tax on 1 July 2004).

29 Circular DPM/DM 2–3 no. 98–429 of 16 July 1998, relating to the recruitment of foreign IT workers.

30 Circular DPM/DMI 2 no. 2004–12 of 13 January 2004.

31 Technically their visa couldn't be refused by the EU consulate except under written justifications.

13

Economic Reform, Further Integration and Enlargement: Can Europe Deliver?

Loukas Tsoukalis

Regional integration in Europe has developed into a complex system with no precedent in history and no rival in other parts of the contemporary world. It is a system with common institutions, rules and significant policy output covering a very wide range of areas, starting from trade and now extending to many other manifestations of cross-border interaction; a political system with shared sovereignty in which nation-states are not expected to wither away, or, indeed, risk doing so. It has served as an instrument for peace and security in a crowded part of the world with a long and turbulent history. It has contributed to greater prosperity; and it has helped to consolidate democracy, while also working as a kind of convergence machine for the benefit of the less developed countries of the European continent.[1]

Since the turn of the century, this European political system has delivered a common currency, replacing twelve national currencies with a long history behind them, opened its doors to ten new members, and negotiated yet another revision of the treaties, this time called a constitution. Whatever the difficulties encountered – and they are, surely, many – it is not a bad record by any standards, especially for a political system usually criticized as being extremely slow, inefficient and overly bureaucratic.

The European political and economic map has changed radically, and for the better. Yet Europe is now going through a phase of self-doubt and pessimism about the future. Has the European project reached its limits? Or, perhaps worse, are we already in reverse gear? The problems we are currently facing have much to do with the poor economic situation and the growing feeling of insecurity among many of our fellow citizens in times of rapid change. They also have to do with the weakening of the old consensus about the main objectives of European integration. This chapter discusses these rather broad issues in relation to economic reform, further integration and enlargement.

Lessons from Lisbon

Regional integration started basically as an economic affair, though with strong political undertones. Economics remains today the back-bone of it all. For many years, integration helped to sustain a succession of virtuous circles, which significantly helped national economic growth while also bolstering the essentially permissive consensus of European citizens about further integration. Love of Europe has always had a strong pecuniary dimension, and it has depended on the ability of European and national institutions to deliver the goods. It was fine as long as it lasted. The performance of several European economies, most notably the three biggest economies in the Eurozone, has been disappointing for a long time. Stagnating economies with few jobs and ageing populations are a recipe for disaster, not only for generous national welfare systems but also for the European project more generally.

We need more growth and more jobs, especially at the upper end of the knowledge scale – it is worth remembering that Europe is losing thousands of postdoctoral researchers to America every year and most of them never come back. And we need to adjust our policies to meet those goals. Neither the internal market nor the EMU has so far succeeded in injecting much-needed dynamism into many of our national economies. For some time, there has been broad agreement among economists and, judging from official rhetoric, also among politicians that Europe needs economic reform, mostly in the direction of supply-side measures, in order to generate more growth and jobs; and this should go beyond the further implementation of the internal market programme.

Economic reform has been on the agenda for several years: it constitutes a key element of the Lisbon Agenda agreed by our political leaders in 2000. But unlike earlier experience with economic integration, the so-called Lisbon process does not rely on common laws and regulations, which have been an integral part of the internal market programme, or on the centralization of policies, as happened with monetary policy, for example, in the context of EMU. And rightly so, it can be argued, since the Lisbon process touches on many aspects of labour market and welfare policy, among other things, where diversity and subsidiarity remain the name of the game; hence the emphasis on the role of the European Union as an external catalyst and facilitator rather than a law-maker.

Some years later, there are lessons to be drawn.[2] Peer pressure, benchmarking and soft coordination, which are all distinguishing features of the Lisbon process, have shown their limitations. The consensus on the general direction of economic reform has proved fragile: when the external catalyst collided with domestic political realities, it was the latter that almost invariably prevailed. Naming and shaming of those countries lagging behind in the implementation of measures solemnly agreed upon at the European level, through the publication of indicators by the Commission, does not work unless the shaming part is internalized by national political systems – and this has hardly happened until now. A few national bureaucrats have been talking to and writing reports for other bureaucrats to read, while politicians and societies in general have remained largely indifferent.

Instead of a catalyst and a facilitator, the Union has often served as a scapegoat for national governments, when those governments finally decided to take unpopular measures at home. There has been a general tendency in recent years for national politicians to appropriate for themselves any measures deemed popular, while passing the responsibility for difficult or unpopular decisions, involving short-term political costs, on to the EU and the Commission in particular. We are now reaping the fruits of such shortsighted behaviour, and not only in France and the Netherlands.

The EU can and should provide a useful forum for debate as well as a basis for comparing national experiences and possibly also a soft version of benchmarking. At the same time, it can and should provide a broad policy framework, and hopefully no longer a scapegoat. It is important, however, to recognize the limitations of such an exercise in which the final responsibility lies with member states, while the role of the EU is limited to 'soft' coordination at best. There is a huge difference between the Lisbon process on the one hand, and the internal market and EMU on the other. It would not be wise for Europe to be seen by citizens as having responsibility for things it has no real power to deliver. Having said that, we want to make more and better use of financial incentives through the common budget as a way of strengthening the Lisbon process.[3] This should include a more direct link with Structural Funds as well as more money for research and development. The proposal to set up the Globalization Adjustment Fund linked to economic restructuring also goes in the right direction.[4]

Integration and different models

There is a wider political issue as well. The big challenge for European countries, individually and collectively, is to try to reconcile international competitiveness and internal structural reforms with the kind of politically stable and compassionate society that West Europeans created in the aftermath of the Second World War. The American model surely has useful lessons for Europe, but it is hardly the kind of model that our societies will want to buy as a package. They still place much greater emphasis on equality and redistribution as well as on collective insurance against risk for individuals.

There is, nowadays, widespread fear of change and pessimism in many European countries. There is also an increasing number of losers, potential or imaginary losers as well, who turn to the old and familiar national institutions for protection. They are the ones who turn against European integration as well, perceived by them as being a vehicle of change and the dreaded globalization. The large majority of blue-collar workers in France voted 'no' in the recent referendum.

Poor economic performance, social angst and weak political leadership often feed into each other, thus creating a vicious circle. This needs to be broken sooner rather than later. There is, however, relatively little that can be done by European institutions alone, except for issuing mild exhortations. The responsibility lies with national governments, and some are bound to move faster than others. However, in times when inequalities are growing within countries and the number of losers is on the rise, a division of labour in which European institutions concentrate on economic liberalization while national institutions retain the (near) monopoly of redistribution and welfare can become politically explosive.[5] More growth would help in this respect, but perhaps it will not be enough on its own.

On the other hand, economic liberalization and the growing international mobility of goods, services, persons and, even more so, capital have reduced the ability of the national state to regulate and tax. Admittedly, the degree to which this has already happened remains a controversial issue among professionals.[6] It has become a political issue as well, mainly because of the perceived distributional effects that globalization and regional integration have within our countries. It is a question of winners and losers.

What kind of minimum common standards or policies we want to adopt at the EU level for a wide range of policy areas related to the functioning of the internal market is also a real, and indeed, legitimate political issue. It may apply to anything from health and safety standards to minimum tax rates and the regulatory framework for financial services. This is what much of European politics will continue to be all about in the years to come.

At the one extreme of this political debate, we will find zealous centralizers, including large parts of the European bureaucracy, old-fashioned integrationists, who still believe in the transfer of powers to Brussels for its own sake, and weak governments who often prefer importing difficult decisions from abroad. We will also find old- and new-style protectionists who believe that Europe can be shielded from the rest of the world and also from change. At the other extreme, we will find globalization missionaries preaching the virtues (and usually the alleged inevitability) of the shrinking world, together with market fundamentalists who want to strike down all barriers in order to unleash the forces of competition. According to them, politics should simply submit to superior economic logic. The majority of Europeans will situate themselves somewhere in between. The point of compromise can only be decided at the political level. We shall have to wait and see whether the political battle on this major issue remains confined to the intergovernmental level.

The Euro as a factor of integration

There is, of course, much more to European integration than the internal market and the Lisbon Agenda. There is economic and monetary union, for example, which has undoubtedly been the biggest step in integration since the very beginning. Currencies are not self-managed. The institutional structure provided for in the Maastricht Treaty is both weak and unbalanced, with rigid rules to compensate for those faults. But this is what was politically feasible at the time. As the European Central Bank becomes wiser and more confident with time and experience, the countries of the Eurozone will need to strengthen the 'E' part of EMU.

A monetary union needs a more effective coordination of fiscal policies, going beyond the restrictions imposed on national budget deficits and the broad economic policy guidelines, which are usually too broad to have a real effect on national policies. It also needs a more symmetrical approach to national fiscal policies, and the common monetary policy also. Ideally, it needs a policy institution that takes a global view of the Eurozone as a whole, collectively agreeing on the main macroeconomic policy priorities while also introducing a more effective coordination of economic policies in the wider sense.[7]

There is a close link between macroeconomic policy and structural reform. Structural reform helps growth, but it is also easier to introduce in a favourable macroeconomic environment. Interestingly enough, most countries that so far lead the pack as regards progress in the implementation of the Lisbon Agenda are those outside the Eurozone. One might have expected otherwise. After all, structural reform is even more necessary in a monetary union, since the latter implies both the loss of important policy instruments at the national level and closer economic interdependence between members.

An effective management of the common currency calls for more integration as far as the smaller group of participating countries is concerned. If and when that happens, it will also have important consequences for relations between 'ins' and 'outs' within the Union. Should we prepare ourselves for one Europe with the internal market in its core and another with the common currency and much more? And if so, where would foreign policy or internal security fit?

Past enlargements as a guide

Let me now turn to a different subject. Regional integration in Europe has been mostly the product of an elitist conspiracy, with good intentions and pretty remarkable results. This is changing fast. The permissive consensus on which regional integration used to rely for many years can no longer be taken for granted. The European project begins to look old and tired, and perhaps also irrelevant for an increasing number of citizens. The signs have been around us for some time, although many of our political leaders apparently choose not to see them: declining public support as registered in surveys of the Eurobarometer, negative or marginal results in earlier referenda in which citizens were invited to approve yet another treaty revision, not to mention the difficulties experienced in mobilizing voters in successive elections to the European Parliament.

The majority of European citizens continue to support integration, although they are now more concerned about the kind of Europe that will be built. Europeans are apparently no longer prepared to give *carte blanche* to their political leaders on further integration or enlargement. Regional integration is becoming more politicized and, I believe, there is no way back. In a more political Europe, identity and borders will be important but also divisive issues. Regional integration so far has been marked by successive and mostly successful enlargements: from six to nine, then to twelve in two instalments, later to fifteen, not counting the very important, though indirect, enlargement following German unification, and finally to twenty-five. The political decision to enlarge further to twenty-seven has already been taken and the relevant treaties signed, although the precise date is not yet known. And there are still more countries waiting to join.

Successive enlargements are the best proof of the strong attraction that the Union continues to exert on its neighbours. And they have also been one of the most successful policies of the Union, an effective way of extending *Pax Europaea* to more countries of the continent. Having helped to establish the conditions for a peaceful and prosperous centre, the old Carolingian core if you wish, today's mission of the Union may indeed be to export democracy, stability and modernity beyond its present borders. Empires have often tried to do something similar in the past, although using much more unpleasant means and, of course, relying less on democracy. It is characteristic that members sharing borders with countries outside the Union are only too keen to bring their neighbours inside the fold: Poland is today the strongest advocate of Ukraine's European perspective, and so is Greece for the countries of South-east Europe, including Turkey.

There is no denying, however, that a European Union with many more members, including Turkey – a country that forms a category of its own for reasons of size and history, if nothing else – will be a very different Union from what we have known so far. And then, the awkward question is being asked, a question that is difficult to answer but also increasingly difficult to avoid: how much diversity can the European political system take before it implodes? And more mundanely, at what speed can European institutions incorporate new members without reaching gridlock, or how much money are taxpayers of member states prepared to pay for the benefit of those Europeans much poorer than themselves and keen to join the club?

The latest enlargement was the biggest enlargement ever and likely to prove the most difficult. It is not just a question of numbers. The new members have relatively low levels of economic development and limited experience of democratic governance. The latest enlargement is therefore similar to the Southern enlargement of the 1980s, if only on a much bigger scale and taking place in a less favourable economic and political environment. The same observation applies to those countries still waiting to join, only more so.

There had been many scare stories preceding the Southern enlargement, stories about dilution of the Community, as it was then, dumping of goods and mass migrations of poor, unemployed people from the new members. The Polish plumber today has replaced the

Spanish tomato grower in the minds of French people and others who are afraid of new, poorer countries joining the Union.

Scare stories were proved wrong in the past. The accession of Greece, Portugal and Spain was accompanied by the further deepening of integration: the internal market programme and the strengthening of the redistributive dimension of the common budget, through the creation of the Structural Funds and the Cohesion Fund, were both closely connected with the enlargement of the 1980s.[8] Enlargement coincided with (and contributed to) higher growth in the EU as a whole, at least in the early years, while Spaniards and Greeks did not invade the labour markets of the more advanced economies in Europe; if anything, many of those already there went back home. The reason is very simple: the new members have enjoyed healthy growth for most of the time since joining and they have therefore succeeded in progressively narrowing the income gap that was separating them from their richer partners. There are several elements there of a positive sum game.

Membership of the EU has meant the opening of national markets, in some cases after a long history of protection. It has meant large inflows of funds, both private and public, the relative distribution varying from country to country. Private inflows, mostly in the form of foreign direct investment, fit nicely with traditional theories: free trade and lower wage costs bring foreign investment, thus leading to higher growth. But there have also been large transfers of public funds: in the case of Greece and Portugal, transfers from the Structural and Cohesion Funds reached 3.5 per cent of GDP per year, as with Ireland until some years ago, going mostly into infrastructural projects and investment in human capital.

There is, admittedly, little agreement among economists about the real contribution of these transfers to economic growth in the recipient countries; some of the money was clearly wasted as a result of inefficiency or corruption. However, the importance of structural funds should not be underestimated. Furthermore, with the exception of Portugal, the poorer countries of the EU have also benefited from transfers of funds through the CAP, although at a price for their consumers. While being net recipients of funds from the EU budget, the three South European countries have been steadily building up their welfare states, which has meant large increases in government expenditure, as part of the process of catching up with the more advanced countries of Western Europe.

There is, of course, more to EU membership for the less developed countries than economic growth and transfers. Membership has meant opening up to the rest of Europe and the world in more than an economic sense; in other words, greater exposure to modernity. It has also meant the consolidation of democracy in countries which had been cut off for shorter or longer periods from Europe's post-war democratic core; and it has meant different benchmarking and the import of higher standards of public and corporate governance. The three South European countries, and also Ireland, are now very different from what they were 15 or 20 years earlier; and they owe much of this transformation to the EU. Of course, modernization has not just been imported; membership of the EU has mostly offered carrots as well as sticks, which helped to change the internal balance of forces in favour of the modernizing elements of the society. Last but not least, these countries have acquired a new role on the European and international stage, and this has been a tremendous boost to self-confidence in countries that had long been objects rather than subjects of international diplomacy.

A strategy for further enlargement

Can this experience be repeated for the benefit of those who have recently joined the EU, and eventually also for others still in the waiting room? The answer to this question depends on several factors, including domestic conditions in countries joining, the European and international economic environment, as well as policies pursued by the EU.

The transformation of the former communist countries of Central and Eastern Europe, now members of the EU, is already quite remarkable. For years the perspective of membership provided the necessary focus and a powerful incentive for domestic change.[9] The growth prospects for the new members now look good; arguably, the most difficult part of the transition is already behind them.

There is, however, a less optimistic reading of the situation, which may suggest that the process of Europeanization of the new members, a process that academics have written so much about, risks being rather long and also painful for all parties concerned. A large number of citizens of the young democracies in Central and Eastern Europe show little trust in their political leaders and even less confidence in the political system in general; many of them are tired of reforms, often perceived as being imposed by Brussels; and having suffered for long under foreign domination, they now attach themselves with religious zeal to some of the formal attributes of sovereignty, having already relinquished many of their real powers, especially in the economic field. There is serious risk of a further rise in populism in those countries, more so than in the old members of the Union, which would, of course, impact negatively on domestic adjustment but also on the functioning of the enlarged EU. It is worth remembering that most of the new members start from a much lower economic level than the three South European countries when they joined.

The EU(25) (and soon 27) may take several years to adjust and find its own pace. The institutional reforms contained in the Constitutional Treaty would have made this adjustment smoother and quicker. They may never be applied; at best, they will come later and, perhaps, they will also be further diluted. In times of slow growth and tight budgetary constraint, there is likely to be a mentality of zero-sum game, and hence less enthusiasm for cross-border transfers among other things.

In such a context, further enlargement is bound to be a slow process at best. Public opinion cannot be left behind, and there is at present precious little enthusiasm for more countries joining in. For further enlargement to happen – and happen successfully – hence without acting as a boomerang against the Union itself, I submit we will need at least four things: Patience, Persuasion, Imagination and Generosity: the PPIG strategy, if you like acronyms. Let me explain.

Our citizens will have to be convinced about the benefits of further enlargement. It cannot be otherwise. At present, many of them seem to have serious doubts. One of the problems is that the benefits of enlargement for existing members are mostly long term and intangible – an investment, in other words, in democracy, security and prosperity in our neighbourhood, while the costs are usually perceived to be more immediate and concrete. This is hardly the combination to mobilize politicians in a democracy. Most of them tried to avoid the subject altogether until recently. It is now out in the public, offering plenty of opportunities for demagogues. Hopefully, they will not be the ones to dominate the debate on further enlargement.

While criteria of eligibility have to be strictly adhered to, the Union may be well advised to make the intermediate stages leading to full membership more substantial in economic and political terms. Gradual adoption of the *acquis communautaire* by the candidates should be complemented with more rapid integration in the European internal market and participation in common programmes and policies. And this will also cost money to the EU budget, let us be honest. *Pax Europaea* does not come cheap.

There is also no point in pretending that the Union can keep on taking new members without this having an effect on its internal cohesion and its ability to deliver the goods. To put it differently, in order to be able to stabilize the periphery, we first of all need a centre that functions. And this is becoming less and less obvious. Internal reforms, implying difficult decisions and compromises, may therefore be an effective precondition for a successful further enlargement.

We need large amounts of patience to carry through the process of further enlargement; strong skills of persuasion in order to convince our fellow citizens of the merits of it; extra doses of imagination to design flexible and more differentiated forms of membership, while also constructing more substantial intermediate stages leading to it; and last but not least, more money in order to help lubricate the process of Europeanization.

Concluding thoughts

There is disillusion with the European project, which manifested itself more clearly than ever before in the French and Dutch referendums on the constitution in 2005. As integration begins to reach the nooks and crannies of our societies, while successive enlargements increase the diversity and also weaken whatever common identity we may have created over the years inside the Union, there are signs of growing indigestion of things European and also the realization that the key question is no longer how much Europe we have, but what kind of Europe.

Important decisions in recent years have been poorly explained or justified to the citizens of our countries. EMU and enlargement are the obvious examples. Others, including the Lisbon Agenda, have simply been oversold. There has been confusion in many national capitals as to what they really want out of the European project, except perhaps for some short-term benefits. This may also explain the dangerous habit of blaming Brussels and the European institutions for unpopular decisions or simply when things go wrong. More clarity and realism about what Europe can in fact deliver would help enormously. So would greater consistency in defining objectives and means. National politicians remain the key stakeholders of the European project; they have too often pretended otherwise. European issues also need to become more political in the traditional sense of the term, instead of being treated as a matter for intergovernmental diplomacy. There are choices to be made.

The internal market is still incomplete, especially in the area of services; much still needs to be done. Greater diversity and a more fragile consensus arguably call for a more selective approach to integration and – why not? – more subsidiarity. We should, however, be under no illusion. Subsidiarity often implies less integration or uneven conditions for economic agents as long as national systems continue to diverge. In other words, subsidiarity does not always come free of charge.

European integration has served as an agent of reform in the past. Nowadays, economic reform, broadly defined, constitutes the big challenge for European societies as they try to cope with technological progress, globalization and changing demography among other things. A distinction needs to be drawn between responsibilities that belong to European institutions and those that belong to member states. The former should no longer provide convenient scapegoats, nor should they create expectations about things they cannot deliver. On the other hand, economic liberalization and the breaking down of national barriers and regulations are not a neutral process. The problem of losers is taking a much bigger dimension at both the national and the European level. To be an effective agent of economic reform, the EU needs to develop a stronger caring dimension. It is a matter of urgency, while significant sections of our populations begin to perceive Europe as a threat rather than a factor of stability and prosperity.

While the new economic environment may call for more flexible and, arguably, less regulation in managing the internal market, the single currency may indeed call for more integration. The combination will create serious problems inside the Union, and difficult decisions will need to be made by participating and non-participating countries in EMU and other manifestations of further integration.

Last but not least, there is further enlargement. It is not realistic or wise to ask those who have recently joined to shut the door behind them. The EU exerts a strong attraction on its neighbours. The pressure for further enlargement is therefore the price the Union has to pay for its own success. However, the EU cannot simply go on taking new members, while it tries to preserve its own internal coherence and fragile identity. This looks like an attempt to square the circle. Perhaps, different and complicated geometric figures will develop in the process; in other words, different kinds of membership. And surely, further enlargement will be a long drawn-out process. The final destination of the European journey still remains unknown.

Notes

1 For further elaboration of some of the arguments developed here in summary form, see L. Tsoukalis, *What Kind of Europe?* (Oxford: Oxford University Press, 2005).

2 W. Kok, *Facing the Challenge*. Report of Wim Kok to the European Commission (The Kok Report) (Brussels, 2004).

3 A. Sapir et al., *An Agenda for a Growing Europe* (The Sapir Report) (Oxford: Oxford University Press, 2004).

4 See also L. Tsoukalis, 'Why we need a Globalisation Adjustment Fund', Discussion paper of the British Presidency, October 2005 <http://fco.gov. uk/Files/kfile/Loukas-final.pdf>.

5 M. Ferrera, *The Boundaries of Welfare. European Integration and the New Spatial Politics of Social Protection* (Oxford: Oxford University Press, 2005).

6 D. Cohen, T. Piketty and G. Saint-Paul, *The Economics of Rising Inequalities* (Oxford: Oxford University Press, 2002).

7 P. de Grauwe and G. Kouretas, eds., 'EMU: Current state and future prospects', Special Issue, *Journal of Common Market Studies*, 42, 4 (2004).

8 See Tsoukalis, *What Kind of Europe?*

9 M. Vachudova, *Europe Undivided. Democracy, Leverage, and Integration After Communism* (Oxford: Oxford University Press, 2005).

14

Friends, Not Foes: European Integration and National Welfare States

Maurizio Ferrera

Solidarity and Europe: A Problematic Relationship?

According to a traditional Swedish saying, 'Per Albin built the people's home and Ingvar Kamprad furnished it'. Albin was the Social Democratic Prime Minister who led Sweden out of the economic depression of the early 1930s and initiated key social welfare legislation. Kamprad is the founder of IKEA, the world-famous maker of affordable furnishing products. The saying's message is clear: high standards of living and 'well-being' rest upon a generous and protective welfare state *and* on a thriving and efficient market economy. In the second half of the twentieth century the Scandinavian countries showed that such a virtuous combination is not only desirable, but also possible. Despite the turbulences of the 1990s, the Nordic 'social model' was still a beacon for all those who cared about social justice and economic growth in the era of globalization. But the thorny question then is: how can the two be reconciled for those countries which had no Albin and no Kamprad – or did not have them in this order? And can the two be reconciled within the EU? The second question is thornier than the first one, for it presupposes an understanding of the 'architectural' rationale and mission of the EU itself. Is the EU a new 'home-in-the-making'? Or is it merely a 'commons' amongst distinct national homes – a level playing field for economic transactions? And in this latter case how can we make sure that the logic of the commons goes hand in hand (or, as a minimum, does not clash) with the logic of the homes?

Such questions lie today at the heart of political debates all over Europe. And they rank at the top of the preoccupations of ordinary people. European citizens are keen supporters of both 'solidarity' and 'Europe'. But they perceive an increasingly problematic link between the two. A quick look at some recent opinion surveys[1] reveals that:

- Solidarity and welfare receive overwhelming mass support as social values and policy goals in all countries. Of EU(15) respondents, 95 per cent think that 'helping others' is very important and significant majorities consider 'social security', 'equality' and 'the spirit of cooperation' to be precious legacies of the twentieth century.
- EU membership and European integration are also the object of widespread support in the vast majority of member states (EU(25) average: 54 per cent). Despite their 'no' to the referendums on the Constitutional Treaty, 51 per cent of the French and 77 per cent of the Dutch still thought in June 2005 that 'EU membership is a good thing'.[2]
- Yet there are fears about the EU as well: more than half the respondents – the EU(25) average – are afraid that European integration may lead to a loss of social benefits, while more than three-quarters are anxious about job losses. The fear that rising numbers of immigrants may pose a threat to the domestic economy and cultural identities is also linked, in mass attitudes, to the integration process.
- Probably as a consequence of such fears, citizens tend to be very jealous of the decision-making prerogatives of their own governments in the core areas of social protection: about two-thirds of Eurobarometer respondents declare that responsibility for 'health care and social security' should remain firmly in the hands of national authorities, without interference from the EU.

These figures do confirm the existence of a tension, uneasiness in linking or reconciling 'solidarity' with 'Europe'. Both receive mass support, but only to the extent that they keep on separate tracks and that solidarity remains a national affair. This popular preference for separation rests on something deeper than a cognitive 'quick fix' – on something that is neatly captured by the Swedish metaphor of the welfare state as the people's home.

Social sharing builds on 'closure'. It presupposes the existence of a clearly demarcated and cohesive community, whose members feel that they belong to the same whole and that they are linked by reciprocity ties vis-à-vis common risks and similar needs. Since the nineteenth century (in some countries since much earlier) the nation-state has provided the closure conditions for the development of sharing sentiments and practices within its own territory.

European integration, on the contrary, rests on 'opening': on weakening or tearing apart those spatial demarcations and closure practices that nation-states have built around themselves. Free movement, free ('undistorted') competition and non-discrimination have been the guiding principles of the integration process. This process has undeniably produced a novel social aggregate – the 'Euro-polity' – whose individual members have become 'equals' in respect of economic and (most) civic transactions. But the establishment of an enlarged level playing field in these spheres has not (yet?) fostered bonding dynamics among the new equals. Based as it is on the logic of economic opening, European integration is programmatically geared towards the expansion of individual options and choices, often challenging those closure conditions that sustain social solidarity. Therefore, it is quite understandable that ordinary citizens remain 'nationalist' when asked about the latter and express a preference for keeping the EU away from this sphere.

The problem is, however, that the 'separate tracks' solution – that is, the insulation of national social protection systems from the dynamic of economic integration and from supranational interference – long ago ceased to be viable. When the integration project was launched in the 1950, behind the federalist discourse on an 'ever closer union' and functional spillovers, the idea was precisely that the European communities would concentrate on economic opening, while the member states would keep for themselves the sphere of solidarity and welfare. Since the 1980s, however, the division of labour has become increasingly untenable: advances in economic integration prompted the introduction of direct or indirect constraints also in the sphere of domestic sharing arrangements. The establishment of Economic and Monetary Union made such constraints very explicit in the course of the 1990s, giving rise to the mass fears that are revealed by opinion surveys.

The 2000s have witnessed a growing politicization of the 'opening' issue and, in some countries more than others, of the integration process as a whole. The most evident manifestation of this politicization occurred in the spring of 2005, during the campaigns for the French and Dutch referendums, which rejected the Constitutional Treaty. Not surprisingly, questions regarding the social sharing dimension (who shares what, and how much? Is it appropriate for the EU to interfere in such decision? More crucially still, is the EU undermining national welfare arrangements and labour markets?) play a central role in this process, while national governments find themselves increasingly sandwiched between the growing constraints imposed by

the EU on the one hand and the national basis of their political legitimacy on the other – a legitimacy which remains highly dependent on
decisions in the social protection domain.

According to many commentators, the best strategy for coping with
this situation is to sweep sensitive questions about the social implications of integration under the carpet, stick to the pre-Convention
status quo (with minor institutional fixes, if absolutely necessary) and
concentrate on what's really important for the future of Europe, i.e.
economic reforms for competitiveness and growth.[3] Competitiveness
and growth are fundamental objectives, no doubt. The fact is,
however, that without providing some answers to the sensitive questions about their social implications, economic reforms are unlikely to
make much progress – at both national and supranational levels. The
French and Dutch examples show that large, pro-status quo coalitions
(whatever the actual motives of their supporters) can rapidly emerge
in domestic political markets. If it is true that solidarity and social
cohesion rank so high in people's preferences and expectations and
that the EU is increasingly perceived as a potential threat to such
values, then it seems wise to openly address these perceptions and
worries, identifying their objective roots and pondering about possible responses. The European Union is not likely ever to turn into a
'people's home' in the thick, Swedish sense of the expression. But
surely it can be made more 'homey' than it is currently perceived by a
growing number of its citizens. As a minimum, efforts are needed to
persuade citizens that the large 'commons' (the Single Market) which
has emerged in their neighbourhood is not a negative threat for their
homes, but a positive opportunity for all the inhabitants of the homes.
As we shall argue below, this does not entail a watering down of the
current agenda for economic reforms, welfare state modernization
and more market liberalization. But it does require a delicate 'nesting'
of such agenda in a wider and more socially friendly institutional and
discursive framework.

The next section of this chapter will suggest a diagnosis of the
objective, institutional roots of the current predicament.[4] The subsequent sections will discuss scenarios and proposals on how to possibly address it.

Opening the people's home: gains and pains

Let us start with a bit of history and some general concepts. As is well
known, the European welfare state was born in the last decades of the

nineteenth century, through the establishment of compulsory public social insurance, a new innovative technique that allowed the pooling of risks among wide social collectivities and thus made redistribution towards the less fortunate enormously more efficient than all prior forms of social protection. Compulsory insurance rests on 'closure' principles: it 'locks' entire segments of the population (or the whole population, in certain cases) into redistributive schemes backed by the authority of the state, which imposes obligations and confers entitlements on those who are 'in', while rigorously keeping out all those who do not qualify, those who do not meet the requirements for admission. Compulsory insurance is a form of 'bounding' that has both a social and a territorial component: it typically envisages rules of affiliation linked to individual status (e.g. being an employee, an unemployed or an elderly person); such rules are binding in respect of a given territory, normally the entire national territory. Social protection schemes are thus 'bounded spaces', with a clearly defined membership and territorial scope. Boundaries and compulsory affiliation play a fundamental role in securing and stabilizing redistribution over time – especially 'vertical' redistribution from stronger to weaker groups and individuals.

The period between the end of the Second World War and the oil crisis of the mid-1970s is known as the 'Golden Age' of national welfare. In those three decades social insurance rapidly expanded its coverage and its generosity and started to offer widespread security (occasionally, even security *cum* comfort) to millions of 'little people' – elderly people, poor people, disabled people, etc. – whose life-chances had traditionally been modest and haphazard.[5] Welfare state-building was accompanied by an unprecedented political and ideological consensus on the role of the state in society and in the economy. This consensus was important not only for its distributive outcomes, but also for its bonding effects: it created strong solidarity bonds (horizontal and vertical) throughout the social structure, as well as strong political bonds between ordinary citizens and state elites, through the mediation of interest groups (especially trade unions) and mass parties. The expansion of welfare programmes has consolidated distinct national 'communities of trust', it has contributed to anchoring democracy to society and to feeding a virtuous circle of economic modernization and growth, political legitimation and stability, social cohesion and solidarity.

During *les trente glorieuses* (1945–75), being a citizen entailed a wide range of civic, political and social rights; but the space of national citizenship was not easy to enter for outsiders and not easy to exit for insiders – at least on a permanent basis and with full access to rights. Vis-à-vis the exterior, citizenship operated as a filtering device, as an *instrument* of closure.[6] But, inside the boundaries, citizens were 'captives' of their nation-states: they had guaranteed freedoms and entitlements, but also the corresponding set of obligations and constraints. Cross-national movements were indeed possible, but at the risk of suffering significant losses in terms of protections. This state of captivity did not affect only the sphere of citizenship. Thick boundaries existed in those decades around most of the other functional spheres of each nation (including the market), and most of these closures reinforced the welfare state. As national tax bases (including capital) and national consumers were 'locked in', the distributive and regulatory costs of the welfare state could be easily reflected in prices without jeopardizing the profitability of capitalist production.[7]

When it was launched in the 1950s, the project of European integration did not intend to challenge the institutional foundations of national social contracts. Quite to the contrary: the Founding Fathers and most of the relevant national elites conceived of European integration as a project capable of creating and sustaining a virtuous circle between *open* economies and outward-looking economic policies on the one hand and *closed* welfare states and inward-looking social policy on the other:[8] according to Gilpin's famous formulation, the maxim then was 'Smith abroad, Keynes at home'.[9] The limited competences assigned by the Rome Treaty to the supranational level in the social policy sphere reflected the explicit objective of a division of labour between national and EC rulers that was seen as virtuous for both the market and the welfare state; it also rested on an implicit *favour*, a positive orientation of the Founding Fathers vis-à-vis social protection, high labour standards and full employment objectives, whose national scope and closure preconditions were taken for granted and thus assumed as inherently non-problematic for a project essentially aimed at creating a customs union. European integration and the welfare state were to remain only 'loosely coupled': the EEC did not need to meddle in welfare issues, because these lay at the core of domestic agendas, buttressed by national political compromises and legal orders already well tuned in socially protective directions.

With the passing of time, however, the scope of the integration process has gradually widened and its momentum has accelerated. Cross-national boundaries have been extensively redefined, differentiated, reduced or altogether cancelled in a growing number of policy fields. An internal market has been established, resting on the free circulation of goods, persons, capitals and services. A common currency has been introduced in the Eurozone, accompanied by rather rigid constraints on domestic fiscal policies. A tightly monitored competition regime forbids national closure practices that are judged as market distortions by supranational authorities. Firms, capitals and more generally 'tax bases' are no longer captives of the nation-state, thus greatly altering the traditional economic context of redistributive arrangements and restricting the margins of manoeuvre for sectoral, occupational and, in general, 'social' cross-subsidizations within domestic labour markets.

European integration has moreover affected in a *direct* way the boundaries of national citizenship spaces and of the institutional core of the welfare state, i.e. compulsory social insurance. The traditional link between rights and territory has become much looser: for most civic and social rights, the filtering role of nationality has been neutralized. In the field of social insurance proper, a detailed set of rules has been established for coordinating social security regimes in case of cross-border movements, while EU competition rules have started to affect certain aspects of these regimes at the national level.[10] The exclusionary or discriminatory prerogatives of national governments vis-à-vis outsiders have been severely restricted and the very 'sovereignty to bound' of the nation-state in the social sphere has been put in question. Social insurance contributions and benefits have become portable across the Union; patients can seek medical treatment in any EU hospital; pension funds have been allowed not only to invest, but also to shop for clients and 'sponsors' in all member states; the treatment of legal immigrants (including third country nationals) has been harmonized across the Union, envisaging access not only to social insurance, but to means-tested social assistance as well; and private (third pillar) insurance has been almost fully liberalized. The principles of compulsory membership and of public monopoly over social insurance schemes are still shielded from the EU competition regime, but only to the extent that certain conditions apply (e.g. the adoption of PAYGO financing).[11] With respect to *les trente glorieuses*, the institutional framework which is currently in force represents a true quantum leap in terms of 'opening' for at least three reasons: (1) the extremely wide scope of coordination rules: both the material scope (i.e. the range of benefits and schemes covered by coordination rules) and its personal scope (i.e. the range of eligible groups and persons); (2) the 'tighter coupling' between social protection and the internal market, which have become increasingly intertwined with each other; (3) the high degree of 'juridification' of both the coordination and the competition regimes of the EU , a juridification emblematically represented by the powers of a supranational court enjoying supremacy over domestic courts. The sovereign 'right to bound' is still there: but it is no longer an absolute right, subject as it is to the limits posed by the EU competition and coordination regimes – which specify the conditions under which it can be legitimately exercised – and by the judicial review of the European Court of Justice.

This opening of the 'people's homes' on the side of the EU was well-meant and has brought enormous advantages. The Single Market project was elaborated in order to respond to the threats of stagnation and Euro-sclerosis, with a view to revamping 'growth, competitiveness and employment'. As underlined by Giddens, the EU GDP is now significantly larger than it would have been without enhanced market integration.[12] Liberalizations have made several goods and services more affordable to consumers (let us think of low-cost air fares), enhancing the range of options available to them; in certain areas (e.g. health and safety) market integration has also brought about more consumer protection and higher labour standards. In addition, the tighter coupling between economic integration and national systems of social protection has prompted several countries to undertake much-needed distributive rationalizations: not all the cross-subsidizations mentioned above served genuine social justice objectives. More generally, the establishment of the EMU has encouraged a thorough re-examination of the financial bases of European welfare states, of the quantity and quality of their spending commitments and modes of financing, also in the light of endogenous transformations and challenges (most notably: demographic challenges). In other words, the deepening of integration has generated tangible benefits and beneficial 'modernizing' spurs to national systems of social protection. Since the early 1990s, important and incisive reforms have already been introduced in most countries – a fact that is less acknowledged in public debates than it deserves.[13]

But 'opening' has caused strains and problems too. Certain sectors, occupations, territorial areas and social groups have gained; others have lost: the opportunity structure of Europe's political economy has witnessed dramatic upheavals since the mid-1980s.[14] Traditional social and political equilibriums that had formed around national redistributive arrangements have been destabilized. Sizeable segments of the electorate have matured growing feelings of insecurity: about jobs, social benefits and, generally, intrusions from outside. In many countries there are clear symptoms of 'Euro-fatigue': for the sacrifices made to join EMU, on the one hand, but also for the gap between Euro-expectations and Euro-deliveries (regarding prices, growth, employment, etc.) on the other. An interesting Eurobarometer survey on globalization reveals that 20 per cent of EU(15) respondents consider their national economy to be 'too open' and 26 per cent consider the European Union to be 'too liberal' – with peaks of

34 per cent in France and Germany.[15] A more recent survey covering Germany, France, Spain, the UK and Poland shows that Europe has come to be perceived as a disappointment and even as a source of worry on the very grounds on which it traditionally based its 'output legitimacy': 75 per cent of respondents are convinced that the Euro has caused a rise in prices, 30 per cent (43 per cent in France and in Poland) declare that EU membership has implied a decline in economic prosperity and 30 per cent are convinced that EU membership makes no difference at all for prosperity.[16] Behind these numbers there is a heterogeneous mix of socioeconomic profiles and ideological orientations. But such numbers cannot be ignored by those national and EU leaders who are currently in charge of Europe's policy agenda. However desirable from an economic point of view, a policy platform predominantly centred on 'opening' risks to generate various forms of 'political backlash', i.e. dynamics of defensive mobilizations around the status quo, increasingly framed in Euro-sceptic terms and accompanied by anti-EU orientations. Are there ways of avoiding this scenario?

Casting Lisbon in a 'social nest': a rebalancing act

As was anticipated at the end of the first section, our proposal is that of 'nesting' the economic reform and 'modernization' objectives in a wider, more socially oriented discursive and institutional framework.[17] The deepening of market integration and the Lisbon goals on competitiveness, growth, labour market and welfare state modernization should remain, no doubt, fundamental priorities of the EU policy agenda. The 'modernization' agenda can be further improved and fine-tuned in programmatic terms and definitely needs to be stepped up in terms of actual implementation, especially in the big continental countries of the Eurozone. But this agenda ought to be widened and enriched. In particular, it should become clearer that these economic objectives are prioritized not per se but as vehicles for social progress, i.e. as instruments for the expansion of the life-chances of Europe's citizens and the consolidation of their 'homes'. The European social model(s) must become more market-compatible and even more competition-friendly: as mentioned above, if intelligently steered, reforms in this direction can bring about sizeable gains on both efficiency and equity grounds. But in its turn the EU must clarify and upgrade its social dimension and more openly reveal to its citizens its solidarity-friendly face.

As the 'nesting' task is urgent, it must be undertaken with building blocks that are already available. These instruments are basically the following: fundamental rights, open policy coordination and, of course, the Constitutional Treaty itself. If it is true that the latter is doomed to remain 'frozen' in the short/medium term, nothing hampers far-sighted EU leaders from discreetly exploiting its discursive and institutional appeal while waiting for political conditions to be ripe again for a full ratification.

A bit of historical reconstruction might be useful, again, to articulate our argument. The issue of how to reconcile economic and social policy objective at the EU level is certainly not new. The idea of a 'social dimension of the internal market' made its appearance in the wake of the Single European Act. Some significant measures of positive integration started to be adopted towards the end of the 1980s, establishing common social standards in a number of spheres (health and safety at work, gender equality, contractual relationships, and so on).[18] In the second half of the 1990s the reconciliation issue appeared explicitly on the EU agenda and the turning point came with the Amsterdam Treaty of 1997. While remaining aloof from any suggestion of regulatory harmonization from above (let alone the promotion of supranational redistributive schemes), the new approach inaugurated with the treaty on the EU goes beyond the traditional mix of cohesion measures and the setting of minimum social standards. This approach was and is intended to embed national systems of social protection within a two-pronged institutional framework: fundamental social rights on the one hand and open policy coordination on the other. The first element is aimed at supplying a positive list of enumerated social freedoms and entitlements recognized and upheld by the EU legal order: the general but common content of EU citizenship in its social dimension. The second element (the open method of coordination or OMC) is aimed at supplying in its turn both a common set of routinized procedures and a common set of policy goals and targets capable of encouraging and supporting reforms at the domestic level while orienting such reforms in a convergent direction.

A catalogue of social rights recognized by the EU has been included within the Charter of Fundamental Rights, first proclaimed by the European Council at the Nice summit of 2000 and subsequently included as Part II of the Treaty Establishing a Constitution for Europe. To be sure, the rights listed under Title IV (devoted to 'Solidarity') of the Charter are nothing new with respect to what already exists in the member states.[19] Moreover, in strictly legal terms the recognition of such rights in the new treaty has not made them directly enforceable rights; rather, they have the status of 'programmatic principles' or 'aspirational rights', and are thus endowed with a much lesser binding character than other civic or political rights such as free movement or non-discrimination.[20] Despite these limitations, the codification and (future) constitutionalization of something akin to a bill of (social) rights must be regarded as a very significant innovation,[21] which could promote a normative and symbolic rebalancing of the Union's overall mission and thus might prompt a gradual redress of the traditional asymmetry between the economic and social dimensions of integration. How could this rebalancing actually unfold? Initially, through jurisprudence. In fact, the codification of fundamental rights offers to the European Court of Justice a novel 'anchor' for (re)orienting its rulings in a more socially oriented direction. In the past on several occasions the ECJ has already played an important role in upholding social sharing objectives – sometimes by confirming the legitimacy of closure (e.g. as regards compulsory affiliation to social insurance), sometimes by confirming the legitimacy of opening (e.g. as regards non-discrimination of immigrants within social protection). The constitutionalization of a bill of rights will allow the court to exercise this function in a more consistent, firm and continuous way. In the longer run, this constitutionalization could contribute to gradually shifting the centre of gravity of the EU political production towards some middle point between the safeguard of 'freedoms' and the stabilization of 'entitlements' – the two sides of life-chances in the European tradition.

The second prong of the new institutional framework is the open method of coordination (OMC), a new instrument of multilevel governance in the social policy sphere, initially inaugurated in the field of labour policy with the European Employment Strategy (EES) in 1997.[22] In the context of the Lisbon Strategy launched in 2000, the OMC has been subsequently extended to the field of social inclusion (2001), pensions (2003) and, more recently, health care. From our perspective, the OMC is promising both from a procedural as well as from a substantive point of view. Procedurally, the OMC is centred on the following steps: (a) the setting of broad objectives and guidelines for each sector of intervention; (b) the translation of these objectives into national action plans periodically prepared by member state governments; (c) the monitoring and evaluation of such plans through peer review and benchmarking exercises; and (d) a comparative assessment (with the possibility of issuing recommendations, in the case of employment policies) performed jointly by the Commission and the Council, feeding back into the first step at each subsequent round. From a substantive point of view, the OMC specifies for each sector the priorities for action with a view to orienting the content and direction of policy change. The substantive priorities for employment, social inclusion, pensions, and health care are set out in table 1.[23] While a few of these priorities reflect the economic and financial preoccupations typical of EMU discourse, most of them do speak a different language. This is particularly the case with the social inclusion objectives. As noted by Mary Daly, in the social inclusion process 'there is a vision of the good society . . . one where people have access to a range of social goods, where family solidarity prevails, where life is not blighted by life crises and where, politically, all relevant bodies (and especially those experiencing poverty and social exclusion) are mobilized. Hence the community is seen as political community.'[24] Though primarily considered a procedural innovation, the OMC does have an important substantive dimension. Its 'homey' symbolic and policy agenda can work in the same rebalancing direction as the Charter of Fundamental Rights.

Based on the experience since the turn of the century, several doubts have emerged in the debate about the adequacy of fundamental rights and the various OMC processes as counterweights to 'the temple of competition'.[25] It may be true that looked at from a 'perfectionist' angle, the social dimension of EU citizenship remains conspicuously 'thin', even in the wake of an eventual defrosting and future ratification of the Constitutional Treaty. But perfectionism is

Table 1   The employment, social inclusion, pension, and health care 'processes': main substantive objectives

Employment: overarching objectives
- full employment
- quality and productivity at work
- social cohesion and inclusion

Social inclusion: common objectives
- to facilitate participation in employment and access by all to the resources, rights, goods and services
- to prevent the risks of exclusion
- to help the most vulnerable
- to mobilize all relevant bodies

Pensions: common objectives (broad headings)
- safeguarding the capacity of systems to meet their social objectives (adequacy)
- maintaining their financial sustainability
- meeting changing social needs (modernization)

Health care and care for the elderly: long-term objectives
- accessibility
- quality
- financial viability

seldom an appropriate yardstick for assessing the nature and prospects of a new institution. Through an intelligent political steering, the institutional configuration outlined by the Constitutional Treaty might incrementally originate several virtuous developments, for example exploiting the interaction between – precisely – fundamental rights and the OMC. Such interaction may in fact trigger two parallel trends: (a) a gradual 'hardening' of the OMC objectives which, through the mediation of fundamental rights and ECJ jurisprudence, may acquire a more binding character vis-à-vis domestic policy environments and choices; and (b) the establishment of systematic procedures for the actual implementation and monitoring of fundamental rights at the domestic level through the mediation of the employment, social inclusion and (to a lesser extent) the pension and health care processes.[26]

The first testing ground for both developments could be the sphere of social inclusion and in particular the 'right to sufficient resources', which features explicitly in the catalogue of fundamental rights and is at least indirectly evoked by the broad objectives of the social inclusion process. As is known, the establishment of a common guarantee of sufficient resources appeared on the EU agenda in the early 1990s.[27] The Commission's proposal was blocked but has since remained part of policy and academic debates.[28] If the narrow path resting on fundamental rights and the OMC remains open or possibly gets wider, then the adoption of an EU minimum income guarantee for 'the most vulnerable' might be its first tangible institutional step. Such a move might also find adequate support from public opinion. We said in the first section that ordinary citizens are jealous of the decision-making prerogatives of their national governments in the core sectors of social protection. But, according to the Eurobarometer, in the field of poverty and social exclusion a majority of 62 per cent would indeed favour joint national–EU decision-making.[29]

Fundamental rights, the OMC and its 'processes' (in particular, the social inclusion process) and the Constitutional Treaty are thus the most obvious and readily available building blocks that can be used in order to embed the 'competitiveness and growth' agenda in a more socially friendly symbolic and institutional framework. Is there a direct and explicit way for visualizing the overall configuration that would originate from such a 'nesting' project? Can a map be drawn that could serve as reference point for policy-makers and the wider public? An attempt at drawing such a map is shown in figure 1.

At the centre of the figure we find the national welfare state (space A): a reformed and 'modernized' welfare state, possibly reconfigured in a decentralized fashion and complemented by a number of

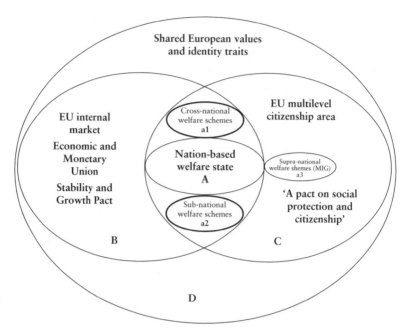

Figure I
Nesting the nation-based welfare state within the EU architecture

novel transnational forms of sharing, such as cross-border pension funds covering certain occupational groups, trans-frontier health care or labour market programmes, and so on. Each national welfare state is nested, however, within two wider and common regulatory spaces. Space B is already in place: it is the Single Market, resting on free-movement provisions and competition rules – and, in the EMU countries, on a common currency, a common monetary policy and common budgetary rules. Space C is the novelty and can be called the emerging 'EU multilevel citizenship space', resting on a common (and adequately 'hardened') catalogue of fundamental civic, political, and social rights – including, if it should prove feasible in the future, an EU 'guarantee to sufficient resources', possibly funded directly by the EU budget.[30] As regards social rights, it should be made clear that the new regulatory space C would *not* force a top-down harmonization of domestic social citizenship regimes. Its function would be twofold: (1) it should explicitly and officially affirm that the European Union recognizes and respects citizens' entitlements to protection against social risks; (2) it should establish general principles about the tasks of EC law and the tasks of national legal orders as regards the actual content and implementation of such entitlements. To a large extent, these two functions are already adumbrated in Article 34, Title IV of the Nice Charter.[31] It really is a pity that during the constitutional debate national publics were not given a chance to grasp the highly innovative character of this article – both as a protective shield for national social protection institutions vis-à-vis the pressure of 'negative integration' and as a spur for more socially friendly jurisprudence and legislation on the side of the EU.

Space C also includes the various OMC processes, in both their substantive and governance dimensions. Space B and space C overlap underneath space A. This overlap is meant to signal two facts: first, some civic rights (typically the four freedoms) by their nature belong to both spaces; second, the economic and budgetary policies of space B are (or ought to be) programmatically linked to the social policies of space C.

There may be other, more sophisticated forms of visualizing the overall institutional framework needed for overcoming the current predicament of the national welfare state and for countering the 'political backlash' scenario outlined at the end of the last section. The purpose of the figure is purely illustrative. What matters are the two important messages that the figure intends to convey:

1 The 'people's home' – i.e. the nation-based welfare states – should remain/be placed at the centre of the institutional architecture of the EU. The centrality of nation-based welfare provision is not only a 'side-payment' that has to be paid in order to avoid political backlash in the wake of increased market integration. National welfare states serve essential integrative functions within European polities and societies. An adequate level of social integration is a pre-requisite for a thriving market performance.

2 A new regulatory space should be developed, with a view to programmatically link the 'competitiveness and growth' agenda with a parallel agenda, centred on the expansion and fair distribution of life-chances for all EU citizens. Life-chances are not only a matter of (market) 'options', but are also a matter of 'ligatures', of normative and social bonds that tie individuals and social groups to one another.[32] Life-chances rest on a delicate (and dynamic) balance of 'opening' and 'closure', a balance that needs constant institutional 'gardening'.

The figure includes a third, outer (and thinner) circle: a sociocultural space consisting of a (limited) 'core' of values, symbols, and identity traits shared by all EU citizens. This space should underpin the other three spaces and provide a basic reservoir of systemic loyalty for the functioning of the whole Euro-polity and the strengthening of its legitimacy. The formation of such a space is inherently difficult and problematic, given the robustness of state-national cultural and institutional legacies. But loyalty-building is a process, which – to the extent that it actually happens – rests on the build-up of incremental changes: in particular, the gradual increase in the mutual relevance and mutual trust among the various European nationalities, in the wake of denser transactions and contacts.[33] Generational replacement is likely to accelerate such process. If we look for them, we do find some empirical signs that already point in this direction. For example, a Eurobarometer survey of 1999 asked respondents the following question: 'Is there a European cultural identity shared by all Europeans?'[34] On average, 49 per cent of EU(15) respondents answered negatively and only 38 per cent answered positively. But, interestingly, the percentage of agreement was higher among educated and especially among young people. The young are also much more likely to feel 'national and European' than the average population. This suggests that generational replacement may indeed work in favour of greater 'we-feelingness'. It must also be noted that a 38 per cent agreement is not negligible at all. There seems to be, in other words, a sizeable 'capital' on which to build.

Urgently needed: political leadership and action

National leaders (including centre-left leaders) have so far manifested little interest in social Europe. They have tended to treat social policies as a preserve of domestic sovereignty, largely detached or detachable from the dynamics of European integration. They have behaved, in other words, as if the original 'division of labour' between the supranational and the national levels were still in place. The political earthquakes that took place in France and the Netherlands in the spring of 2005 should, however, have alerted them that 'loose coupling' is no longer viable and that some explicit compromise must be found at the highest political level, with a view to reconciling within the EU institutional framework the reasons and 'logics' of the two prime drivers of progress in the European tradition, i.e. the marketplace and the welfare state. Once again, like in the 1950s, the integration project must be (re)cast with a view to rescuing the financial and institutional foundations of the national social models, in the face of changed internal and external transformations.

As argued above, the obvious springboards for such recasting are the instruments that are already available, and in particular the 'open coordination' processes in the field of social protection and social inclusion.

The existing EU agenda offers a unique opportunity for catching up. In the wake of decisions taken during the 2005 spring European Council, a new departure is now envisaged for 'open coordination' in the fields of social protection and social inclusion. The Commission has already issued a Communication outlining a reformed and 'stream-lined' institutional framework for this new departure.[35] European leaders thus have an immediate chance for making the caring side of Lisbon more visible and more vigorous.

At the national level, this could be achieved by turning the prepa-ration of the various National Action Plans into a serious occasion for elaborating and discussing domestic strategies for reconciling competitiveness and cohesion, the market and the welfare state (a modernized welfare state) in the framework of the broad objectives jointly defined at the supranational level. The strongest criticism against the OMC has been so far its low political salience within domestic policy systems and public spheres, the lack of involvement of national parliaments and key stakeholder groups. Research has indicated that the actual picture is perhaps less gloomy than gener-ally perceived: a growing mobilization of social actors is indeed taking place around both the employment and the social inclusion process. But more efforts must be made in this direction, through the deployment of appropriate procedural and possibly financial incentives.

At the EU level, national leaders could give a strong and visible political signal about the importance of the social dimension: for example, by issuing a joint official statement or declaration (which might take the symbolic form of a 'Pact on Social Protection and Citizenship': see figure 1 above) supporting the relaunch of open policy coordination in the field of social protection and especially social inclusion. The latter is indeed the 'process' that has the highest legitimizing potential for the EU. A specific mandate for reconciling the economic and social sides of the Lisbon Strategy and making con-crete proposals (on procedures and substance: e.g. improved bench-marking and more tangible, financial incentives) could be given to the newly established committee of 'Ministers for Lisbon'.

Such a political signal would be decisive: precisely because its sym-bolic and policy potential has not been adequately exploited so far, the OMC may soon be condemned to evaporation and oblivion. There are no other instruments at hand in the short and medium run to respond, politically, to the 'anti-opening' (anti-market, anti-capitalist, anti-immigrants, anti-enlargements, etc.) tide which is rapidly surging in many member states. Revamping the 'caring' dimension of Europe through an instrument such as the OMC may itself prove inadequate or insufficient. After all, social Europe already has an *acqui* of hard law, which needs to be fine-tuned and further developed. But now we need a swift political move: the reform of soft coordination in the fields of social protection and social inclusion has the advantage of being already on the agenda – and is a flexible and promising instrument, which deserves to be given a real chance.

Let us conclude with a final remark, less centred on current political conjunctures and deadlines than on the *longue durée* of the integration project. At the beginning of this chapter we said that the early steps of supranational integration were accompanied by an ambitious discourse about an 'ever closer union' of a quasi-federal type between six relatively homogeneous founding member states. But de facto, the project was that of 'rescuing the nation-state' after the catastrophes of two wars. The expansion of domestic social protection systems (the national social models) was made possible by the dividends of economic growth – an exceptionally rapid growth triggered and sustained by market integration and intensifying cross-border trade flow. Fifty years on, we have to wonder whether the original project should not be turned on its head. If the diagnosis of this analysis is correct, it may in fact be wise to tone down explicit federal ambitions and recast European integration as a project explicitly aimed at rescuing what has in the meantime become a core ingredient of the nation-state itself, namely the social protection systems. In this perspective, the common and coordinated policies of the EU (especially space B of figure 1) should be adjusted and publicly justified as the most effective instruments for sustaining and fostering these (modernized) systems, through more efficient and more integrated markets, higher growth and employment levels. The 'ever closer union' may still come, with its own slow pace and possibly a variable geometry: but it would come as a silent and non-intrusive by-product of this new and critical rescue operation.

Notes

A shorter version of this chapter – and, in particular, its conclusions – was included within the 'discussion papers' distributed by the UK Presidency at the European Council held at Hampton Court on 27 October 2005.

1 European Commission, *How Europeans See Themselves* (Luxembourg, 2001) and *Eurobarometer no. 62* (Luxembourg, 2004).

2 The UK is the only member state where a plurality of respondents declares that EU membership is 'a bad thing'.

3 The following quote is from an article of the *Financial Times* published prior to the Hampton Court European Council of October 2005 and represents well this point of view: 'The EU has become a scapegoat for failures in national politics. It has as a result been weakened in its ability to do the things it must do: ensure trade and competition that force adjustment on companies and countries. If the summit were to agree that this is indeed the role of the EU, with the rest up to the member states, it would have achieved something not just important, but surprising' (*Financial Times*, 20 October, p. 4). The negative tone in which the Anglophone press discusses the issue of 'social models' is also epitomized by the title of a 'Charlemagne' editorial which appeared in *The Economist* (1–7 October 2005): 'Choose your poison' – the poisons being, precisely, national social models.

4 For a more general and articulated formulation of the diagnosis, see Maurizio Ferrera, *The Boundaries of Welfare. European Integration and the New Spatial Politics of Social Protection* (Oxford: Oxford University Press, 2005).

5 See G. Esping-Andersen, *The Three Worlds of Welfare Capitalism* (Cambridge: Polity, 1990).

6 Rogers Brubaker, *Citizenship and Nationhood in France and Germany* (Cambridge, MA: Harvard University Press, 1992).

7 See F. Scharpf, *Governing in Europe* (Oxford: Oxford University Press, 1999), and F. Scharpf and V. Schmidt, eds., *Welfare and Work in Open Economies*, 2 vols. (Oxford: Oxford University Press, 2000).

8 See A. Milward, *The European Rescue of the Nation State*, 2nd edn (London: Routledge, 2000), which argues that in the 1950s and 1960s European integration 'rescued' the nation-states of Europe.

9 See R. Gilpin, *The Political Economy of International Relations* (Princeton: Princeton University Press, 1987).

10 See S. Leibfreid and P. Pierson, 'Social policy', in H. Wallace and W. Wallace, eds., *Policy-Making in the European Union*, 4th edn (Oxford: Oxford University Press, 2000).

11 These conditions have been specified by various ECJ rulings. There is no principle in the treaties that explicitly shields public social insurance from competition law. See Ferrera, *The Boundaries of Welfare*.

12 Anthony Giddens, chapter 1 in this volume.

13 See M. Ferrera and A. Hemerijck, 'Recalibrating European welfare regimes', in J. Zeitlin and D. Trubeck, eds., *Governing Work and Welfare in a New Economy* (Oxford: Oxford University Press, 2003); A. Hemerijck, 'The self-transformation of the European social model', in G. Esping-Andersen et al., *Why We need a New Welfare State*.

14 See S. Bartolini, *Restructuring Europe* (Oxford: Oxford University Press, 2005).

15 European Commission, *Globalization, Eurobarometer no.151b* (Luxembourg, 2004)

16 See TNS-SOFRES, *L'Europe vue par les Européens*, Paris, 2005 (<www.tns-sofres.com/etudes/pol/051005_europe_n.htm>).

17 On the concept and theory of 'nesting' in institutional configurations, see V. Aggarwal, ed., *Institutional Designs for a Complex World* (Cornell: Cornell University Press, 1998).

18 See D. Hine and H. Kassim, eds., *Beyond the Market: The EU and National Social Policy* (London: Routledge, 1998); M. Rhodes, 'Defending the social contract', in Hine and Kassim, eds., *Beyond the Market*.

19 The list includes: workers' right to information and consultation within the undertaking (art. 27); right of collective bargaining and action (art. 28); right of access to placement services (art. 29); protection in the event of unjustified dismissal (art. 30); fair and just working conditions (art. 31); prohibition of child labour and protection of young people at work (art. 32); protection of family and professional life (art. 33); rights to social security and assistance (art. 34); right to health care (art. 35); right of access to services of general economic interest (art. 36); right to environmental protection (art. 37) and to consumer protection (art. 38).

20 The Treaty establishing a Constitution for Europe signed in Rome on 29 October 2004 treats most of the social provisions of the Charter of Fundamental Rights as 'principles'. In art. II-112.5 it specifies that 'The provisions of the Charter which contain principles *may* be implemented by legislative and executive acts taken by institutions, bodies, offices and agencies of the Union, and by acts of member states when they are implementing Union law, in the exercise of their respective powers. *They shall be judicially cognizable only in the interpretation of such acts and in the ruling on their legality*' (emphasis added). This article (and in particular the emphasized passages) confers on social rights a weaker binding character, subject to the mediation of other law-making bodies.

21 Some have said 'spectacular': J. Ziller, '*La nuova costituzione europea*', Bologna, Il Mulino (2003).

22 See M. Ferrera, A. Hemerijck and M. Rhodes, *The Future of Social Europe: Recasting Work and Welfare in the New Economy* (Oeiras: Celta Editora, 2000); C. De la Porte, P. Pochet and G. Room, 'Social benchmarking, policy-making and new governance in the EU', *Journal of European Social Policy*, 11, 1, (2001), pp. 297–307; M. J. Rodrigues, 'The open method of coordination as a new governance tool', *Europa Europe*, 2, 3 (special issue, 'L'evoluzione della governance europea', ed. Mario Telò) (Rome: Fondazione Istituto Gramsci, 2001); J. Zeitlin and P. Pochet, eds., *The Open Method of Coordination in Action* (Brussels: Peter Lang, 2005).

23 A redefinition of these objectives is expected to take place in 2006. See European Commission, *Working Together, Working Better: A New*

Framework for the Open Coordination of Social Protection and Inclusion Policies in the European Union (Brussels: COM, 2005, 706 final).

24 See Mary Daly, 'EU Social Policy after Lisbon', paper presented for the ESPAnet Conference, Oxford, September 2004.

25 See the discussion in L. Tsoukalis, 'Economic reform, further integration and enlargement: can Europe deliver?', in this volume (chapter 13).

26 See S. Sciarra, 'La constitutionnalisation de l'Europe Sociale entre droits sociaux fondamentaux et soft law', in O. De Schutter and P. Nihoul, eds., *Une Constitution pour l'Europe. Reflexions sur les Transformations du Droit de l'Union Européenne* (Brussels: Larcier, 2004); S. Smisman, 'EU Employment Policy', *WP Law*, 1 (Florence: EUI, 2004). An embryonic development in this direction is likely to unfold in the field of non-discrimination rights of disabled people: the OMC employment might become the instrument for monitoring the actual compliance with such rights within national labour markets and active employment policies. See EMCO (Employment Committee), *Disability Mainstreaming in the European Employment Strategy* (Brussels, EMCO 11/290605, 2005).

27 See M. Ferrera, M. Matsaganis and S. Sacchi, 'Open coordination against poverty: the new EU "Social Inclusion Process"', *Journal of European Social Policy*, 12 (2001), pp. 227–39.

28 See for example, T. Boeri and H. Bruecker, *The Impact of Eastern Enlargement on Employment and Wages in the EU Member States* (Brussels: DG Employment and Social Affairs, 2001). P. C. Schmitter and M. W. Bauer, 'A (modest) proposal for expanding social citizenship in the European Union', *Journal of European Social Policy*, 11, 1, (2001), pp. 55–66.

29 Only in Denmark and Sweden do slight majorities prefer exclusively national decision-making. See European Commission, *How Europeans See Themselves* (Luxembourg, 2001).

30 Space C also includes a pact for 'social protection and citizenship' as a possible counterweight to the pact on growth and stability: see below. The Social Agenda 2005–10 does mention initiatives in the poverty field and on minimum income schemes in particular: see European Commission, *Communication from the Commission on the Social Agenda* (Brussels: COM, 2005, 33 final).

31 'The Union recognizes and respects the entitlement to social security benefits and social services providing protection in cases such as maternity, illness, industrial accident, dependency and old age, and in the case of loss of employment, in accordance with the rules laid down by Community law and national laws and practices' (art. 34, para. 1).

32 See R. Dahrendorf, *The New Liberty* (London: Routledge, 1975).

33 See J. Delhey, *European Social Integration. From Convergence of Countries to Transnational Relations Between Peoples*, Discussion Paper SP1 2004–201 (Berlin: Wissenschaftszentrum, 2004).

34 European Commission, *How Europeans See Themselves* (Luxembourg: EC, 2001)

35 European Commission, *Working Together, Working Better: A New Framework for the Open Coordination of Social Protection and Inclusion Policies in the European Union* (Brussels: COM, 2005, 706 final).

15

A Common Social Justice Policy for Europe

Roger Liddle

'Social Europe' has long been a highly contested field. The vision commands wide consensus. It is seen as part and parcel of the concept of 'European values'. The debate over what 'social Europe' means received impetus from an unexpected quarter when in June 2005 Tony Blair declared to the European Parliament: 'I believe in Europe as a political project. I believe in a Europe with a strong and caring social dimension. I would never accept a Europe that was simply an economic market.' And he went on: 'Of course we need a social Europe. But it must be a social Europe that works.'

The only groups to dispute this vision would be right-wing apostles of a business environment untrammelled by 'corporatist' social dialogue, flexible labour markets and a narrow conception of fundamental rights, combined with those who take a strict 'subsidiarity' or 'hierarchy of competences' view of the division of powers between the EU and its member states. These of course were views that motivated John Major's government in successfully pressing for a UK opt-out from the Maastricht Treaty's Social Chapter in 1991 and they appear still to be held by the new Conservative leadership elected in Britain in 2005.

Giving social Europe policy substance, however, is not so easy or so consensual. Member states – and not just the UK – regard aspects of their national industrial relations systems as firmly in the reserved garden of national competences. Witness the German determination to prevent European interference with co-determination. EU social legislation has, with some difficulty, succeeded in establishing a minimum floor of employment rights. Some progress has been made in coordinating the standards necessary to the free movement of labour, such as social security rights. But social Europe has stalled in an unending conflict between two traditional models of European integration: the 'negative integration' model of removing barriers to the market, which is insufficient in the social field, except for measures that advance the free movement of labour, and a 'positive integration' model of legislative harmonization at EU level that is difficult to envisage in a diverse Union of 25.

This chapter argues that the EU needs both a new level of social ambition and a new model of European integration – not negative or positive, but a model of 'enabling integration'. The new level of ambition should be motivated by social justice, which, as the Introduction to this volume argues, is 'the key to unlocking the reforms that Europe needs to make but has so far found difficult to achieve'. The enabling integration model for the role of the EU sees it as an exemplar and a catalyst to supplement and incentivize reform efforts by member states. The European institutions can only play this role if there is success in establishing a common agenda among member states which represents both an effective compromise between the ideologies of right and left, but also between differing conceptions of national sovereignty and shared European interest: not an easy task given what appears to be a loss of confidence in European integration in many member states.

This chapter recommends the following steps. The Commission should devise a comprehensive social justice roadmap for member states to follow, which the European Council would endorse. An enabling Europe would assist the delivery of this roadmap through a modernized and expanded European budget to fulfil new tasks at European level, a revamped and strengthened open method of coordination with priority benchmarks and new budgetary instruments to incentivize reform. The modalities of these new instruments should be part of the comprehensive review of the European budget that the Commission has been invited to put forward in 2008.[1]

None of this will be easy. But if the European institutions give up on the attempt to be relevant to the central concerns of its citizens, and 'batten down the hatches' in a tactical retreat to their 'core competences', then globalization may not simply sweep aside old jobs in uncompetitive industries, but also cause such profound social and political dislocation in the member states as to undermine the historic achievements of European integration in the last half century.

Why has the current 'economic reform' agenda met with limited success?

The European Commission has been proclaiming the necessity of 'economic reform' since the 1994 Delors White Paper on Jobs.[2] The European employment strategy was launched in 1997 followed by the Lisbon Strategy in March 2000 'to make Europe the most economically dynamic and socially inclusive knowledge economy in the world by 2010'.[3]

Amongst policy-makers there is, superficially at least, remarkable consensus: that with fiscal and monetary policy constrained by first the Maastricht convergence criteria and then by the stability-oriented rules of EMU, a crucial means to tackle unemployment and raise growth potential lies through 'supply-side' reforms to product, capital and labour markets and welfare systems. The question of whether Europe has managed demand optimally is, of course, hotly debated, but few would argue that the supply-side agenda is not unimportant.

Many thought the coming of the Euro would exert a strong 'reform discipline'; unfortunately, its immediate impact appears to have had the opposite effect. Member states with weak currencies prior to the Euro have escaped the capital market discipline of fixed parities within the EMS; and their competitiveness has deteriorated. Clearly, this deterioration cannot continue indefinitely; high deficits threaten both the sustainability of public debt and the long-term sustainability of the social and political cohesion of member states in the grip of low growth and high structural unemployment.

Reform efforts have met with mixed success and have had little visible impact on economic performance in 'core Europe'. Since the mid-1990s, productivity growth in Europe has lagged further behind the United States, even though productivity per hour worked remains higher in countries like France and Belgium than the US average.[4] The overall employment participation rate in the EU(15) stood at 64.7 per cent in 2004, up a mere 1.3 per cent since 2000, and far away from Lisbon's 70 per cent target for 2010.[5]

Analyses of the EU's disappointing performance have shown that many reforms have actually taken place, though not always in a consistent direction,[6] but their impact has been muted. One possible explanation is the length of the 'incubation period' for reforms. Another is that reforms have been partial and not comprehensive in their scope;[7] for example, Germany's labour market reforms to improve incentives to work were not accompanied by sufficient deregulation of product and financial markets that would have stimulated the demand for jobs.

But there are also unresolved questions of policy design. How much is structural reform defined simply in terms of liberalization, flexibilization and, by implication, a smaller state – what some define as the OECD consensus, 'deregulate and in time, all will be well'?[8] What is envisaged as the role of public investment in both strengthening long-term competitiveness and creating new sources of competitive advantage (education, research, etc) and in financing welfare state reform to promote activation and new opportunity? Do the Euro's fiscal rules stifle such reforms, or can they be designed to facilitate them? These are not just questions of technical policy design, but ideological choice. At the time, Lisbon was seen as representing a modern 'third way' consensus for reform because it stressed the importance of investment in knowledge and social inclusion alongside open markets and labour market flexibility. But the third way consensus papered over these deeper questions.

In its review of Lisbon, the Kok Group[9] chose not to highlight these issues, but instead recommended a sharper focus on priorities and the 'naming and shaming' of member states. The newly appointed Barroso Commission endorsed a much sharper focus on 'Growth and Jobs',[10] but rejected 'naming and shaming' after objections from Germany. This highlighted a weakness at the heart of Lisbon: the European Union had proclaimed a reform strategy that in large measure only its member states could deliver. To resolve that dilemma, Barroso called for a 'partnership' between member states and the EU institutions that the European Council endorsed in March 2005, but observers were sceptical whether this partnership would be robust, meaningful and deliver results.[11] Yet all member states have at least submitted to the Commission, as required, their National Reform Programmes: the structures for a comprehensive system of multilateral surveillance have been put in place and can in future be built upon.

There will be many who argue that as reforms primarily involve national action, it is a mistake to imply an EU level of responsibility. But EU member states have a common interest in each other's prosperity: we share a highly integrated economic space. Even in the case of a big country like Britain, which is geographically separate from the continent and famously not a member of the Euro, well over half UK trade is with the Single Market. According to UK Treasury estimates, a 1 per cent improvement in the growth rate in the Eurozone would add one quarter of a percentage point to the UK growth rate.

In practice, it is impossible to separate the workings of the EU's core competence for the Single Market from social policies that are mainly the responsibility of member states. There is an unavoidable two-way relationship. Pressure to protect the social model at national level increases opposition to market opening reforms at EU level: witness the fevered debate over the proposed Services Directive. Conversely, failures to achieve economic reforms at EU level that raise Europe's growth potential undermine the financial sustainability of national social models.

Euro members are also in a special position of interdependence because of the interlinkages between welfare and labour market reforms and the common monetary policy. Successful reforms that increase labour market flexibility allow in principle a more accommodative monetary policy. However, incentives for individual Euro members to pursue politically difficult reforms are reduced, if other Euro members fail to follow suit, and the common interest rate remains unaffected.[12]

The obvious problem is the political saleability of Lisbon-type reforms. As Luxembourg's Prime Minister Jean-Claude Juncker memorably put it, 'We all know what we should do, but none of us knows how to get re-elected if we do it.'[13] The European discourse has been reform-heavy; the practice reform-light, or at best partial and incremental. Governments of both left and right have found it difficult to build effective political coalitions for reform. Some believe that only a cathartic political crisis at national level will force the pace of reform: the 'waiting for a Mrs Thatcher' argument. But it is arguable that British experience in the 1980s was unique – as well as partial and flawed – and unlikely to be repeated in continental Europe.[14] Notions of 'social dialogue' and proceeding by consensus still command widespread assent on the centre-right as well as the centre-left. Centre-right parties in government have found it extremely difficult to implement market-based structural reforms, because an underlying reform consensus is lacking and too many of their own natural supporters feel they stand to lose out. This is particularly true in countries with large public sectors and weak and overstaffed national administrations.

But it is not just a problem that the political will is there but the political challenge too great; there is a weakness of will as well. Far too many European politicians treat their social model as an icon: a much beloved trophy on the mantelpiece, constantly to be admired, occasionally taken down and polished, but never questioned or still less criticized. It stands as the great achievement of post-Second World War Christian and social democracy. This is true when French politicians talk about their social model or Germans about the social market economy. In this, there is no British exceptionalism. On the left, the creation of the National Health Service by the post-war

Labour government or comprehensive schooling in the 1960s has taken on an almost spiritual significance, despite the stark evidence of widespread inequities and the reality of two-tier provision. This mindset is dangerous, allowing the classic confusion of ends and means. It blinds citizens to the need for reform when the social justice case for reform is compelling.

Leadership at European level could therefore play a useful role in reinforcing mutual commitments to reform. This must not undermine the primary national responsibility for reform. Europe's social models have deep historical roots and are part and parcel of national identities. Europe cannot substitute for strong domestic leadership. But the Commission could help clarify where member state social models are 'inefficient'[15] and what needs to change so that member states can make their own legitimate political choices about the degree of redistribution and social solidarity they favour. In social policy, 'Brussels' should never become the enemy of national political choice, but it can be the facilitator and incentivizer of more effective choice.

Europe's present social justice deficit

To be an effective catalyst for change, the EU – and in particular the Commission – should make the case for reform from a principled position.[16] Typically, the current reform debate focuses on the question of 'sustainability': we 'modernize or die'. Of course, a message based on the argument 'there is no alternative' can at times be powerful. But tough-minded pragmatism always runs the risk of surrendering the territory of values to opponents of reform. For this, there is no need or justification.

None of Europe's models of welfare capitalism presently matches up to the basic instinct for social justice to which most Europeans would subscribe. First, there are severe employment problems in many member states. In Germany, unemployment has never been higher since the last days of the Weimar Republic. In France, unemployment has hovered around 10 per cent for the best part of two decades, with more than a quarter of young people unable to find jobs. Even high employment countries like the Netherlands, Sweden and the UK have difficulties with significant pockets of working-age inactivity.[17]

Second, security against social risks is now partial. Welfare systems continue to insure, with varying levels of generosity, against the risks of nineteenth-century industrialization – unemployment, sickness, industrial injury and poverty in old age (with the exception of some gaps in Southern Europe where young people remain the responsibility of the family until they find a proper job). But European welfare states face difficult challenges in coping with the new social risks of modern life such as single parenthood, relationship breakdown, mental illness and extreme frailty and incapacity in old age.

Third, fairness between the generations has broken down. The elderly have done well in the EU(15). Pensioner poverty is much reduced and confined as a large-scale problem to the new member states. However, in the 1990s child poverty became more of a problem in several European countries. In others, young people bear the brunt of unemployment.

Fourth, there is an increasing insider/outsider division in European labour markets. The old structures of employment law and industrial relations that were supposed to guarantee fair treatment at work no longer protect the weak against the powerful. Some groups remain well protected as a result of social partnership, strong trade unions, collective agreements and legally enforceable employee rights, but they are privileged because they do not represent the majority of the workforce and those excluded from it.

Fifth, the commonly held aspiration that 'every child should have an equal chance in life' is less within reach than it was a generation ago; the disadvantages of social inheritance, as Epsing-Andersen has graphically labelled it, are more embedded.

Sixth, the quality of universal public services in many continental countries is beginning to corrode after years of public spending restraint caused by slow growth. Many member states have an endowment of high-quality infrastructures built in a more economically dynamic era, but this will increasingly fray at the edges if growth remains slow and public finances tight. The composition of public spending in many member states remains frozen in old patterns. High levels of social transfers squeeze out resources for investment in a successful knowledge economy – not just mainstream programmes of education and research, but also innovative social expenditures that improve life-chances and enhance labour market participation.

Where have Europe's social models worked and why?

However, Europe can do more than point out social model shortcomings. Contrary to much of the public discourse on the inherent contradictions of the European social model, the Nordic countries demonstrate that equity and efficiency are compatible. In terms of economic growth, high employment and commonly accepted indicators of social inclusion, the Nordic member states have performed best amongst Europeans in the last decade – and as good as, if not better than, the United States in terms of employment and growth and of course vastly superior in terms of social inclusion.[18] How is this to be explained?

First, in the Nordic countries, active government has sought to build new sources of comparative advantage. This is not only a question of investment in R&D, which in Sweden as a percentage of GDP is the highest in the world. It also applies to the speed of diffusion of IT, and investment more generally in education: again, not just a question of the priority afforded to higher education, but a comprehensive approach to investment in children from a very young age in order to overcome inherited disadvantages and enable them to fulfil their potential. The Nordics have not simply sought to deregulate and liberalize and then sit back and wait for the results: they have pursued active public policies to secure fresh comparative advantage.

Second, the Nordics have shown a commitment to market flexibility based on a recognition that small countries have little alternative but to compete in an open, increasingly global economy. The example of Denmark demonstrates that high employment and an egalitarian welfare state can coexist with high labour market flexibility. It is one of the member states that has most successfully improved its labour market performance in the last decade. Here, 'hire and fire' rules were relaxed, but investment in an 'active welfare state' increased. Social benefits for the unemployed remain generous by any standard, but recipients have to accept personal responsibility for undergoing retraining and relocation. In this way the high public spending costs of welfare become 'productive'. Danish success is *not* an argument for across-the-board deregulation of employment rights. (In *some* areas, individual rights may need to be strengthened – for example, to combat discrimination or facilitate family-friendly work.) But employment rights that delay economic adjustment may be counterproductive to the employees they aim to protect, if they persuade people that old jobs can be saved when the real issue is to equip people for new jobs.

Third, all the Nordic countries have reformed their welfare states. They have maintained generous social benefits but by adding conditionalities that involve responsibilities as well as rights, they have tackled the disincentive effects. They have put in place effective state-sponsored systems of training and work placement. They have recognized that modern welfare states need to be built on a norm of two-earner households and have made the availability of affordable childcare a central pillar of family living standards and cohesion as well as women's opportunities for self-fulfilment. They have introduced public service reforms that offer choice and diversity of provision.

Of course, the Nordic model faces tough challenges for the future. For example, the spread of stress and mental illness resulting in mounting claims for sickness and invalidity benefits; and the sustainability of pension provision in an ageing society. The most serious challenge to their advanced welfare state may well be the rising relative costs of public provision, as a result of pressure for real wage increases from a large public service workforce where productivity growth is low. But one can be optimistic, because in the recent past all three 'Nordics' implemented welfare reforms in response to economic crisis: they have a social model with a proven capacity to adjust.

Social policy analysts have traditionally taken the view that the Nordic experience has little to teach the rest of Europe. They theorize a Nordic exceptionalism by reference to the fact that in small countries with a high degree of social homogeneity and solidarity, it has been possible to build a lasting social consensus around the need for high taxes. However, the more interesting conclusion for the rest of Europe is surely that there is little evidence of inherent conflict between competitiveness and a generous social model. Nothing supports the view that to be competitive, countries need to have low 'tax and spend'. There is more room for political choice about levels of tax if public spending is seen to be 'efficient', with the benefits broadly spread in line with the preferences of the majority of the electorate.

Europe's member states have much to learn from the Nordic experience. They should go with the grain of more open markets. They have to find the resources to invest in the knowledge economy. The 'knowledge economy deficit' is growing (with UK performing little better than the European average): Europe as a whole is not just lagging behind the US, but China/India are rapidly catching up. The reform of higher education sectors across EU member states is equally urgent: at present, universities are rapidly falling behind and the inadequacy of dependence on state funding is a key issue. And like the Nordics, member states have to modernize their social welfare systems to address the realities of a two-earner labour market; to support parenthood with childcare and family-friendly employment; and to address child poverty and inherited social disadvantage.

The deepening challenge of globalization to social justice

Europe as a whole would be a more prosperous and fairer place if member states were to follow the Nordic example. But is that enough to face the challenge of globalization?

In principle, all facets of economic openness – the Single Market, EU enlargement and globalization – should be positive in raising Europe's growth potential because of the forces of economic competition and the intensified search for comparative advantage that they unleash. But the benefits are generalized across the population at large (and in the case of globalization, across the world at large) – in lower consumer prices and rising incomes, while the costs are highly specific to the workers affected by industrial change. For example, delocalization – the offshoring of parts of the production chain to the new member states – is positive for European competitiveness[19] by enabling European companies to take advantage of lower labour costs and an unused pool of skills in the new member states. It makes it more likely that European companies will keep capital in Europe, rather than see it invested overseas. But there are social 'losers' as a result of the loss of lower-skilled jobs in Western Europe.

Similarly, European industry is reasonably well positioned to meet the competitive 'threat' from Asia, principally the emergence of China and India. As a supplier of 'top-quality' goods and services,[20] European companies can move away from mass production to highly specialized, custom-designed supply, tailored to high-value segments of new emerging markets. But this is bound to have an impact on the occupational structure of firms, reducing dramatically the number of traditional blue-collar jobs. At the same time, service industry offshoring and outsourcing will have an impact on jobs higher up the social scale.

In the mass-manufacturing economy of the previous generation, many of the low-skilled workers were protected by trade union power and collective bargaining: the impact was to equalize rewards within the firm and raise wages/employment benefits for the low paid above what market forces themselves would have determined. But this is not true in the competitive service economy which Europe is rapidly becoming. Low-skilled workers lack these previous protections. Trade union organization in services is weak, outside the privileged protected position of the public sector, but including public sector contractors. There are issues of job quality and gender discrimination. Private sector service firms lack the ability to pass on costs to the consumer.

Structural change in the labour market, which economic reform reinforces, thereby deepens inequalities and heightens insecurity.

These processes are clearly under way at present. But given the global mobility of capital, the full impact of the emergence of China and India on Europe's economy lies in the future and will be on a much vaster scale. For their societies combine a long-term comparative advantage in wages, given the existence of a vast 'reserve army of labour' from the countryside, with the potential ability, through their societies' passion for education, to match Western levels of capability, skill and productivity per head. And China remains an authoritarian state without free trade unions able to secure rising real wages.

So for Europeans, the era of relatively better-paid manual jobs will not return. This raises three key questions for those concerned about widening pre-tax inequalities. How does public policy ensure that low-productivity, low-paid service sector jobs do not become poverty jobs of low quality and with few future prospects? How does one maximize the possibilities of quality 'knowledge' jobs with highly skilled quality people to fill them? And how does one ensure that the occupational structure of the knowledge and service economy, which is Europe's only future, does not become the basis for new rigidities of social stratification, where families with poor-quality jobs are locked in a life-cycle of relative poverty and low expectations?

The Barroso Commission's focus on jobs is absolutely correct. Europe desperately needs more jobs. The insider/outsider barriers that prevent Europe from achieving high employment need to be broken down. Outdated concepts of 'fair wages', resulting in high national minimum wages and uniform national rates of public sector pay, are not appropriate where regional economic variations are sharp. Also, false notions of equity impose high social insurance costs on the low paid in the belief that, in an insurance system, every citizen should make a proportionate contribution according to their means, which amounts to a tax on low-paid work.

Furthermore, critics of the Commission's approach need to recognize that market liberalization will help create more jobs. It has done so in sectors like air travel and telecommunications. It has a strong potential to do so if an effective EU Services Directive comes into effect. And rigorous enforcement of competition policy is essential to allow job-creating SMEs to grow. Externally, a turn to protectionism would isolate Europe from global markets just as they are being revolutionized by Asia's rising productive strength, with disastrous long-term consequences for Europe's ability to compete and its firms to provide the quality jobs of the future.

But from a social justice perspective, more jobs in themselves are not enough. They are necessary but not sufficient. Some fear Europe faces an 'America–Europe' choice between high employment with accelerating inequality on the one hand, and high unemployment with more social cohesion, on the other.[21] But this is a terrible and unnecessary concession to pessimism. Jobs can be created for low-productivity, low-wage workers. In place of social benefits set so high as to disincentivize work, new policies are required that 'top up' the earnings of the low paid to a living wage and in time increase workers' productive potential so that they can earn more. This demands a broader concept of the state's responsibility to promote employability than simply finding jobs for the unemployed. Otherwise, low-skilled and low-paid workers will simply join a revolving carousel of bad jobs and spells of unemployment.

At the same time, public policy needs to focus on what can be done to stimulate the 'quality' jobs of the future by promoting research, improving skills and extending opportunities for enterprise.

A dynamic economy will see constant job losses as well as employment gains. Europe's post-war economic history is no stranger to restructuring. A traditional strength of the European social model has been seen as its capacity to enable workers to accept and adjust to rapid economic change. This is in contrast to the United States, where to lose one's job is often to lose one's health insurance, pension and other social benefits, which accounts for the strength of protectionism among union sympathizers and Democrats in the US Congress. The heyday of *les trente glorieuses* saw, on the Continent, a massive shift of jobs from the land. Across the whole EU, the coal, steel, shipbuilding and textiles industries underwent sharp decline. But in that earlier era, problems of adjustment were managed by active government intervention such as regional policy, redundancy payments and industrial retraining schemes. Instruments were developed at EU level to supplement these efforts, such as the Regional and Social Funds and, of course, the CAP. The policy challenge is what new forms of active government can be developed for our times to manage economic change with social justice.

Neoliberalism is not the only choice for Europe

Some yearn for a EU Keynesian state that recreates and brings back the powers of economic intervention that nation-states were once able to exercise at the height of the post-war consensus: capital and exchange controls; pro-expansionary fiscal policies; industrial interventionism backed by preferential public procurement and state aids; and the capacity to impose external tariffs and import quotas on overseas competition, especially overseas competition that is perceived to be unfair because of low wages or the absence of trade union rights. But this hankering to recreate at European level a set of interventionist policies that at best had a mixed record at the level of the nation-state is not enticing.

A lesser variant of this call for greater interventionism at EU level is the concept of an EU regulatory state, where employment and social regulation would attempt to fill the gap caused by the collapse of the old constraints on capitalism. But in a diverse Union, EU regulation either finds it difficult to raise itself above the lowest common denominator or risks holding back innovation and strengthening the insider/outsider divide in the labour market. Regulation has costs: it cannot provide effective social intervention 'on the cheap'.

The real alternative is a developmental, empowering welfare state. Europe needs a 'Lisbon-plus' model of economic and social development that counters the adverse effects that globalization can have on inequality and the low skilled, but at the same time is open to the world and invests in the future. The basic structures of the welfare state are already in place in Europe. These foundations need to be transformed from the distribution of passive benefits to the creation of active opportunity. And on those modernized foundations need to be built a range of new policies for empowerment to counter the danger that globalization will widen and entrench unacceptable inequalities.

The European social model was traditionally seen as imposing rules, institutions and cultures that are designed to *shape* market outcomes, in addition to simply attempting to *correct* socially adverse market outcomes through a strong safety net and a measure of redistribution from rich to poor. For example, the mechanisms of social partnership, employment protection laws and the entrenched position of trade unions in the workplace (in some countries), far from making Europe uncompetitive, were seen as a positive productive factor. Restrictions on firms' rights to 'hire and fire' were seen to encourage cooperative arrangements at the workplace and investment by firms in the long-term commitment of their employees. This was a cornerstone belief of those who argued that the rest of Europe had much to learn from the stakeholder capitalism of the 'Rhineland model'.

But the old rules and cultures that in the past have attempted to shape market outcomes are now being stripped away in the belief that these hold back growth and innovation. Tight employment protection laws can encourage the creation of 'dual' insider/outsider labour markets and discourage employers from taking on new employees or offering non-standard forms of employment contract. They may make change more difficult for employers with damaging consequences for jobs in Europe in the long run in a world of mobile capital. The old model may only have worked in more stable economic conditions, where incremental change to product standards was all that was required. When, as today, product market competition is subject to radical change, and when the requirements of competitive success switch from on-the-job quality improvement to rapid exploitation of breakthroughs in innovation, then firms may need more flexible employment relations.[22]

In these circumstances, new policies that *shape* market outcomes have to be developed, along with reformed welfare state policies that *correct* the latter. A developmental welfare state goes beyond correcting for the social injustices of the market. It shapes the market as well; for example, by paying a great deal of attention to maximizing its supply of quality human capital. It will regard the removal of the inherited disadvantages that prevent individuals from realizing their full potential through education and training as a big task for public policy – as big as breaking down the barriers to free markets. A developmental welfare state will focus its efforts on the right framework conditions for economic development in regions and parts of regions where demand for labour is weak through enterprise incentives, the provision of knowledge-based infrastructures and the promotion of university spin-offs. A development welfare state will create the maximum opportunities for partnerships between public and private sectors, so that each sector is imbued with the best values of both, for example in encouraging a workplace culture of training and workforce development.

How the EU can help member states to pursue social justice strategies for reform

At present the EU has both an incomplete set of policies and an inadequate set of instruments to pursue a social justice strategy for reform. The absence of a comprehensive set of policies reflects the limits of EU competence and the traditional reluctance of member states to allow the European institutions to engage in issues that are seen as primarily national responsibilities. However, in the last ten years the EU has established employment guidelines (now part of the integrated broad economic policy guidelines) that range fully over the terrain of welfare and labour market reform. As a result of Lisbon, a peer review process was established on social inclusion. And other coordination processes cover pensions, care for the elderly and education. The Hampton Court Summit gave the Commission a wide-ranging mandate to explore the potential of further European initiatives in higher education, research, migration and issues to do with demography.

From this patchwork of mandates and processes, it should be possible for the Commission to prepare a comprehensive social justice road map for reform, if Europe's political leaders are prepared to give the Commission the mandate to do so. A modern conception of social justice is about much more than income distribution and employment rights. A strategy for 'quality' jobs for the future has to embrace questions of research, higher education, skills, knowledge diffusion and enterprise promotion. A strategy for maximizing opportunity has to include questions of access to childcare, raising standards throughout the school system, training for new skills at all stages of life, a more equal spread of opportunities for university education, fresh ladders of opportunity for those in dead-end jobs and help with mid-life adjustment to economic change. These are the necessary credible components of a social justice strategy for social model reforms that improve work incentives and flexibilize labour markets. They should be presented as a charter to tackle the new inequalities and equip European citizens with new entitlements for the future.

Three types of instrument should be developed to encourage member states to follow this social justice roadmap. The first is effective peer review through a strengthened open method of coordination.[23] The policy vehicle is already available – the National Reform Programmes which member states have bound themselves to submit under the revised 2005 Lisbon Strategy. The Commission should attempt to obtain a stronger political commitment from key member states to this process. To assist this task, a new, higher-profile multilateral surveillance procedure should be instituted for assessing National Reform Programmes. An advisory council for social modernization could be established at EU level to assist the Commission in this task. This would consist of experts whose intellectual qualities and independence are without question: it would not represent interests. It would be charged with preparing its own assessment for each member state of the reforms that they should undertake to conform to the social justice roadmap. To make this work will require a greater political commitment than at present from the European Council. There should be a pre-agreement by the European Council to give national prominence and priority to the social justice roadmap and launch national debates on the recommendations of the advisory council on social modernization. A special council of ministers could be set up to coordinate and debate the assessments. Heads should be urged to appoint to this special council a senior cabinet minister who would be given a cross-cutting national responsibility for this agenda.

Second, new criteria need to be established at EU level to assess the quality of national public expenditure. The broad economic policy guidelines should give greater weight to rigorous analysis of the composition of member states's public expenditure and how far it meets the criteria of productive social investment, and the social justice roadmap. The EU might consider, for example, setting a target for public investment in the knowledge that it would include all forms of public expenditure on research, higher education, the promotion of IT and R&D-based enterprise: this would be more meaningful than the current 3 per cent R&D target for each member state which embraces private expenditures over which public policy has at best weak influence (though it would be worth exploring a European framework for R&D tax credits); and is bound to be more achievable in some member states than others because of their variable industry structure.[24]

Public spending is high in many member states – but it does not achieve the objectives of social justice, because it is spent inappropriately, or wasted in over-centralized bureaucracy. For all the need for fiscal discipline, the operation of the Stability and Growth Pact has been perverse: it has narrowed the scope for additional public expenditures that promote structural reforms. Yet without structural reform, growth potential remains constrained. The risk is that the fiscal rules entrench the forces of 'reform immobilisme'. More flexibility should be allowed in the Stability and Growth Pact for genuine reform programmes that have high initial costs. This is already acknowledged for pensions reform – but why pensions and not other desirable reforms?

Third, the Commission's comprehensive review of the EU budget, to be completed by 2008, should involve consideration of new EU budget incentives for reform. This is not the place to set out in detail ideas for EU budget reform. Suffice it to say that the conclusions of the Sapir Report remain relevant: 'As it stands today, the EU budget is a historical relic';[25] '[h]ence the EU budget reform should be an integral part of a strategy of moving towards a more incentive based approach.'[26] Sapir proposed regrouping the EU budget around three new instruments:

- a fund for economic growth, principally R&D and innovation, education and training and infrastructure;
- a convergence fund for poorer countries, focusing on institution building and physical and human capital;

- a restructuring fund aimed at facilitating the process of resource reallocation, including aid to displaced workers.

While all of these expenditures have a modern social justice dimension, Sapir is strongly of the view that criteria of efficiency and equity should not be confused in the allocation of funding. Research funding, for instance, should be spent where the greatest research productivity is likely to be achieved, not in an attempt to equalize capabilities between regions or member states. If the purpose of spending is equity, then research projects that are considered unsuitable for the growth fund should compete for limited funds against other desirable objectives of convergence spending.

While the logic of assigning a single instrument to a single clear objective is well understood, there is surely a case for establishing an additional category for EU funding that incentivizes new social policies that serve the purposes of efficiency and equity, economic reform and social justice. As the purpose of taking such an initiative at EU level would be both presentational as well as substantive, it might be best to concentrate funding on a small number of emblematic policies that would catch the popular imagination. The Global Adjustment Fund, the funding for which President Barroso fought successfully in the December 2005 agreement on the 2007–13 Financial Perspectives, is an example of an approach that might be further developed. Help for displaced workers losing their jobs as a result of global economic shocks might be extended into a generally available financial entitlement for redundant workers that could be spent flexibly on clearly defined purposes such as retraining, moving home or setting up a business. Similar socially progressive entitlements might be established at EU level in priority areas for economic modernization such as childcare, scholarships for higher education and adult learning entitlements. It would be for consideration whether these entitlements are universal or focused on those with limited means; how much matching funding would be expected from member states; whether they would be related to the establishment of individual targets for member states; and whether financial contributions would be rebated for member states that already exceed these targets.

Conclusion

One cannot be complacent about the present conjuncture in Europe. High unemployment in several key member states, growing numbers of people who feel 'losers' in the world around them – detached from hope of change from conventional domestic politics and still less any positive idea of Europe – and ethnic and racial tensions never far below the surface in many communities raise the possibility that acute social strains will develop in several European countries. We have already seen a resurgence of populism on the right and the left. This could easily descend into ugly nationalism and xenophobia.

The warning signs were present in the French and Dutch 'no' votes in their referenda on the Constitutional Treaty at the end of May 2005. In both countries, it was not the perceived inadequacies of the constitutional text that voters rejected, but the context of an economically underperforming Europe centred on a Brussels that felt increasingly alien – associated with a liberalization agenda that was seen to threaten job security and an enlargement agenda that would intensify migration and threaten traditional solidarities. Instead of being the source of hope that European integration once meant to continental citizens, Europe has become a source of fear.

These economic and social discontents flow directly from the failure of Europe's political leaders to make a convincing case for necessary economic and social reform. Europe and its member states need a new social justice consensus for reform – not just a new 'spin', but new substance as well. This discussion is intended as a contribution to that debate.

Notes

1 Brussels European Council Conclusions, December 2005
2 Delors White Paper, 1994.
3 Lisbon European Council Conclusions, March 2000
4 R. Liddle and M. J. Rodrigues, eds., *Economic Reform in Europe: Priorities for the Next Five Years* (London: Policy Network, 2004).
5 *European Employment Report 2004*
6 For example, the early decisions by the incoming left-wing governments in France and Germany in 1997 and 1998, respectively to introduce a 35-hour week and abolish provision for low-paid jobs exempted from social insurance contributions, have since been substantially unwound.
7 The IMF view, for example, is that Germany's Agenda 2010 reforms to the welfare system have not had as much impact on employment as they would have done had parallel liberalization of product markets taken place at the same time, such as the liberalization of shop opening hours.
8 I am grateful to Dr Karl Aiginger for forcefully driving home this viewpoint.
9 Mid-Term Review of the Lisbon Strategy. Report of a High Level Group chaired by Wim Kok, formerly Prime Minister of The Netherlands, October 2004.

10 European Commission, *Growth and Jobs Strategy for Europe* (European Commission, February 2005).

11 See, for example, the columns of Wolfgang Munchau in the *Financial Times*.

12 I am grateful to Jean Pisani Ferry of Breughel for this point.

13 A remark Juncker reportedly made at the European Council in March 2005.

14 By 1979, the experience of British decline had been so acute that there was widespread acceptance that 'there is no alternative'. The social democratic (and moderate Conservative) strategy of governing Britain on the basis of social consensus had collapsed in the 1978–9 Winter of Discontent. Mrs Thatcher was able to pursue extremely tough and radical policies, because little else credible was seen to be on offer, and because the significant numbers of 'losers' from her policies were heavily concentrated amongst supporters of the Opposition parties. The rest of Europe is not, even today, in this position.

15 The concept of which social models are 'efficient', and why, is admirably expounded in the paper that André Sapir presented to European Finance Ministers at the Informal ECOFIN meeting in Manchester in September 2005.

16 This critique of Europe's present social justice deficit draws heavily on the work of Gøsta-Epsing Andersen. See his *Why We Need a New Welfare State* (Oxford: Oxford University Press, 2002). This is turn arose from an initiative of the Belgian Presidency in 2001 and its then Social Affairs Minister Frank Vandenbroucke.

17 According to the statistics presented in *Employment in Europe 2005* (European Commission, September 2005) the inactivity rate for 55–64 year olds was 29.9 per cent in the UK as against 31.6 per cent in the EU as a whole.

18 I am grateful here to several analytical papers by Dr Karl Aiginger of WIFO, the Austrian Institute of Economic Research, including his contribution to this volume.

19 This is the conclusion of a comprehensive analysis of the available research evidence conducted on behalf of the President of the European Commission by his Group of European Policy Advisers in 2005.

20 According to DG Trade analysis contained in its working paper 'The External Dimension of Competitiveness' (September 2005), the EU is significantly better positioned as a 'top-quality' supplier than the United States, though weaker as a supplier of high-tech products.

21 The contrasting experience of Europe and America is well set out in André Sapir et al., *Agenda for a Growing Europe* (Oxford: Oxford University Press, 2004), p. 119.

22 This analysis was bravely set out in Sapir, *Agenda for a Growing Europe*, pp. 35–8.

23 The best analyses of the effectiveness of the Lisbon experience with the Open Method of Coordination are to be found in papers by Maria Joao Rodrigues. See, for instance, 'The debate over Europe and the Lisbon Strategy for growth and jobs'.
24 This point I owe to Luc Soete, and is contained in the paper published in his name by the British Presidency prior to the Hampton Court Summit in October 2005.
25 Sapir, *Agenda for a Growing Europe*, p. 197.
26 Ibid., p. 153.

Index